GOLDY'S KITCHEN COOKBOOK

ALSO BY DIANE MOTT DAVIDSON

Catering to Nobody

Dying for Chocolate

The Cereal Murders

The Last Suppers

Killer Pancake

The Main Corpse

The Grilling Season

Prime Cut

Tough Cookie

Sticks & Scones

Chopping Spree

Double Shot

Dark Tort

Sweet Revenge

Fatally Flaky

Crunch Time

The Whole Enchilada

Diane Mott Davidson

Presents

GOLDY'S KITCHEN COOKBOOK

Cooking, Writing, Family, Life

WILLIAM MORROW

An Imprint of HarperCollins*Publishers*

FIRST EDITION

Designed by Shannon Nicole Plunkett

Library of Congress Cataloging-in-Publication Data has been applied for.

ISBN 978-0-06-219404-6

15 16 17 18 19 OV/RRD 10 9 8 7 6 5 4 3 2 1

To all the marvelously supportive
booksellers who have
helped bring Goldy to readers

Contents

Acknowledgments

The author gratefully acknowledges the assistance of the following people: Jim Davidson; Jeff, Rosa, Ryan, Nick, and Josh Davidson; J. Z. Davidson; Joey Davidson; Sandra Dijkstra, Elise Capron, Andrea Cavallaro, Thao Le, Elisabeth James, and the rest of the superb team at the Sandra Dijkstra Literary Agency; Brian Murray, Michael Morrison, Liate Stehlik, Carolyn Marino, Kaitlyn Kennedy, Tavia Kowalchuk, Joseph Papa, and the entire brilliant team at Morrow; the St. Anne's-Belfield community in Charlottesville, Virginia, especially Kay Butterfield and Gunda Hiebert, with special remembrance of the passing of our beloved Pamela Malone and Emyl Jenkins; Professor Diana Kleiner of Yale University; Kathy Saideman; Carol Alexander, for testing the recipes and making many valuable suggestions; Jasmine Cresswell; Linda and David Ranz, M.D.; Shirley Carnahan, Ph.D.; Carole Kornreich, M.D.; Julie Kaewert; Dylan Burdick and Tiffany Green; Lyndsay White; Pamela Eaton; J.R. and John Suess; the Reverends Andi Suess Taylor, Jay Rock, David Evans, and John Hall, all of St. Boniface Episcopal Church in Sarasota, Florida;

Judith Rock, Nancy Evans, Betsie Danner, Carolyn Walker, and all the parishioners and staff at St. Boniface; Harriët van Elburg and Jason Heckman; the Reverend Nancy Malloy, Bill and Carole Hörger, and all the parishioners at St. Laurence Episcopal Church in Conifer, Colorado; my far-flung family: Adam Mott, Janie Mott Fritz, Lucy Mott Faison, Sally Mott Freeman, and William C. Mott, Jr., plus all their wonderful spouses and dear children, with remembrance again of the passing of our beloved Tom Fritz; John William Schenk and Karen Johnson Kennedy, who taught me how to cater; Marty O'Leary and the staff at Sur La Table in Sarasota, Florida, for numerous helpful suggestions; and thanks forever to Triena Harper and Sergeant Richard Millsapps, now retired from the Jefferson County Sheriff's Department, Golden, Colorado.

Introduction

In the early 1980s, I started to write about a character named Goldy. She would be a caterer, I decided. At that time, I only knew three things about her: She loved to cook; she had a troubled eleven-year-old son; she was a survivor of domestic abuse. Her ex-husband, whom I named the Jerk, was a wealthy doctor who had repeatedly beaten her. But as I wrote more about Goldy, I realized that she had thrown him out. Her grit, hard work, and ability to find support from friends, church, and her mentor at a Denver restaurant enabled her to put her life back together. She did more than survive. She thrived. She took the lemon that life had given her and made not just lemonade but Lemon Chicken, Lemon Bars, Lemon Cookies, and Lemon Meringue Pie.

By 1987, I had finished writing what became *Catering to Nobody.* My critique group, to which I often brought cookies, told me I should put some recipes in the book. So I did. In 1988, the wonderful literary agent Sandra Dijkstra took me on. She sold the book to St. Martin's Press, which published it in 1990. Over the next twenty-plus years, Goldy, her family, and I have continued to grow, and it has been a fabulous journey.

Like Goldy, I enjoy working in the kitchen. This was not always so. The night before I married my husband, Jim (who is nothing like the Jerk; I say this only because people have repeatedly asked), I broke down.

"I can't marry you!" I cried, as we sat in the front seat of our Chevy Nova (which turned out to be a lemon of a different kind).

Jim asked, "We can't get married? Why not?"

"I can't cook!"

Jim said, "We'll be fine."

And we were. I learned to have fun cooking. How I decided to write about Goldy is another, parallel story.

But let's start in the kitchen. I am the oldest of four children. Our mother disliked—*despised* would not be too strong a word—the necessity of preparing the family's evening meal. My guess is that this resentment coincided with a mishap with the pressure cooker.

I was nine. My mother had mastered making beef, potatoes, and carrots in her cooker, so that was what we ate almost every night. This would usually be accompanied by leaves of iceberg lettuce dabbed with mayonnaise from a jar. Based on our experiences at friends' houses, my siblings and I knew that some mothers liked to cook and did it well. But if we dared to complain, we would be sent to our rooms without dinner. So we learned to keep our mouths shut, as they say in the South, *right quick*.

Occasionally, my mother varied what she served, perhaps out of a sense of duty. She was from New England. On St. Patrick's Day, she made corned beef and cabbage. Even though we were Protestants, she always served fish sticks on Friday—just in case. We also had the occasional dinner of (canned) Boston baked beans and (canned) New England brown bread. On the weekends, my father worked off stress by making yeast breads, which he kneaded with great vigor. We kids dug into the corned beef and cabbage and pressure-cooked beef, potatoes, and carrots and slathered margarine—all we knew in those days—on Dad's bread, and things hummed along.

Then she accidentally blew the lid off the pressure cooker. I remember the *ker-bang*. No one was hurt, thank God. But the kitchen ceiling bore a permanent imprint from the lid. The beef, potatoes, and carrots left stains that never came out. (Before they sold the house, my parents scrubbed the ceiling and painted over the stains.)

After the pressure cooker incident, my mother threw in the kitchen towel and pretty much handed the job off to me. She didn't mind shopping, so I would use the ingredients she bought: packages of chicken pieces, pounds of ground beef, those sticks of margarine, plus more heads of iceberg lettuce, boxes of Shake 'n Bake seasoning, Rice-A-Roni, Betty Crocker Noodles Romanoff, Kraft Macaroni & Cheese, instant mashed potatoes, instant mushroom gravy, instant salad dressing mix.

So in fact I had done plenty of "cooking" before Jim and I were due to get married. But I knew it wasn't *real* cooking. The mothers of my friends and my siblings' friends when we were growing up outside Washington, D.C., were great cooks, and they made everything from lasagna to tzimmes with what looked like ease and dedication. When I would plead to have my friends over for a meal, my mother would bake a ham. I made Kraft Macaroni & Cheese to go with it, plus iceberg lettuce mixed with mayonnaise.

During those early years, I also was fortunate enough to witness a real cook in her element. When my siblings and I were young, our parents would go on vacations without us, which was common among middle-class households in the fifties and sixties. An older woman would stay with us. I'm sure she's passed away, but still: Let's call her Mrs. Jones.

Mrs. Jones made everything from scratch. As long as I was willing to listen sympathetically to her laments about her son, Jeremiah, I could watch. Mrs. Jones would make luscious chicken pot pies. She cut real butter—never margarine—into flour, sprinkled on iced spring water, and rolled out pie crust while telling me how Jeremiah had been acting up. Mrs. Jones made spice cookies, chocolate cookies, and sugar cookies while bemoaning the fact that Jeremiah was in jail. Mrs. Jones's real specialty was candy. The problem with Jeremiah, she said as she rolled chocolate into luscious globes, was that he had a chemical imbalance. I listened and nodded, all while recognizing that Mrs. Jones, like the mothers of our friends, was the genuine article in the kitchen.

I had just turned twenty, and Jim had just turned twenty-two, when we were about to get married and I was sobbing and saying that there would not, *could not,* in fact, be a wedding the next day, because I couldn't cook. I knew the "Mrs. Jones standard" would be the one by which I would be assessed. Those were the days when women, and only women, were judged—usually harshly—based on their ability to cook. My mother had escaped this judgment, but I knew "the truth," and that was that we had Instant Everything.

When our parents had cocktail parties, they served frozen egg rolls that my sisters and I heated up. For their rare dinner parties, my father would place a raw egg beside his place and expertly whisk it into a dressing for Caesar salad, which would be served with ham and baked potatoes. Other times, when they needed to entertain guests for a meal, they took them to a restaurant.

So before the pressure cooker exploded, I had enjoyed the beef, potatoes, and carrots, the occasional New England dish, the ham, and fish sticks. Then I'd had my adventures with Shake 'n Bake and other time-and-effort-saving dishes. When I was twelve, though, I quite unexpectedly received a profound lesson in differing regional cuisines.

That year, I received a scholarship that enabled me to attend a girls' boarding school, St. Anne's, in Charlottesville, Virginia. (It is now a coed school called St. Anne's-Belfield, known by the acronym STAB. When I purchased a pair of sweat-pants with *STAB* embroidered on them, our youngest son thought I'd bought them at a crime writers' convention.)

At St. Anne's, I was blessed to have outstanding teachers, one of whom, Emyl Jenkins, told me I should be a writer, a compliment that I held in my back pocket for eighteen years, while going to college, working at other jobs, and raising a family.

In the food department, Charlottesville might as well have been a continent away from Washington. At St. Anne's, we had real Southern cooking: grits and sausage; biscuits and gravy; perfect fried chicken; black-eyed peas and stewed tomatoes. According to my sisters (they were too young to cook, and my brother was only a year old), our mother resignedly took over making the Shake 'n Bake chicken and Rice-A-Roni. One hundred ten miles away, I thought I'd died and gone to Food Heaven.

Eight years later, when Jim and I were, despite my pre-wedding meltdown, married, we were both full-time scholarship students, this time at Stanford. Jim was a Navy ensign and ensconced in a graduate engineering program. I was finishing my undergraduate degree and had a limited budget to prepare meals. At first, I served Jim Instant Everything. Surprised, he lavished compliments on me.

While relying on Instant Everything—which was expensive but not time-consuming—I read Peg Bracken's hilarious, wonderful *I Hate to Cook Book*. It seemed even I could follow her simple instructions. I learned the Art of the Casserole, which usually involved canned creamed soups mixed with a variety of other ingredients.

We hummed along until the day I splurged and bought a steak. Since I only knew the Art of the Casserole, I put that sorry piece of beef in the oven at 350°F for an hour.

Jim ate every bite.

I did not immediately set my sights on becoming a writer. I studied hard, protested the war in Vietnam, and developed affection for the subject of art history. (Most of the professional foodies I've met majored in art history—an interesting coincidence. And art historians themselves are usually wonderful cooks.) While in school, my desire to become a better cook deepened, owing to two sources.

When we were newlyweds, Jim and I lived in a tiny apartment in Menlo Park, right near the offices of *Sunset* magazine. I bought their cookbooks at the Moffatt Naval Air Station commissary. When I had the time, I worked my way through some of them. Encountering a problem, I would call the *Sunset* test kitchens. The people who talked to me were unfailingly helpful and encouraging. But I remained timid, and when I was tired, would opt for tuna casserole.

The other, and longest-lasting, reason I came to love cooking was an epiphany that took place during a particularly exhausting exam period that year. Unable to face the prospect of opening yet another can of tuna, I turned on the television and saw

Julia Child on PBS. I shook my head as she gave straightforward, simple instructions on making a roux that didn't taste of flour. That night, I made my first béchamel sauce. She was right. The food was luscious, and I felt energized, not drained.

I bought *The French Chef Cookbook,* based on the TV show, and soon I was stuffing mushrooms, poaching chicken, and whipping up *bavarois à l'orange.* Julia Child's assertion was a revelation: *I can teach you to prepare French food.* Many women of my generation followed her into the kitchen. To this day, I feel Julia Child's helpful, guiding presence at the stove.

Once we finished school, the Navy sent Jim off on back-to-back eighteen-month deployments. The first seven years we were married, we moved thirteen times. When Jim finally finished his obligation to the Navy, he landed a job in Colorado. We moved to a small mountain town that bears a marked resemblance to the Aspen Meadow of the Goldy books. Our family grew to include three sons. I did volunteer work at our local church, in our diocese, and for our political party. I tutored in a correctional facility and counseled rape victims. I helped raise funds for various community projects, cared for the kids and the house, cooked up a storm, and in what there was of my spare time, I read. I never forgot Emyl Jenkins's advice, but I did not yet know how to use it.

The problem with doing scads of volunteer work is that, as with any profession, you can get burned out. When you are a volunteer, the hours are long, appreciation is minimal, and gratitude, if it's doled out at all, is sparse. And of course you are not being paid. Our three kids had to go to college *somehow.* Denver, an hour away, offered scant employment opportunities, none of them part-time.

At thirty-two, I still had not tried to become a professional writer, although as a volunteer I had done plenty of writing. I felt directionless, so I took a writing class.

I loved it. I took another class and then another. And I wrote—a lot. Often frustrated, I'd finished and rewritten three novels before *Catering to Nobody* was accepted for publication.

But where do you get your ideas? is a question writers frequently hear at bookstores and libraries.

What I reply is that a cook goes to the refrigerator to take out ingredients to prepare a meal; a writer goes to the *emotional* refrigerator to cook up a book. The first ingredient for the Goldy series that got stored in my emotional refrigerator came from my volunteer work. There, I had repeatedly seen a phenomenon that nobody seemed to be talking or writing about in those days: the middle-class—and sometimes wealthy—physically abused spouse. (This was pre-O.J., when nationwide consciousness was suddenly raised.)

I had heard that women stuck in poverty were sometimes beaten up by their husbands or boyfriends. But the abused women I was encountering were my fellow volunteers and committee members. One woman said, "Look at where my husband broke my thumb in three places with a hammer." He was a social worker. Back then, a woman had to be willing to testify against her husband, and many women simply could not afford to do this.

The laws have since changed, but abused spouses and partners, ex and otherwise, are still not safe. If you need help, please call the National Domestic Violence Hotline at 1-800-799-7233. Trust your intuition regarding threats from a partner. If you doubt your intuition, please read *The Gift of Fear* by Gavin de Becker.

From the stories I'd heard, I created Goldy's ex-husband, the Jerk. From my own experience raising our three sons, Arch and Julian were born. The characters are composites. But I had plenty of material. A typical Arch story might come from the true story of going clothes-shopping with one of our adolescent sons. (I always seemed to embarrass our sons.)

"Mom," our son said, this time in a low voice, "when we go into this store, do not call my name. Do not show me any clothes. Do not point out any girls you think are cute. In fact, *pretend that you don't know me.*"

Some readers have commented that Arch speaks to his mother in a disrespectful manner. When *they* were growing up, these readers say, that kind of language and behavior would not have been tolerated. Well, that was when *they* were growing up. And by the way, all of our sons were viewed by their teachers and peers as being exceptionally well-mannered. So there.

The character of Tom comes, of course, from being married to a hardworking but easygoing spouse. Numerous women have asked me, “Where do I meet someone like Tom?” I was lucky.

The character of Julian, Goldy’s helper, arose from when one of our sons was going through a particularly challenging period. When *Dying for Chocolate* was published in 1992, Julian was introduced as a rebellious teen who was a scholarship student at a local prep school. To relieve his frustration, he swam. Because my agent is a vegetarian who had requested more vegetarian recipes, Julian became a vegetarian who loved to cook.

The evolution of the character of Marla, Goldy’s wealthy best friend, is harder to pinpoint. Sometimes it’s better not to try to figure out where characters originate. This is especially true when a bejeweled woman in a designer outfit sashays into a scene you’re writing, drops her Louis Vuitton bag on the kitchen table, and announces, “I’m the Jerk’s other ex-wife.”

This cookbook contains almost all of the recipes from the seventeen books in the Goldy series. (Only a very few have been omitted.) Most of them came from playing around with dishes I’d tasted in restaurants. Others are family favorites: Dad’s Bread (see page 174), for example, is in *The Whole Enchilada*. There are also recipes that came from friends we knew in one of the many places where Jim was stationed, and that I copied down on three-by-five cards, only to make numerous changes to them over the ensuing decades. These recipes then became dishes the family decided they couldn’t live without.

Others, finally, were happy accidents. I relate a story in *Dying for Chocolate* that came from a neighbor’s visit. I was making Julia Child’s *gâteau de crêpes à la Florentine,* while my friend and I chatted. The recipe calls for two fillings between the crêpes: one mushroom, one spinach. The neighbor and I somehow got to talking too long. I mixed up the proportions and ended up with much more of the spinach filling than the mushroom. Since my neighbor was still sitting at the kitchen table and it was getting on to dinnertime, I thinned out the extra spinach filling with chicken broth, and served the family and my neighbor what became Goldilocks’ Gourmet Spinach Soup. Here is the recipe:

Goldilocks' Gourmet Spinach Soup

—DYING FOR CHOCOLATE—

5 tablespoons unsalted butter

4 ounces fresh button mushrooms, cleaned, dried, trimmed, and diced

1 scallion, chopped

5 tablespoons all-purpose flour

2 cups canned chicken broth, or homemade chicken stock (see page 30)

2 cups milk, preferably whole

½ teaspoon salt (optional)

Freshly ground black pepper

Freshly grated nutmeg (optional)

4 ounces cream cheese, at room temperature, cut into cubes

1 cup grated Gruyère cheese

¾ pound fresh spinach, trimmed, washed, cooked, and chopped

In a large saucepan, melt the butter. Add the mushrooms and scallion and slowly sauté until tender. Add the flour and stir just until the flour is cooked, a couple of minutes. Whisk in first the chicken broth and then the milk, stirring until thickened. Add the salt (if using), pepper to taste, nutmeg to taste (if using), cream cheese, and Gruyère, stirring until melted. Then stir in the spinach. Taste and correct the seasoning. Heat and stir very gently. Serve hot.

Makes 4 to 6 servings

The neighbor adored it and wrote down the recipe. And our three sons actually loved a soup that *involves fresh spinach.*

So . . . the Goldy books began from taking a second look at events in my own life to which I had had a strong emotional reaction. Then I worked (and reworked, it must be said—many times) those experiences into stories. In the chapters that follow, I talk about cooking and writing, and what I discovered about both. Cooking began out of necessity and became fun. My vocation is writing. I am extremely grateful to have had the good fortune to enjoy doing both.

Chapter 1

Appetizers and Soups *or* How Do I Look?

(AND OTHER STORIES ABOUT FOOD AND APPEARANCE)

I learned about catering in the kitchen of J. William's, the now unfortunately closed bistro and catering operation owned and operated by John William Schenk. I volunteered to work in his kitchen and with his team for catered events. He agreed, for which I am endlessly thankful. At the outset, I asked John and his wonderful assistant, Karen Johnson Kennedy (that is actually her name), if they had a lot of secret recipes. Karen collapsed in giggles and John, to my surprise, said the cookbooks he used were not the most important aspect of food service. The primary guideline for catering was not "How does the food taste?" but "How does it look?" This is the reason cookbooks with photographs of food are:

1. Expensive to produce
2. More fun to look at than cookbooks with no pictures

(Sorry, this cookbook has no photographs.)

We eat first with our eyes, John would say. Over the years, he always reminded me to take note of a dish's appearance on the plate or platter. For parties, John would serve a large, shallow rectangular basket so bulging with crudités that it virtually invited one to dive in. A salade composée was just that. The cakes were not only made with butter but elegantly iced with ruffles of buttercream frosting, sometimes held in perfect place by the addition of melted gelatin.

This applies to writing in a number of ways. When I was first published, I found that people who came to bookstore events wanted to have fun. Their desire was to meet the author, get their book signed, maybe eat a cookie, and have a laugh. So far, so good.

Being out promoting a book can generate ideas for other books. The genesis of my fifth book began in Scottsdale, Arizona, in 1992. I was visiting a bookstore to sign *Dying for Chocolate.* A woman in line looked at my author photograph on the book flap, took a step forward, then glanced at me. She turned her gaze back to the photograph. Then she stared at me. When she arrived at the front of the line, she tapped the picture and said, "This is an extremely flattering photograph."

I was already working on the third Goldy book, *The Cereal Murders,* back at home. I also had the broad outline of what would become the fourth, *The Last Suppers.* So I wasn't exactly looking for a book idea when I returned to Colorado and raced down to The Denver, an elegant department store that used to be *the* place to go in the city for fashion and beauty. No, the thought that I looked *much less attractive than my photo* did that. No question about it: I needed a makeover.

The very nice young woman who patted first one cream, then some concealer, then dabs of other products on my face asked, "What do you do for a living?"

"I write murder mysteries," said I.

"My, my," she murmured, "I sure could write a murder mystery about *this* place."

"Oh?" I asked. "How's that?"

And she proceeded to tell me about the tactics used to sell cosmetics. At that time, the top Colorado saleswoman for the leading cosmetics company in the nation was fortyish. She would sell enormous amounts of something called Age-Defying Cream. And this lady would defy her age, all right, by telling women that she used the cream every night, and she was *seventy* years old. The cream had taken a miraculous thirty years off her face!

Cosmetics sales at that time were—and perhaps still are—largely commission-based. My young resource told me that the cards clients fill out with their contact information are like gold to the saleswomen. And since they are like that precious metal, they were often stolen . . . by other sales associates. Not only that, but if a particularly well-heeled client showed up unexpectedly and asked for say, Jennifer, and Jennifer had just left for lunch, the competitive associate would say, "Jennifer doesn't work here anymore. Can I help you?"

There was also industrial spying. A fellow from a local facial-care and cosmetics-manufacturing company used to chat up the young women who worked behind the counter. He would take them out for lunch, give them coupons for free facials and lipsticks . . . and interrogate them on the new lines emerging from corporate HQ in New York. What was the packaging on the compacts going to look like? (White compacts were viewed as "old-fashioned," whereas navy or black compacts were thought to be hip. Since then, silver compacts have become chic, and at some future point white compacts will probably stage a comeback.) The spy would also want to know the names of new products, sales projections, dates and contents of giveaways, and gift-with-purchase events. If an associate became suddenly tight-lipped, the spy would chat with someone else, sometimes offering a higher-paying job to that associate . . . as long as she gave helpful information and was wanting a new gig.

Suddenly, the cosmetics counter looked a lot more interesting. After The Denver closed (the local cosmetics company also closed), I continued my trips to that cosmetics counter, then housed at Lord & Taylor. I had a source who worked there, the daughter of a friend. I called her Deep Neck.

The book became *Killer Pancake,* a title our youngest son, then in first grade, invented. After my editor said she loved it, our son, delighted, insisted that he also wanted to do the jacket art. He bolted to his room and later proudly handed me a drawing of a giant pancake with an angry face, running on stick legs and holding up a bloody knife with one stick arm, while a man a third the size of the pancake raced away in panic.

The publishing company declined his kind offering.

Now, as to Appetizers and Soups. These days, people usually serve one or the other, because each entails making a separate course that is not supposed to fill people up before dinner. So if you are having people over and are serving wine or drinks, it is a good idea to bring out several types of cheese with crackers if you are serving a soup. Or you can serve an appetizer. Catered events that feature drinks on empty stomachs can quickly descend to disaster. Sometimes *hosts* began imbibing (and fighting) before John and our catering team ever arrived. There are many reasons catering is challenging, and this is one of them.

Now, as to guacamole: When I began writing the Goldy books, there was no refrigerated guacamole available at the grocery store . . . much less one that you could freeze and then thaw and bring forth at serving time. You used to have to make it from scratch. The recipes that follow often call for making guacamole from scratch, but feel free to substitute the store-bought variety, as it is usually excellent. Still, if you want to make your own, go for it.

Holy Moly Guacamole

—CATERING TO NOBODY—

This is our family's gold standard guacamole recipe, and is obligatory for the watching of all televised sporting events. It is easy to make ahead, too, as the mayonnaise keeps the avocado from turning brown, and can be mixed in at serving time.

1 large or 2 small avocados

1 tablespoon picante sauce

1½ teaspoons fresh lemon juice

1 teaspoon freshly grated onion

¼ teaspoon salt

¼ cup mayonnaise

Corn chips or tortilla chips, for serving

Peel, pit, and mash the avocado(s). You should have 1 cup. Place the mashed avocado in a nonmetal bowl and mix in the picante sauce, lemon juice, onion, and salt until well blended. Spread the mayonnaise over the top to the edges, cover the bowl, and refrigerate. At serving time, uncover the bowl and thoroughly mix in the mayonnaise. Taste and add more picante sauce if desired. Serve with corn chips or tortilla chips.

Makes 1¼ cups

Nachos Schulz

—THE CEREAL MURDERS—

Tex-Mex food, which you will find throughout this book, is extremely popular in Colorado. This is the version our family enjoys when we watch football games and discuss why the Bronco offense is lined up in the spread, the I, the split, or the shotgun. (If you have a husband and three sons who love football, these are things you need to learn.) This dish is easy to prepare in advance, too. The bean mixture can be made ahead, covered with plastic wrap, and refrigerated; the cheese can be grated; the scallions, tomatoes, and olives chopped. You can make the guacamole while the nachos heat, or you can substitute store-bought guacamole.

Contents of one 15-ounce can chili beans in chili sauce, such as Kuner's

½ cup plus 1 tablespoon picante sauce

One 15-ounce bag tortilla chips

4 cups grated Cheddar cheese

1 avocado

1 tablespoon fresh lemon juice

1½ cups regular or light sour cream

1 tablespoon freshly grated onion

4 scallions, chopped (including tops)

1 cup canned pitted black olives, chopped

1 tomato, chopped

1. Preheat the oven to 400°F. Grease two 9 x 13-inch baking pans.

2. In a medium bowl, mash the beans with their sauce and ½ cup of the picante sauce until well mixed. Divide the tortilla chips between the baking pans, then spoon the bean mixture over them. Sprinkle the Cheddar on top. Bake for 10 minutes, or until the cheese is melted and the beans are bubbling.

3. Meanwhile, make the guacamole: Peel, pit, and scoop the avocado into a bowl. Mash it, then mash in the lemon juice, ½ cup of the sour cream, the grated onion, and remaining 1 tablespoon picante sauce.

4. Garnish the nachos with the guacamole, the remaining 1 cup sour cream, scallions, olives, and tomato.

Makes 6 to 8 servings

Bacon-Wrapped Artichokes with Dijon Cream Sauce

—THE MAIN CORPSE—

One learns quickly in catering that any appetizer including bacon is going to disappear quickly. Artichoke hearts can be difficult to deal with, since the chokes are hairy. So using the artichoke bottoms can make life easier. But if your grocery store does not sell artichoke bottoms, you can substitute canned artichoke hearts or the frozen variety that you steam until just tender. Always drain the artichokes and pat them dry.

6 artichoke bottoms (contents of one 14-ounce can; see Note), drained and patted dry, or 14 ounces artichoke hearts, drained and patted dry

9 slices center-cut bacon

3 tablespoons Dijon mustard

¼ cup half-and-half or heavy (whipping) cream

1. Preheat the oven to 400°F.

2. Cut each artichoke bottom into 6 equal wedges. (If you are using artichoke hearts, cut large ones in half, or use whole small ones. You need 36 pieces.) Cut each bacon slice into fourths. Wrap a piece of bacon around each piece of artichoke (it will not completely surround the piece of artichoke), secure with a toothpick, and place on a rimmed baking sheet.

3. Bake for 20 to 30 minutes, or until the bacon is crisp. Drain thoroughly on paper towels.

4. In a small bowl, stir together the mustard and cream and serve as a dipping sauce.

Makes 36

Note: Occasionally cans of artichoke bottoms will contain 5, rather than 6 pieces. In that case, use 7½ slices of bacon to make 30 appetizers.

Tom's Layered Mexican Dip

—PRIME CUT—

When you're going to someone else's *house to watch the football game, this is a good recipe to take. Enjoy it within 24 hours of making it, because the guacamole and tomato layers are perishable.*

- 2 avocados
- 2 tablespoons fresh lemon juice
- 2 tablespoons medium or hot picante sauce
- 2 tablespoons freshly grated onion
- 2½ cups regular or light sour cream
- Contents of one 16-ounce jar spicy black bean dip (or the contents of one 16-ounce can of refried beans, mixed with an additional ¼ cup picante)
- 2 tomatoes, chopped (about 3 cups)
- 6 scallions, chopped (including tops)
- 1½ cups sliced pitted black olives
- ½ pound Cheddar cheese, grated
- Tortilla chips, for serving

1. To make the guacamole, peel, pit, and scoop the avocados into a bowl. Mash with the lemon juice, picante sauce, grated onion, and ½ cup of the sour cream until the mixture is smooth. Set aside. (Or you can use 2 cups store-bought guacamole.)

2. Using a large platter or a 9 x 13-inch glass pan, place the bean dip into the bottom of the pan. Carefully smooth the guacamole on top of the bean layer. Place the sour cream on top of the guacamole layer.

3. Layer the tomatoes, scallions, olives, and Cheddar on top.

4. Chill the platter or pan and serve with tortilla chips.

Makes 24 servings

Mexican Egg Rolls with Spicy Guacamole Dipping Sauce

—TOUGH COOKIE—

This is a fancy, somewhat labor-intensive recipe, so you might want to reserve it for when you're having people over. Once again, you can make your life easier by using prepared refrigerated guacamole from the grocery store.

2 tablespoons vegetable oil, plus more for shallow-frying

1½ pounds chicken breast, trimmed of fat and chopped into ½-inch cubes

2½ cups chopped onions

1 to 2 tablespoons prepared dry chili mix, to taste

1 cup canned black beans, well drained

Contents of one 4-ounce can chopped green chiles

1 cup grated Cheddar cheese

1 cup grated Monterey jack cheese

½ cup finely chopped fresh cilantro

½ jalapeño chile, seeded and finely chopped

3 tablespoons picante sauce

1 teaspoon salt

16 egg-roll wrappers (from a 1-pound package)

Spicy Guacamole Dipping Sauce (recipe follows) or store-bought guacamole (see Note)

1. In a large skillet, heat the 2 tablespoons oil over medium-high heat until the oil ripples, and is hot but not smoking. Add the chicken and onions, stir well, then add the dry chili mixture and stir again. Stir for several minutes, until the onions turn translucent and the chicken has turned white and is just cooked. Remove the pan from the heat and add the beans, chiles, cheeses, cilantro, jalapeño, picante sauce, and salt.

2. On a very lightly floured surface, working with 1 egg-roll wrapper at a time, spoon ¼ cup of the filling into each egg roll. Roll up, following the package directions. Repeat for all 16 egg rolls.

3. Pour vegetable oil into a large skillet to a depth of ½ inch. Using a deep-fry thermometer that does not touch the bottom of the pan, heat the oil to 370°F. Place no more than three egg rolls at a time into the oil and fry until the egg rolls are golden brown, about 3 minutes per side. Drain on paper towels. Serve with the dipping sauce.

Makes 16 egg rolls

Spicy Guacamole Dipping Sauce

1 avocado

Juice of 1 lime

1 cup regular or light sour cream

½ cup medium-hot picante sauce

⅓ cup finely chopped fresh cilantro

1 tablespoon freshly grated onion

½ seeded jalapeño chile, finely chopped and whirled in a small blender or food processor

Peel, pit, and scoop the avocado into a bowl or food processor. Add the rest of the ingredients and either mash or process until well combined and smooth. Chill before serving.

Makes 1¾ cups

Note: If you are using store-bought refrigerated guacamole, use 1 cup of it. Then stir in ½ cup sour cream, ¼ cup picante sauce, ⅓ cup cilantro, freshly grated onion to taste, and one-quarter of a very finely chopped jalapeño. Stir well.

Chile Con Queso Dip

—CHOPPING SPREE—

This is Goldy's (and my) take on a very simple recipe, good for kids who like Tex-Mex food.

- 1 pound lean ground beef
- 12 ounces Velveeta, sharp Cheddar flavor or regular, cut into 1-inch cubes
- ½ cup medium picante sauce
- Corn chips and/or crudités, for serving

1. In a large skillet, cook the ground beef over medium-high heat, stirring frequently, until browned but not overcooked.

2. Add the Velveeta cubes, reduce the heat to medium-low, and stir until the Velveeta has melted. Turn the heat to low and add the picante sauce. Heat just until bubbling and serve with chips and/or crudités.

Makes 8 to 12 servings

Diamond Lovers' Hot Crab Dip

—CHOPPING SPREE—

People love substantial, hot dips that contain crab and artichokes; they seem very exotic. The buttered bread crumbs provide a crunchy foil for the creamy dip. I developed this recipe when Goldy was called upon to cater a jewelry show.

2 shallots, peeled and finely chopped

6 tablespoons (¾ stick) unsalted butter, divided

Contents of one 14-ounce can artichoke bottoms, drained and patted dry *or* contents of one 14-ounce can of artichoke hearts, drained and patted dry

24 ounces cream cheese, at room temperature

1 tablespoon Dijon mustard

⅓ cup regular or light sour cream or crème fraîche (for homemade crème fraîche, see page 127)

1 cup freshly grated Parmesan cheese

1 pound pasteurized crabmeat, flaked and picked over to remove any stray bits of cartilage

1. Preheat the oven to 350°F. Butter an attractive 2-quart gratin dish, preferably a dark-colored one (to contrast with the whiteness of the dip).

2. Place the shallots in a mini food processor and blend until juicy, less than 1 minute. In a medium-size skillet, melt 1 tablespoon of the butter over medium-low heat. Add the shallots and sauté just until the shallots begin to turn golden. This should take less than 10 minutes. Remove from the heat and set aside.

3. Chop the artichokes into ½-inch dice. Set aside until you are ready to assemble the dip.

4. In a large bowl, with an electric mixer, beat the cream cheese until very smooth. Add the mustard, sour cream or crème fraîche, and Parmesan and beat on low speed just until combined. Stir in the crab, shallots, and artichoke bottoms until well combined. Turn the crab mixture into the gratin dish.

- 2 cups fresh bread crumbs, preferably made from homemade bread (brioche is best)
- ½ cup finely chopped fresh parsley
- Corn chips and crackers, for serving

5. In a medium sauté pan, melt the remaining 5 tablespoons butter and stir in the bread crumbs. Cook and stir just until the butter is absorbed and the crumbs are beginning to turn golden. Remove from the heat, stir in the parsley, and distribute this mixture over the top of the crab dip.

6. Place the dip in the oven and bake for 30 minutes, or until the topping is golden brown and a small spoonful of dip scooped up from the center tastes very hot. Serve immediately with a choice of chips and crackers.

Makes 24 or more servings

Handcuff Croissants

—DOUBLE SHOT—

This is technically an hors d'oeuvre, because you serve individual portions (croissant halves) with a topping. You can use miniature croissants, if you like, and the portions will be smaller. The herbed crumb crust is divine. I thought the finished product looked like handcuffs, appropriate for a Goldy mystery.

4 large butter croissants, split horizontally (see Note)

1 cup mayonnaise

Contents of one 6½-ounce jar marinated artichoke hearts, drained, patted dry, and chopped

1 cup flaked pasteurized crabmeat, picked over to remove any stray bits of cartilage

⅓ cup freshly grated Parmesan cheese

⅓ cup grated Gruyère cheese

4 scallions, chopped (including tops)

1. Preheat the oven to 350°F. Line a baking sheet with a silicone baking mat.

2. Place the 8 croissant halves cut side up on the baking sheet. In a bowl, mix the mayonnaise, artichokes, crab, Parmesan, Gruyère, and scallions. Spread this mixture on top of the croissant halves.

Crumb crust:

2 tablespoons unsalted butter

1 garlic clove, crushed through a press

1 cup fresh bread crumbs

2 tablespoons finely chopped fresh parsley

¼ teaspoon dried rosemary, crushed

¼ teaspoon dried thyme

¼ teaspoon dried oregano

¼ teaspoon dried marjoram

For the crumb crust:

1. In a small skillet, melt the butter over low heat. Add the garlic and sweat (cook without browning) until translucent.

2. In a bowl, combine the bread crumbs, parsley, and dried herbs. Pour in the garlic and butter and mix well.

3. Top each croissant with the crumb mixture and bake for 15 to 20 minutes, or until heated through, with the crumb crust turning golden brown.

Makes 8 servings

Note: Croissants now come in three sizes: large, medium, and small (or "cocktail"). This recipe is tailored for the large croissants. However, if you can only get medium or cocktail-size croissants, merely adjust the portions as necessary, making sure that the mayonnaise mixture is spread to the edge of each croissant half.

Prosciutto Bites

—DARK TORT—

This is another croissant-based hors d'oeuvre. The crumbly, buttery flavor of the croissant balances perfectly with the prosciutto, plum preserves, and goat cheese.

- 4 medium butter croissants (see Note on page 25)
- ¾ cup best-quality plum preserves, drained of liquid, with plums reserved
- 6 slices prosciutto
- ½ cup soft goat cheese or cream cheese

Makes 32 small "bites"

1. Preheat the oven to 375°F.

2. Carefully slice the croissants horizontally. Place the 8 croissant halves, cut side up, on an ungreased baking sheet.

3. Spread each croissant half with 4 teaspoons of the strained preserves, spreading just to the edge.

4. Slice the reserved plums into fourths. Evenly divide them among the croissant halves, placing the plum slices at regular intervals on top of the preserves.

5. Trim the fat from the prosciutto slices. Place the prosciutto slices over the preserves and plums. Trim any overhang. Chop and crumble the goat cheese or cream cheese into ½-teaspoon portions. Evenly dot the prosciutto with the cheese.

6. Bake for 10 minutes, or until the cheese is just beginning to brown. Remove from the oven and allow to cool for at least 5 minutes. Using tongs, carefully place each croissant half onto a cutting board. Using a sharp serrated knife, cut each croissant half into four "bites."

Not-So-Skinny Spinach Dip

—THE WHOLE ENCHILADA—

At the request of one of our sons, I worked for months on perfecting a hot spinach dip. Unfortunately, the results never came out the same. Ever. This recipe appeared from several sources on the Internet. With very few adjustments, it tested perfectly, and Julian (!) put it here for your enjoyment.

1 tablespoon unsalted butter

1 tablespoon minced garlic

One 10-ounce package frozen chopped spinach, thawed, drained, and patted dry with paper towels

8 ounces cream cheese, at room temperature

One 10-ounce container refrigerated Alfredo sauce

⅓ cup finely grated Parmesan cheese

1 cup grated fontina cheese

Freshly ground black pepper

Chips and crackers, for serving

In a large sauté pan, melt the butter over low heat. Add the garlic and cook and stir until it is translucent. Add the spinach and cream cheese, stirring until very well combined. Add the Alfredo sauce, Parmesan, and fontina. Stir until the cheeses have melted and the mixture is hot. Taste and season carefully with pepper. Serve immediately with chips or crackers.

Makes about 3 cups

Hoisin Turkey with Roasted Pine Nuts in Lettuce Cups

—KILLER PANCAKE—

I first encountered stuffed lettuce cups at a fancy Vietnamese restaurant in Denver, now closed. I did some experimenting, and this recipe is the result. If you are on a low-carb diet, you can leave out the wild rice; just adjust the proportions of hoisin sauce and lettuce accordingly.

½ cup pine nuts

1 pound ground turkey

1 teaspoon cornstarch

¾ cup (7 ounces) hoisin sauce (available on the Asian foods aisle)

2½ cups cooked wild rice

8 large iceberg lettuce leaves

1. Preheat the oven to 400°F.

2. On a rimmed baking sheet, toast the pine nuts for 5 to 10 minutes, or until golden brown. Set aside.

3. In a large skillet, cook the ground turkey over medium-high heat, stirring, until it changes color and is cooked through. Drain well and return to the pan. Stir in the cornstarch and hoisin sauce. Heat and stir over medium heat until bubbling. Add the pine nuts and the wild rice and stir until heated through.

4. Spoon a generous ⅓ cup of the hot turkey mixture onto each lettuce leaf. Roll up and place, seam side down, on a platter. Serve immediately with tongs.

Serves 8 as an appetizer

Not-So-Secret Cheese Spread

This is a bonus recipe, not in any of the Goldy books. It began at a dinner with a member of my family who shall remain anonymous for his own safety. I asked what was in a recently arrived jar on the kitchen counter. My relative said it was a Cheddar spread that his whole family loved. It had been brought over by a friend who refused to share the recipe. And by the way, Diane, could you please figure out what's in it?

I said, "Got a spoon?"

Deciphering what was in that spread took more time than I would have thought. You do need to let it sit in the refrigerator several hours or overnight before serving.

½ cup flat wheat beer

½ pound best-quality grated mild Cheddar cheese

2 tablespoons finely chopped scallions (including tops)

2 tablespoons finely chopped fresh parsley

1 teaspoon mustard powder

10 to 14 drops Tabasco sauce

Crackers, celery sticks, cauliflowerets, and/or broccoli spears

1. Stir the beer before measuring to make sure it no longer has bubbles.

2. In a large bowl, stir together the Cheddar, scallions, parsley, mustard powder, lesser amount of hot sauce, and beer. Stir until completely mixed.

3. Cover the bowl with plastic wrap and refrigerate for 2 hours. Scoop some onto a plain cracker and taste. If you would like more heat, add the extra Tabasco sauce. Chill at least 2 more hours, or overnight.

4. Serve with crackers, celery sticks, cauliflowerets, and/or broccoli spears.

Low-Fat Chicken Stock

—KILLER PANCAKE—

When low-fat cooking was all the rage, readers begged me for low-fat recipes. I performed experiments over many months, and ended up throwing away most of the numerous failures. They just didn't pass the taste test. Now the scientific experts are telling us that it is simple carbohydrates, not fat, that are the problem. (My immediate thought upon learning this was, You mean I drank all that disgusting fat-free milk for nothing?*) That said, homemade chicken stock—which you take the time to de-fat—is an absolutely essential part of any serious cook's kitchen. For this recipe, I now use all canned chicken broth as the liquid in the stock. I have to pour the finished stock into two or sometimes three large metal or glass bowls, then let it cool, then find room in one or two refrigerators. (When our old refrigerator became too small for our growing needs, we put it in the garage, which has proven very handy for extra refrigeration.) Thorough chilling will make the fat solidify so it can be lifted off. Stir the de-fatted stock before you use it or before pouring it into plastic freezer containers.*

2 tablespoons extra-virgin olive oil

1 large onion, chopped

1 carrot, chopped

3 to 3½ pounds bone-in, skin-on chicken drumsticks and thighs

12⅓ cups chicken broth (contents of two 49.5-ounce cans) plus 12⅓ cups spring water (or use 25 cups canned chicken broth)

1. On the stove, heat a very large stockpot over medium heat. (If you do not have a very large stockpot, you can divide the ingredients and make the stock in 2 stockpots.) Add the oil and heat until it shimmers. Toss in the onion and carrot, reduce the heat to low, and cover the pot. Cook, stirring frequently, until the onion is translucent. (This can take up to 15 minutes.) Increase the heat to medium-high. Add the chicken, and cook, stirring frequently, until the chicken skin is browned on both sides, about 5 minutes. Pour in the chicken broth and water,

- 1 celery stalk with leaves, cut up
- 2 bay leaves
- 2 teaspoons dried thyme, or more to taste
- ½ teaspoon freshly ground black pepper, or more to taste

add the celery and bay leaves, and bring to a boil. Boil for 5 minutes. As foam accumulates, skim it off and discard.

2. Reduce the heat to a simmer and stir in the thyme and pepper. Simmer, partially covered, for 2 hours. Add water as necessary to keep the chicken covered with liquid.

3. Remove the pot from the heat. Remove the chicken and allow it to cool, then pick the meat from the bones and reserve for another use. Strain the stock and discard the vegetables and bay leaves. *Cool to room temperature.*

4. Cover and refrigerate overnight, or until the fat has congealed in a single layer. (This can take up to 2 days.) Lift the layer of fat from the stock and discard. Store the stock for 2 or 3 days in the refrigerator or freeze in covered plastic containers for longer storage.

Makes about 25 cups

Models' Mushroom Soup

—PRIME CUT—

This is a hearty soup, lusciously thickened with puréed vegetables.

5 tablespoons unsalted butter, divided

1 large carrot, chopped

1 large onion, chopped

2 celery stalks, chopped

8 ounces fresh button mushrooms, cleaned, trimmed, and thinly sliced

4 tablespoons all-purpose flour

6 cups chicken stock, preferably homemade (page 30)

2 tablespoons chopped fresh thyme

1 tablespoon chopped fresh marjoram

2 tablespoons heavy (whipping) cream

6 tablespoons dry white vermouth

Salt and freshly ground black pepper

1. In a large skillet, melt 2 tablespoons of the butter over medium-low heat. Add the carrot, onion, and celery and cook, covered, stirring frequently, until the vegetables soften, 15 to 25 minutes. Set aside to cool.

2. In a small skillet, melt 1 tablespoon of the butter over medium-low heat. Add the mushrooms and cook briefly, until they are cooked through and begin to yield some juice. This takes less than 5 minutes. Set the mushrooms aside.

3. In a blender, purée the cooked carrot, onion, celery, and any accumulated liquid.

4. In a large skillet, melt the remaining 2 tablespoons butter over low heat. Stir in the flour and cook this paste, stirring constantly, until the flour bubbles. Slowly whisk in the stock. Increase the heat to medium. Cook and stir until hot and thickened, about 10 minutes. Stir in the thyme, marjoram, cream, mushrooms, vermouth, and puréed vegetables until hot and bubbling, about 5 minutes. Season with salt and pepper to taste. Serve immediately.

Makes 6 servings

Homemade Cream of Mushroom Soup

—CRUNCH TIME—

This is one of our family's favorite soups. It combines the complex flavors of wild and fresh mushrooms. Homemade chicken stock makes it sing, and the cream and sherry make it fancy.

1 ounce dried wild mushrooms (porcini, cremini, morels, or a mixture)

2½ cups spring water

8 tablespoons (1 stick) unsalted butter, plus an additional 2 tablespoons, if needed

1 shallot, peeled and finely diced

8 ounces fresh button mushrooms, cleaned, trimmed, patted dry with paper towels, and finely diced

7 tablespoons all-purpose flour

4 cups (1 quart) homemade chicken stock (page 30)

2 cups heavy (whipping) cream

¼ cup dry sherry

Sea salt or kosher salt and freshly ground black pepper

1. Place the dried mushrooms in a large heatproof bowl. Bring the water to a boil and pour it over the dried mushrooms. Allow to sit for 30 minutes. Remove the reconstituted mushrooms with a slotted spoon. Remove the stems and discard. Pat the mushrooms dry, finely chop, and set aside. Strain the mushroom soaking liquid through dampened cheesecloth or a sieve lined with a paper coffee filter into a bowl. You should have about 2 cups of mushroom liquid. Set aside.

2. In a stockpot, melt the 8 tablespoons butter over low heat. Add the shallots and fresh mushrooms and cook, stirring frequently, until soft, about 10 minutes. Increase the heat to medium, sprinkle in the flour, and stir constantly until the mixture bubbles and the flour is cooked, about 3 minutes. (If the mixture is completely dry, add up to 2 extra tablespoons of butter. Stir the mixture until the butter is completely melted, then stir and cook until the flour is cooked.)

3. Add the chicken stock and reserved mushroom liquid, increase the heat to medium-high, and cook, stirring constantly, until the mixture thickens and bubbles. Reduce the heat and add the chopped wild mushrooms, the cream, sherry, and salt and pepper to taste. Cook, stirring frequently, for another 15 minutes, to blend the flavors. Remove from the heat to cool slightly.

4. Working in batches, purée the soup in a blender. Place the puréed batches into a large heatproof bowl. When the soup is completely puréed, pour it back into the stockpot, taste, and correct the seasoning. Bring the soup back to a simmer and serve.

6 to 8 servings

Rainy Season Chicken Soup

—THE MAIN CORPSE—

This soup is for those times when you need a good chicken soup for a sick child, neighbor, or friend. The fideo *makes it exotic. Don't worry about adding dry white vermouth, as the alcohol cooks out. Feel free to use regular sour cream, as we now know it's not the sour cream that makes you fat, it's the pasta . . . but kids will look askance at you if you give them what is basically a glammed-up chicken noodle soup, with no noodles. So go ahead and put them in.*

2 dried porcini mushrooms

2 tablespoons butter

2 leeks, white part only, split, rinsed, and diced

1 medium carrot, diced

1 medium onion, diced

1 large celery stalk, diced

2 boneless, skinless chicken breast halves

2 tablespoons all-purpose flour

2 tablespoons dry white vermouth

4 cups chicken stock, preferably homemade (page 30)

1 cup regular or light sour cream

1 cup *fideo* (fine egg noodle strands)

Salt and freshly ground black pepper

1. In a small saucepan, bring 1 cup spring water to a boil and drop in the porcini mushrooms. (If you live in a place with bad-tasting tap water, use spring water.) Cook uncovered over medium-high heat for 10 minutes. Drain the mushrooms, pat them dry, and thinly slice. Set aside.

2. In a large sauté pan, melt the butter over low heat. Add the leeks, carrot, onion, celery, and chicken, stir gently, cover, and cook for 5 minutes. Uncover, stir the vegetables, turn the chicken, and check for doneness. (The chicken should be about half done.) Cover and cook until chicken is *just* done—not overdone—about another 5 minutes. Remove the chicken from the pan and set aside to cool.

3. Sprinkle the flour over the melted butter, vegetables, and pan juices and stir to cook the flour over low heat for 2 minutes. Slowly add the white vermouth and 2 cups of the chicken stock. Stir and cook until bubbling and thickened. Add the sour cream very slowly, and allow to cook gently while you cut the chicken into thin, bite-size pieces.

4. In a large skillet, bring the remaining 2 cups stock to a boil. Add the *fideo* and cook 4 minutes, or until almost done. Do not drain. Slowly add the noodle mixture to the hot vegetables and sour cream mixture. Add the chicken and the mushrooms and bring back to a boil. Serve immediately.

Makes 4 servings

Chapter 2

Eggs and Cheese *or* My Agent Is Still a Vegetarian

Highbrow (and even some lowbrow) food writers disparage quiche. But anyone who enjoys lunch at the neighborhood bistro will tell you that the Quiche of the Day has remained a menu staple for over thirty years. People, including real men, *like* a rich mélange of eggs, cream, cheese, and other ingredients.

I came by quiches in California, where an older student in one class—she was French and was married to a professor in the French Department—invited some classmates to lunch. As I'd learned from observing Mrs. Jones, I helped out in the kitchen beforehand: gathering dishes, silverware, and glasses, as my friend whisked eggs with cream and poured it over chopped cooked bacon and grated cheese already in a crust. Not long afterward, we all dug into a velvety, cheesy, crunchy concoction our hostess told us was Quiche Lorraine. Forty-plus years later, I still remember it.

Yes, quiches became overdone, because they were made poorly, contained inferior ingredients, or were forced to sit until they (and we) wept. But with a little attention, that simultaneously feathery and hearty dish is still scrumptious.

So . . . once I started taking my agent's admonition to create more vegetarian dishes, I began to work on quiches and other egg and cheese dishes. The ones in this chapter became our family's, and thus Goldy's, favorites. I find others delicious, such as Julia Child's Quiche au Roquefort, but when I tried to develop a blue cheese pizza, our family rebelled. I had to palm off that particular creation on an obliging neighbor.

Now, the parallel to writing is this: A similar dynamic can take place with character development (which does not mean you are palming off anything on an unsuspecting neighbor). *Au contraire,* sometimes you create a recipe or character whom you love, but no one else does (see: Blue Cheese Pizza). Say you think the character is charmingly naïve. Your critique group (your writing family) says that person is boring, stupid, or both. Other times, you create a character you think is, well, enthusiastic. The group unanimously says, "Bombast and rudeness don't work."

Okay, lesson learned. But there is something else I learned from paying attention to my friend making the Quiche Lorraine. Observing one's own emotional reaction to people can help create characters. My example here is General Farquhar, an unplanned character who walked onto the pages of *Dying for Chocolate.*

The story of the inspiration for the unplanned character begins with my enjoyment of discovering the etymology of commonly used words. Take *glamour.* We think of a person as glamorous if she or he is chic, or dresses fashionably. But a *glamour* originally meant a spell. By those lights, a person who is truly glamorous casts a spell.

So, if you're in the writing business, it behooves you to pay attention when a person you encounter seems to cast a spell. Race home, write it all down, see how it works, rewrite it, then rewrite once more. You might have something you can get past your writers' group.

How this relates to my recently learned etymology of *glamour* (and General Farquhar) came about in 1990, when I attended my first mystery convention, Malice Domestic, in Bethesda, Maryland. My parents were staying in Washington and took me out for lunch at the Army-Navy Club.

We were enjoying a pleasant (read: nonpolitical) conversation when my father, a retired admiral, suddenly said, "Come here, there's someone I want you to meet."

I am sorry to say that I did not reply, "Sure, Dad!" My father and I were not of the same political persuasion. I had met enough of his friends to know that they weren't likely to be of my political persuasion, either.

So instead I said, "Please. I don't want to meet any of your friends."

My father lowered his formidable eyebrows and said, "Don't embarrass me."

My mother sighed.

At that point, I was already embarrassing Jim's and my adolescent son. Now I was embarrassing my father. It seemed I couldn't win.

So I followed my father—you'll have to imagine the clinking of silver, china, and crystal—to the far side of the dining room, where my father said, "Colonel North, I'd like you to meet my daughter, Diane."

I blinked and blinked again as Oliver North very graciously responded to my father's introduction. He asked me a question or two—he and Jim had been a year apart at the Naval Academy, as it turned out—but all I could say was "Uh, uh, uh."

It was hard for me to find my voice, because Oliver North was glamorous in the old-fashioned sense: He cast a spell. I finally answered one of his questions regarding the Academy. ("What company was your husband in?" Oliver North asked. "The thirtieth!" I finally replied.) But I went home thinking, *I have to use this.* My emotional reaction to this spellbinding man, my theory went, could create a character.

And thus was General Farquhar born. Goldy takes refuge in the Farquhars' house when the Jerk begins stalking her. After the Jerk argues with Goldy and begins throwing clay pots at the Farquhars' house, the general sneaks up silently behind him, grasps him in a stranglehold, and torques his head around to force eye contact. General Farquhar warns the Jerk to keep away from Goldy, and adds,

"I'll show you how the Special Forces can kill people without making any noise. Is that clear?"

General Farquhar is a real man. And he eats quiche.

Note on equipment: Some of these recipes call for using a 10-inch pie plate, but these can be hard to find these days. In its place, I now use an Emile Henry 11-inch pie plate, and no, I don't get any money from Emile Henry. It works perfectly in place of the old 10-inch pie plate.

Chile Relleno Torta

—DYING FOR CHOCOLATE—

I first tasted a recipe similar to this at a Mexican restaurant in Denver. The flavors of chiles rellenos melded with a creamy custard? Heaven! I begged the chef for the recipe. But what she gave me didn't quite work, maybe because it was for a hundred people, and what became Goldilocks' Gourmet Spinach Soup had already proven I had issues with food fractions. (A typical dialogue in our kitchen used to go like this: Diane: "Jim, what's three-fourths of 3½ cups?" *Jim:* "Diane, you should be able to do that in your head." *We don't have those kinds of conversations anymore, because even I can figure out how to use a calculator on a smartphone.) Anyway, I was confident I could come up with a dish that approximated the tastes I wanted. Thankfully, the family was willing to try anything Tex-Mex. In this dish, the picante sauce rises to the top of the custard, giving, once the torta is cut into, a scumbled surface—one readers of the Goldy series know can be handily and undetectably laced with poison.*

½ pound Cheddar cheese, grated

½ pound Monterey jack cheese, grated

5 large eggs

⅓ cup all-purpose flour

1⅔ cups half-and-half

Contents of one 4-ounce can diced green chiles, drained

¼ cup picante sauce

1. Preheat the oven to 375°F. Butter a 10- or 11-inch pie plate.

2. Mix the Cheddar and jack cheeses and spread evenly in the pie plate. In a bowl, beat the eggs, add the flour slowly, and then beat in the half-and-half. If the mixture is lumpy, strain it. Pour the egg mixture over the cheeses in the pie plate. Carefully spoon the chiles over the surface, then spoon the picante sauce over all. Bake for 45 minutes, or until the center is set.

Makes 8 to 10 servings

Crustless Jarlsberg Quiche

—DYING FOR CHOCOLATE—

This is technically a ramequin, *which is also one of the names for an oval-shaped casserole in which you can bake your recipe. The virtue of this dish is that it can be assembled in advance and refrigerated.*

8 tablespoons (1 stick) unsalted butter, plus more for the pan

½ cup all-purpose flour

1½ cups whole milk

11 ounces cream cheese, at room temperature

2½ cups (24 ounces) small-curd cottage cheese

1 teaspoon baking powder

1 teaspoon Dijon mustard

1 teaspoon kosher salt

9 large eggs

3¼ cups grated Jarlsberg or Gruyère cheese (¾ pound)

⅓ cup freshly grated Parmesan cheese

Makes 8 servings

1. Preheat the oven to 350°F. Butter a 9 x 13-inch glass baking dish or a 10-cup capacity gratin pan.

2. In a large skillet, melt the 8 tablespoons of butter over medium-low heat. Add the flour and stir just until the mixture bubbles. Slowly add the milk, stirring constantly. Stir this cream sauce until it thickens. Add the softened cream cheese and whisk the mixture well, until smooth. Set aside to cool.

3. In a medium bowl, stir together the cottage cheese, baking powder, mustard, and salt. In a large bowl, beat the eggs well, then beat in the cottage cheese mixture. Slowly beat in the cream sauce, then thoroughly incorporate the Jarlsberg and Parmesan. Stir well to combine. Pour into the prepared baking dish. At this point you can cool the dish, cover with plastic wrap, and place in the refrigerator.

4. If you have refrigerated the dish, allow it to come to room temperature before baking. Bake for 35 to 45 minutes, or until puffed and golden brown.

Julian's Cheese Manicotti

—THE CEREAL MURDERS—

This was another recipe that I thought would be super for my vegetarian agent. I threw myself into making manicotti—every night. After five nights of this, the family rebelled. "No more manicotti," they cried. So I started bringing it to nighttime church meetings, where everyone always seemed to arrive both irritated and hungry. Julian's Cheese Manicotti, in its final form, soothed tempers and got meetings finished.

Sauce:

2 tablespoons extra-virgin olive oil

1 large onion, chopped

4 garlic cloves, crushed through a press (preferable) or minced

Contents of two 6-ounce cans tomato paste

2 tablespoons finely chopped fresh oregano or 1½ teaspoons dried oregano, crushed

1 small bay leaf

1 teaspoon salt

½ teaspoon freshly ground black pepper

Preheat the oven to 350°F.

For the sauce:
In a large sauté pan, heat the oil over medium heat. Add the onion and gently sauté, stirring frequently, until the onion is translucent, about 5 minutes. Reduce the heat to low and stir in the garlic. Cook slowly until the garlic is also translucent. Add the tomato paste and stir until well combined. Fill each of the tomato paste cans 2 times with spring water and add to the pan. Add the oregano, bay leaf, salt, and pepper and let the sauce simmer while you prepare the manicotti and filling.

Pasta:

1 teaspoon extra-virgin olive oil

14 manicotti noodles

Filling:

1½ cups ricotta cheese

6 large eggs

¾ pound fontina cheese, grated

¼ pound mozzarella cheese, grated

⅔ cup freshly grated Parmesan cheese, divided

6 tablespoons unsalted butter, at room temperature

1 teaspoon salt

¾ teaspoon freshly ground black pepper

2 tablespoons finely chopped fresh basil

For the pasta:
Bring a large pot of spring water to a boil. Add the olive oil and drop in the manicotti. Cook just until al dente, according to package directions. Drain in a colander and run cold water over the manicotti just for a moment, to cool it.

For the filling:
1. In a large bowl, with an electric mixer, beat the ricotta with the eggs until combined. Add the fontina and mozzarella, ⅓ cup of the Parmesan, and the butter, and beat until combined. Add the salt, pepper, and basil and beat on low speed just until everything is combined.

2. Butter two 9 x 13-inch glass baking dishes. Gently fill the cooked manicotti with the cheese mixture and arrange in the dishes. Cover the pasta in each dish with the sauce. Sprinkle half of the remaining ⅓ cup Parmesan on top of the sauce in each dish. Bake for 20 minutes, or until the cheese is throughtly melted and the sauce is bubbling.

Makes 7 servings

Mexican Pizzas

—THE LAST SUPPERS—

This was one of those recipes I came up with when I wanted to give a Tex-Mex twist to Pizza Margherita, which is the tomato sauce with mozzarella pizza we primarily know in America. Baking these pizzas in springform pans was a no-brainer, and made them look pretty, too. With Schulz's Guacamole Salad (page 82), they make a complete Tex-Mex meal. Our family of five polished off four of these in one sitting.

Two ¼-ounce envelopes active dry yeast (4½ teaspoons)

2 cups warm spring water

1 teaspoon sugar

1 teaspoon salt

1 tablespoon plus 1 teaspoon extra-virgin olive oil

5 to 6 cups all-purpose or bread flour

Extra-virgin olive oil and cornmeal, for the pans

1⅓ cups picante sauce

6 cups grated Cheddar cheese

1. In a large bowl, sprinkle the yeast over the warm water. Add the sugar, stir, and set aside until the mixture is bubbly, about 10 minutes. Stir in the salt and olive oil. Beat in 5 cups of the flour, then add as much extra flour as needed to make a dough that is not too sticky to knead. Knead on a floured surface until the dough is smooth and satiny, 5 to 10 minutes. (Or place the dough in the bowl of a stand mixer fitted with the dough hook and knead until the dough cleans the sides of the bowl, about 5 minutes.) Place the dough in an oiled bowl, turn to oil the top, cover with a kitchen towel, and let rise in a warm place until doubled in bulk, about 1 hour.

2. Preheat the oven to 425°F.

3. Brush a little olive oil over the bottom and sides of four 9- or 10-inch springform pans. Sprinkle cornmeal over the oiled bottoms and sides. Punch the dough down and divide it into quarters. Press each piece of dough out to fit the bottom of a pan, making a small raised rim around the edges. Spread ⅓ cup picante sauce on top of the dough rounds and top each pizza with 1½ cups Cheddar. Bake for 10 to 20 minutes, or until the dough is cooked through and the cheese is completely melted. Remove the sides of the pans, and cut each pizza into wedges.

Makes four 9- or 10-inch pizzas

Quiche Me Quick

—CHOPPING SPREE—

This is my go-to quiche. The trick to avoiding soggy crusts for any pie with a baked filling is to bake the crust in advance. Buy a roll of parchment paper at your grocery store. Cut out a piece somewhat larger than your unbaked crust, then carefully place the parchment on top of the pie shell, fill it with uncooked beans or uncooked rice, then bake the crust for anywhere from 5 to 15 minutes in a 350°F oven. Remove the parchment and the beans or rice before proceeding with the recipe. This is the recipe that is most like that original Quiche Lorraine I tasted all those years ago. If you want the dish to be vegetarian, omit the bacon.

7 slices thick-sliced bacon

4 ounces Gruyère cheese, grated

One 8-inch pie shell, baked (a baked 9-inch frozen pie crust is fine)

3 large eggs

1 cup heavy (whipping) cream

¼ teaspoon freshly grated nutmeg

1. In a skillet, if you are using the bacon, cook it until crisp. Drain thoroughly and pat with paper towels. Cut each slice of bacon into 4 equal pieces.

2. Evenly distribute first the bacon, then the Gruyère, over the pie crust. Set aside.

3. Preheat the oven to 350°F. In a large bowl, beat the eggs until they are thoroughly combined. Beat in the cream, then sprinkle on the nutmeg and stir until combined. Pour this mixture over the bacon and cheese, and set carefully in the oven.

4. Bake for 30 to 40 minutes, or until the quiche has puffed and browned slightly and is set in the middle. (Check with a spoon to make sure there is no uncooked liquid in the center of the quiche.) Serve immediately.

Makes 6 servings

Tomato-Brie Pie

—THE MAIN CORPSE—

Baking Brie or Camembert with fresh tomatoes and basil is one of my favorite things to do in summer. This recipe is also rich with eggs and cheese. A flight attendant once confessed to me that when she was on a particularly bumpy flight, she sat with a hysterical passenger and read her this recipe, which calmed both of them. Such is the power of comfort food.

Crust:

1¾ cups all-purpose flour

¾ teaspoon sugar

¼ teaspoon salt

¼ cup lard, cut into pieces and chilled

6 tablespoons cold unsalted butter, cut into pieces

1 to 3 tablespoons iced spring water

Filling:

1½ pounds (5 medium) ripe tomatoes, trimmed but not peeled, cut into eight equal wedges, seed pockets removed

5 ounces Brie cheese, rind scraped off, cut into small cubes

Butter a 9-inch pie plate.

For the crust:

1. In the bowl of a food processor fitted with the steel blade, combine the flour, sugar, and salt and process 5 seconds. Add the lard and process until the mixture is like cornmeal, about 10 seconds. Add the butter and process until the mixture resembles large crumbs, about 10 seconds. Add the water 1 tablespoon at a time, pulsing quickly, adding just enough so the mixture holds together. Roll the dough out between sheets of wax paper to fit into the pie plate. Prick the dough and flute the edges.

2. Chill the plate for at least 1 hour, but for no longer than 4 hours.

3. When you are ready to bake the pie, preheat the oven to 350°F. Remove from the refrigerator and place a large piece of parchment over the dough. Weigh down the parchment with uncooked rice, dried beans, or ceramic pie weights.

2 ounces best-quality fresh mozzarella cheese, cut into small cubes

1 ounce Fontinella cheese, cut into small cubes

⅓ cup chopped fresh basil

3 large eggs

⅓ cup heavy (whipping) cream

⅓ cup milk, preferably whole

4. Bake the crust for 5 to 7 minutes, or until it is an even, pale gold. Remove the parchment and the rice, beans, or weights. Set aside on a rack to cool slightly. (Leave the oven on.)

For the filling:

1. Drain the tomatoes thoroughly on paper towels. Place the cheese cubes evenly around the pie crust. Place the tomatoes on top of the cheese and top with the basil.

2. In a bowl, beat together the eggs, cream, and milk. Pour this mixture over the tomatoes, basil, and cheese. Bake for 35 to 50 minutes, or until the center is set. Let cool for 10 minutes before serving.

Makes 6 servings

Provençal Pizza

—THE MAIN CORPSE—

One ¼-ounce envelope active dry yeast (2¼ teaspoons)

1 cup warm spring water

½ teaspoon sugar

½ teaspoon salt

2 teaspoons extra-virgin olive oil

2½ to 3 cups all-purpose or bread flour

½ cup prepared pesto

¾ pound ripe tomatoes, thinly sliced and seed pockets removed

3½ ounces chèvre (French goat cheese)

4 ounces best-quality fresh mozzarella cheese, grated

Makes 6 servings

1. In a large bowl, sprinkle the yeast over the warm water. Add the sugar, stir, and set aside until the mixture is bubbly, about 10 minutes. Stir in the salt and olive oil. Beat in 2½ cups of the flour, then add as much extra flour as needed to make a dough that is not too sticky to knead. Knead on a floured surface until the dough is smooth and satiny. (Or place the dough in the bowl of a stand mixer fitted with the dough hook and knead until the dough cleans the sides of the bowl, about 5 minutes.) Place the dough in an oiled bowl, turn to oil the top, cover with a kitchen towel, and let rise in a warm place until doubled in bulk, about 1 hour.

2. Preheat the oven to 425°F.

3. Brush a little olive oil over the bottom and sides of a 10 x 15-inch baking pan or rimmed baking sheet. Punch the dough down and press it into the bottom of the pan. Spread the pesto over the dough. Lay the tomato slices in even rows over the pesto. Dot the surface evenly with pieces of chèvre, and sprinkle the mozzarella over the entire surface. Bake for 15 to 25 minutes, or until the mozzarella is bubbling and the dough has cooked through. Cut into 12 squares. Serve immediately.

Doll Show Shrimp and Eggs

—THE GRILLING SEASON—

Okay, this has shrimp in it. Many vegetarians I know eat seafood. Julian eats seafood. But you can leave it out if you want. This is a hearty dish for breakfast, brunch, or lunch.

1 teaspoon Old Bay seasoning

8 frozen large easy-peel shrimp

3 tablespoons butter

¼ cup chopped leek, white part only

⅓ cup chopped fresh tomato (seeded)

6 large eggs, lightly beaten

Salt and freshly ground black pepper

3 ounces cream cheese, cut into ¼-inch cubes

1. Preheat the oven to 400°F.

2. In a saucepan, bring 2 cups water to a boil. Add the Old Bay and the shrimp. Cook the shrimp until *just pink,* usually less than 2 minutes. *Do not overcook.* Drain and peel the shrimp, then cut each one in half.

3. In an ovenproof skillet, melt the butter over medium-low heat. Add the leek and tomato and sauté gently until the leek is softened, about 5 minutes. Pour the eggs into the leek-tomato mixture, season with salt and freshly ground pepper to taste, and cook over medium-low heat, stirring occasionally to prevent browning, until the eggs have almost set but still have some liquid left. Stir in the shrimp and cream cheese.

4. Transfer to the oven and bake for about 10 minutes, or until the cream cheese is melted and the eggs are completely set.

Makes 2 or 3 servings

Collector's Camembert Pie

—THE GRILLING SEASON—

This dish also has shrimp in it, which you can leave out and still have a hearty vegetarian entrée. Yes, the brioche topping makes it time-consuming. But it is a lovely, intensely flavorful dish that is a real hit at holiday potlucks. Your pals will thank you.

Crust:

⅓ cup milk, preferably whole

2 tablespoons butter

2 teaspoons sugar

One ¼-ounce envelope active dry yeast (2¼ teaspoons)

¾ teaspoon salt

1 large egg, lightly beaten

1½ teaspoons vegetable oil

1¼ cups all-purpose or bread flour, or more as needed

Filling:

1 tablespoon Old Bay seasoning

36 large easy-peel shrimp (1½ pounds)

½ pound fresh asparagus, tough ends trimmed

1 pound canned artichoke bottoms or an equivalent amount of artichoke hearts

1 pound fresh tomatoes

Two 12-ounce wheels Camembert cheese

1 cup mayonnaise

⅔ cup freshly grated Parmesan cheese

2 teaspoons pressed garlic (4 to 6 cloves crushed through a press)

¾ teaspoon dried thyme, crumbled

¾ teaspoon dried rosemary, crumbled

¾ teaspoon dried oregano, crumbled

For the crust:

1. In a saucepan, heat the milk, butter, and sugar until the butter is melted. Remove from the heat and set aside to cool to 105° to 115°F (use a digital thermometer to check the temperature). Transfer the warm milk mixture to a large bowl, stir in the yeast, and let it stand for 10 minutes. Stir in the salt, egg, and oil. Add the flour ¼ cup at a time, stirring well, until each addition is thoroughly incorporated and the dough holds together.

2. Turn the dough out onto a lightly floured board and knead for 10 minutes, adding small amounts of flour if necessary, until the dough is smooth and satiny. (Or use a stand mixer fitted with the dough hook and knead for the same amount of time.) Place the dough in an oiled bowl and turn it once to oil the top. Cover the bowl with a kitchen towel and set aside to rise at room temperature until tripled in bulk, about 2 hours.

3. Punch the dough down, roll it into a rectangle about 9 by 13 inches, and place it in a jumbo-size (2-gallon) zippered plastic bag. Keep the dough in a rectangular shape. Refrigerate for up to 6 hours.

4. When you begin to prepare the pie, remove the bag from the refrigerator to allow the dough to come to room temperature.

For the filling:

1. In a large skillet, bring 1 quart of spring water to a boil and add the Old Bay. Add the shrimp and cook until *just pink,* usually no more than 2 minutes. *Do not overcook.* Drain the shrimp and discard the cooking water. Peel the shrimp and set aside.

2. Cut the asparagus spears crosswise into thirds. Drain the artichoke bottoms, trim them of any rough edges, and cut each artichoke bottom into sixths (or do the same with artichoke hearts). Core the tomatoes, cut each into 8 wedges, and remove the seed pockets. Scrape most of the rind off the Camembert and slice each wheel into 16 wedges. (You will have 32 small wedges of cheese.) In a small bowl, thoroughly combine the mayonnaise, Parmesan, garlic, and dried herbs.

3. Preheat the oven to 350°F. Butter a 9 x 13-inch glass baking dish.

Assemble the pie:

1. Place half of the shrimp in the bottom of the baking dish (3 rows of 6 shrimp each), then evenly layer half the asparagus, half the tomatoes, half the artichoke bottoms, and half the Camembert over the shrimp. Using a small spoon, dab half of the mayonnaise mixture over the Camembert layer. Repeat the layers in this order: asparagus, tomatoes, artichokes, Camembert, and shrimp.

2. Carefully place the brioche dough over the top and cut several vents to allow steam to escape.

3. Bake for 45 minutes, or until the crust is golden brown and the filling is very hot and bubbling. Allow to cool 5 to 10 minutes before serving.

Makes 6 to 8 servings

Savory Florentine Cheesecake

—PRIME CUT—

This is an elegant take on spinach quiche. If you desire a bit more spice, try adding more Dijon mustard and cayenne pepper than the recipe calls for. This is what I did for another of those church potlucks, where I always find an eager bunch of hungry tasters.

Serve with sliced fresh fruit, a green salad with vinaigrette dressing, and hot rolls.

2 cups bread crumbs that have been dried in the oven, preferably made from brioche bread

8 tablespoons (1 stick) unsalted butter, melted

One 10-ounce package frozen chopped spinach

24 ounces cream cheese, at room temperature

¼ cup heavy (whipping) cream

1 teaspoon Dijon mustard, or more to taste

½ teaspoon salt

4 large eggs

1¼ cups grated Gruyère cheese (about 4 ounces)

¼ cup freshly grated Parmesan cheese

¼ cup chopped scallions (including tops)

¼ teaspoon paprika

¼ teaspoon cayenne pepper, or more to taste

1. Preheat the oven to 350°F. Butter a 9-inch springform pan.

2. In a bowl, combine the bread crumbs and melted butter and press on the bottom and sides of the springform pan. Bake for 8 to 12 minutes, or until very lightly browned. Set aside to cool. (Leave the oven on.)

3. Cook the spinach according to the package directions, place in a strainer, and press out all the liquid. In a large bowl, with an electric mixer, beat together the cream cheese, heavy cream, mustard, and salt until smooth. Add the eggs, one at a time, and beat well after each addition.

Add the spinach, grated cheeses, scallions, paprika, and cayenne. Beat on low speed until well combined.

4. Pour the mixture into the prepared crust and bake for about 1 hour 5 minutes, or until the filling is set and browned. Cool for 15 minutes on a rack.

Makes 12 servings

Huevos Palacios

—STICKS AND SCONES—

The Boulder Chili that accompanies this dish is not vegetarian. You can use vegetarian chili, if you wish.

- 1 cup Boulder Chili (recipe follows) or canned vegetarian chili (if making all-vegetarian)
- 4 large eggs
- ¼ cup heavy (whipping) cream
- ½ teaspoon salt
- ¼ teaspoon freshly ground black pepper
- 2 tablespoons unsalted butter
- ½ cup regular or light sour cream
- 1 cup grated Cheddar cheese
- 1 medium tomato, seed pockets removed, and chopped
- 2 scallions, chopped (including tops)

1. If using the Boulder Chili, make it and allow it to cool.

2. In a bowl, lightly beat the eggs with the cream, salt, and pepper. In a broilerproof nonstick medium skillet, melt the butter over medium-low heat. When the pan is hot, pour in the egg mixture. Cook over low heat until the edges begin to set. With a heatproof silicone spatula, gently push the edges of the cooked egg into the center of the pan, using a minimum number of strokes. Tilt the pan so that the uncooked portion of egg flows out into the bottom of the pan, making an almost-even overall layer of egg.

3. Position a rack 6 inches from the heat and preheat the broiler.

4. In a small bowl, mix the sour cream and Cheddar and set aside. When the eggs are about halfway done (i.e., when they are about half liquid and half solid), spoon on the chili in 3 spokelike lines that divide the eggs into 6 equal sections. (The eggs will look like a pie.) Scatter the chopped tomato and scallions between the

lines of chili. Carefully spoon the sour cream–Cheddar mixture on top of the chili spokes. Do not worry if some spreads off the chili.

5. Place the pan under the broiler and broil, watching carefully, for 5 to 7 minutes, or until the eggs are done and the cheese has melted and puffed slightly. Serve immediately.

Makes 4 large servings

Boulder Chili

1½ pounds lean ground beef

1 large onion, chopped

2 large or 3 small garlic cloves, crushed through a press

5 tablespoons tomato paste

1 tablespoon prepared powdered chili mix

1 tablespoon Dijon mustard

1½ teaspoons salt

Contents of one 14.5-ounce can chopped tomatoes

1 tablespoon Italian seasoning

Contents of one 15-ounce can chili beans in chili sauce, undrained, such as Kuner's

2 tablespoons Pinot Noir or other dry red wine

In a large sauté pan, sauté the beef, onion, and garlic over medium heat until the beef is just browned and the onion and garlic are tender. Reduce the heat to low and add the tomato paste, powdered chili mix, mustard, salt, tomatoes, Italian seasoning, and beans. Add 2 tablespoons spring water and the wine to the chili bean can and scrape down the sides, then pour into the beef mixture. If the mixture is too thick, add up to 2 tablespoons more water. Heat over medium-low heat, stirring occasionally, until bubbling.

Chuzzlewit Cheese Pie

—SWEET REVENGE—

I set one mystery in a public library, which inspired dishes named from Charles Dickens's works. *(See also the Bleak House Bars on page 250.)*

2 cups half-and-half

8 tablespoons (1 stick) unsalted butter

½ cup all-purpose flour

1 teaspoon baking powder

½ teaspoon kosher salt

¼ teaspoon cayenne pepper

2 teaspoons Dijon mustard

8 large eggs

½ pound extra-sharp Cheddar cheese, grated

½ pound Gruyère cheese, grated

1. In a small saucepan, heat the half-and-half over medium-low heat until very hot but not boiling. Remove from the heat.

2. In a large saucepan, melt the butter over medium-low heat, add the flour, and whisk a couple of minutes, until it bubbles. Slowly add the half-and-half, whisking constantly. Cook and stir this cream sauce until it thickens and is very smooth. Remove from the heat and set aside, stirring frequently, until cool enough to touch with your (clean) finger.

3. Preheat the oven to 350°F. Butter a 9 x 13-inch glass baking dish.

4. In a small bowl, whisk together the baking powder, salt, and cayenne. Stir this mixture into the cream sauce along with the mustard. Whisk until smooth. (Do not reheat.)

5. In a large bowl, with an electric mixer, beat the eggs until they are frothy. Keeping the beaters going, slowly add the cooled cream sauce and beat on low speed until completely combined. Toss the cheeses together, then thoroughly stir them into the egg-cream sauce mixture. Pour into the prepared baking dish.

6. Bake for 40 to 45 minutes, or until the pie is puffed, brown, and set in the middle. Serve immediately, as the pie deflates as quickly as a soufflé.

Makes 8 large servings

Asparagus Quiche

—DARK TORT—

When local fresh asparagus appears in the grocery store and at farmers' markets, it's time to pounce. This dish turns that lovely vegetable into an entrée.

½ pound fresh asparagus, tough ends trimmed, cut into 1½-inch lengths

4 large eggs

¼ cup heavy (whipping) cream

1 teaspoon Dijon mustard

½ teaspoon salt

¼ teaspoon paprika

⅛ teaspoon cayenne pepper, or more to taste

1 cup small-curd cottage cheese

1 cup grated Gruyère cheese

¼ cup freshly grated Parmesan cheese

Makes 8 servings

1. Preheat the oven to 350°F. Butter a 9-inch deep-dish pie plate.

2. In a small sauté pan with a lid, heat about ½ cup spring water just to a boil. Pour in the cut asparagus, cover, and remove from the heat. Allow the asparagus to steam, off the heat, while you prepare the other ingredients.

3. In a large bowl, with an electric mixer, beat the eggs on medium speed until they are very well blended. Beat in the cream, mustard, salt, paprika, and cayenne on low speed until well combined. Using a heavy wooden spoon, stir in the cheeses, stirring until well combined.

4. Drain the asparagus. (It should still be bright green, with a tender, slightly crunchy texture.) Arrange it over the bottom of the pie plate. Pour the egg mixture over the asparagus and place the quiche in the oven.

5. Bake for 35 to 40 minutes, or until the quiche has puffed, browned, and set in the center. Allow to cool 5 minutes before slicing.

Note: Since this is a crust-less quiche, it should be served with rolls or other bread.

Julian's Summer Frittata

—FATALLY FLAKY—

Maybe a frittata is indeed a fancy name for an omelet. Who cares? The kids will undoubtedly call it "scrambled eggs" anyhow.

½ pound fresh broccoli

6 tablespoons extra-virgin olive oil

1 red onion, sliced

8 ounces fresh baby spinach

8 ounces fresh button mushrooms, cleaned, trimmed, and finely chopped

2 tablespoons unsalted butter

½ cup finely sliced scallions (including tops)

12 large eggs

1 cup heavy (whipping) cream

1 teaspoon kosher salt

½ teaspoon freshly ground black pepper

½ cup finely chopped or grated Havarti cheese

½ cup freshly grated Parmesan cheese, divided

1. Preheat the oven to 350°F. Line a rimmed baking sheet with foil.

2. Rinse the broccoli, remove the stalks and discard. On a large cutting board, chop it into florets. Measure out 2 cups and reserve the remainder for another use.

3. Place the broccoli on the baking sheet and toss with 1 tablespoon of the olive oil, then put the onion on top of the broccoli and pour 2 more tablespoons of oil on top. Bake for 10 minutes, stir, then return to the oven for 15 minutes, or until the broccoli is tender. Remove from the oven and allow to cool slightly. (Leave the oven on.)

4. While the broccoli and onion are cooling, rinse the spinach and, in a medium covered saucepan over medium heat, use only the water clinging to the leaves to steam until wilted. This only takes a couple of minutes. Watch carefully; do not scorch. Drain and allow the spinach to cool. When the spinach is cool enough to handle, use paper towels to carefully wring out all liquid. Remove the spinach to a cutting board and chop it.

5. Using a clean cloth towel that can be stained, or paper towels, wring all the liquid out of the mushrooms.

6. In a large ovenproof skillet, melt the butter over medium-low heat. Add the scallions and mushroom pieces and cook until the mushrooms begin to separate. Remove from the heat and place the scallion-mushroom mixture, along with any liquid, into a bowl. Wipe out the skillet.

7. In a large bowl, beat the eggs until they are well blended, then blend in the cream, salt, pepper, Havarti, and ¼ cup of the Parmesan. Mix the cooled spinach, broccoli, and onion into the egg-cheese mixture. Heat the remaining 3 tablespoons of oil in the skillet over medium heat, just until it ripples. Carefully pour the egg-cheese-vegetable mixture and the scallion-mushroom mixture into the skillet. Stir to combine.

8. Sprinkle the remaining ¼ cup Parmesan on top.

9. Place the pan in the oven and bake for about 25 minutes, or until the center is set.

Makes 8 servings

Ferdinanda's Florentine Quiche

—CRUNCH TIME—

This is our family's favorite quiche. The original recipe, over which I would make changes through the ensuing forty years, came from a fellow art history graduate student, Deb Berek, to whom I am forever grateful.

To my dismay, Ferdinanda's Florentine Quiche is the one recipe in a Goldy book that was printed with an error in the first printing of the hardcover of Crunch Time. *I'd doubled the recipe when I was testing it, so I could take two of them to a church function. Unfortunately, I forgot to cut the cottage cheese back in half when I typed up the recipe for the book. Later versions of the published recipe (including this one) contain the correction.*

Rice crust:

1 large egg

2 cups cooked rice, at room temperature

⅔ cup grated Gruyère cheese

Filling:

One 10-ounce package frozen chopped spinach

2 tablespoons unsalted butter, melted

3 large eggs

1 cup small-curd cottage cheese

2 tablespoons heavy (whipping) cream

For the rice crust:

1. Butter a 9-inch glass pie plate.

2. In a bowl, beat the egg until frothy. Add the rice and Gruyère and stir well. Press this mixture into the buttered pie plate. Set aside, or refrigerate, covered, until you are ready to make the quiche.

3. When you are ready to make the quiche, preheat the oven to 350°F.

For the filling:

1. Cook the spinach according to the package directions. Drain thoroughly, place in a sieve, and press out all the liquid. Place the spinach in a bowl and stir in the melted butter.

- 1 teaspoon Dijon mustard
- ½ teaspoon kosher salt
- ⅛ teaspoon paprika
- ⅛ teaspoon cayenne pepper
- ⅓ cup grated Gruyère cheese
- ¼ cup freshly grated Parmesan cheese

2. In a large bowl, beat the eggs until frothy. Stir in the cottage cheese, cream, mustard, salt, paprika, cayenne, and grated cheeses. Stir until well mixed. Add the buttered spinach and stir again, until well mixed. Pour the spinach mixture into the rice crust.

3. Bake for 35 to 40 minutes, or until puffed, golden brown, and set in the center. (Check the center with a spoon to be sure it is no longer liquid.) Allow to cool 5 minutes. Slice and serve.

Makes 8 servings

Chapter 3

Spuds, Salads, Etc. *or* My Editor Is Also a Vegetarian

Yes, it's true. It would seem as if vegetarians are taking over the world, or at least the publishing industry. Carolyn Marino, who was an editor for *Catering to Nobody* and has edited my last six novels, and, bless her, this cookbook, is a vegetarian who also requested more meatless dishes.

But there is another reason why this chapter of *Goldy's Kitchen Cookbook* is titled *Spuds, Salads, Etc.* While learning how to cater, I noticed something interesting: Green vegetables, everything from broccoli to haricots verts, were rarely served hot at a party for, say, forty people or more. The reason was that you could not keep the vegetables at a high enough temperature to feed all those folks *hot* vegetables without overcooking said vegetables. You could serve vegetables if you cooked them between layers of cheese, because the cheese would keep them hot. But cheesy green beans don't quite work with steak and the inevitable cheesy

potato dish, which is what catering clients clamor for. So green salads, in their many forms, are usually what caterers serve with the protein and starch.

Some of these spud and salad recipes were originally published with bacon, ham, chicken, etc. That said, you will probably have at least one vegetarian at your next party. But the carnivores will not be happy if you omit meat from their meals. My advice is to fix your dishes in a vegetarian manner (i.e., omitting the meat), and buy one of those spiral-cut hams to serve at the end of the buffet.

Since I receive many, many more questions about the writing and editorial processes than I do about cooking, I want to add that an editor does more than ask for recipes. She can help a writer figure out what needs to be taken out, put in, or—even more fun—be developed.

I adored the movie *Shakespeare in Love*. Hearing of this, my editor at the time, Kate Miciak, insisted that Goldy cater a Tudor feast. To do this, I had to go to England for research. (Please don't throw me in that there briar patch!) And as it happens, the Tudor kitchens at Hampton Court are almost perfectly preserved. Given that many castles were destroyed by fire, this alone is a miracle. For example: a Tudor pastry chef created a cake topped with actual miniature cannon. When the cake was served, the cannon blew real gunshot that ignited a blaze that destroyed an entire section of the castle. The dangerous activity of baking bread for any castle was often relegated to beehive-shaped ovens located *beside the river,* so that sudden conflagrations could be doused.

Doing the research was fun. That said, I came to the conclusion that folks of today would not particularly relish foods served during the Tudor era, even at the royal table. Why? At court, the spectacle was the thing. A peacock would be skinned in such a way that the head, raw skin, feathers, and feet could be set to the side in one piece. Then the bird itself would be roasted. The head, raw skin, feathers, etc. would then be *put back on* the roast, so that servants could hold the peacock aloft, feathers fanned, as they processed into the banquet hall, where the peacock would be served. Food poisoning, anyone?

Knowing all this, perhaps it's no wonder that so many people in publishing eschew meat.

My writing parallel here is that good editors can help you realize when you're going down a rabbit hole. Even though people ask where writers get ideas, the truth of the matter is that writers have many more ideas than they can possibly develop. Sometimes you have an idea, from an article you read, or something funny that happened in the gym. (Nothing funny has ever happened to me in a gym, but never mind.) You think, Wow! Great story here! And then you work on it for a couple of weeks or months—or years, if you're very unlucky—and send it to your editor, who says that in fact, it is not a great idea, because it has no zing. She will ask, where's the oomph, the vigor, the emotional power? And you reluctantly admit that there is none of the above. Best to start over.

As with characters, the key that will unlock a writer's motivation on a story is the energy—good or bad, light or dark—that one finds in that energy. Once the story takes on a life of its own, you're golden. Or at least, you have a chunk of ore.

It seems I have many issues that are fraught. (Who doesn't?) But issues that involve one's children are the most fraught of all. And since I always have Goldy's voice in my head, I experience those challenges with her reaction as well as mine. A chance conversation created a Goldy-in-my-head moment that led to *The Cereal Murders*.

The necessary background to this story is that Jim and I pulled one of our children from an overcrowded public school, then took out loans to get him an expensive college preparatory education. We discovered too late that without the money to support a country-club lifestyle—including fancy cars for tenth graders and yearly trips to Europe—our nonathletic son would not be considered cool. Unfortunately, those rich kids chewed up our offspring and spit him out in little pieces.

But we knew none of this when we took on massive debt to send this son through middle and high school at a place where the joke was, *How many parents does the headmaster trip over on his way to a member of the Coors family?*

Our child was subject to numerous physical and emotional humiliations. (This was before there was the awareness of bullying that there is now.) Still, when we brought the horrible kids' behavior to the attention of the head of the middle school, he scoffed. "I can't legislate morality," he announced. Goldy (and I) thought, *Then why are you here?*

Of course, if school administrators anywhere are doing their jobs, then they should *kick out,* or at least suspend with required remediation, kids who are bullies. Children should have to take responsibility for their actions, and endure consequences. Then, perhaps, things would not escalate as they all too tragically do and did. But back then, as we repeatedly saw, administrators (and parents) tended to look the other way, or wash their hands, of bullying. We hope that Columbine, which is part of our school district, has changed that.

So, negative things that happened to us and our kids appear in disguised form when Goldy's son Arch is at Elk Park Prep. With Goldy's voice in my head, I could tap into all kinds of dark energy.

Let's take the time Jim and I were at a parent get-together that was billed as "an informal meeting over wine and appetizers to discuss college counseling." The country-club parents came with their talons extended. We never dressed up enough for these events, but we went anyway. After all, we were spending a lot of (borrowed) money to send our child to the school, and one of the supposed perks was the vaunted college counseling program.

One mother looked down from where she towered over me in her very high heels. She took in my clothes and sniffed. She said, "Our other son is at Columbia."

I said, "Oh?"

She said, "That's in New York."

And of course the Goldy voice in my head said, "I thought it was in South America." (This line was later stolen and appeared in a movie, the title for which I have conveniently forgotten.)

One tidbit I picked up along the way was that the country-club parents were deeply offended that Stanford never sent a representative to the school to drum up enthusiasm for applications. I think Stanford is doing the right thing. As has been well documented, many selective schools will lead high school seniors to believe they can get into their university. These recruiters will whip kids into a frenzy to apply. In fact, those universities are using these kids, the great majority of whom they will reject, as a way to inflate their acceptance rate statistics.

But what was really distressing was seeing how a class—and I witnessed this repeatedly—that had been made up of *friends*, disintegrated under the competitive pressure of Who Is Going Where, or even, Who Is Applying Where. This is how I came up with the first line for *The Cereal Murders*: "I'd kill to get into Stanford."

I wrote the book. But before sending it to my editor, I had to test out my Killer Competition hypothesis. So I scooted down to a Denver meeting of college admissions deans. I put the manuscript in the hands of the director of admission at Stanford, and said if he had any problems, please to let me know. (I never heard from him.)

At that same Denver meeting, though, I heard an anecdote that actually proved my hypothesis, although not in the life-or-death terms of my story. During one of the breaks, I talked with the dean of admissions at Bowdoin. (Yes, some are called directors, some are called deans. It probably won't help your child's case if she addresses her letters to the *Chief Gatekeeper.*) When I told the very kind man from Bowdoin what I was writing about, he responded with a story: When he'd previously been dean of undergraduate admissions at Duke, his office had received a letter from a highly valued applicant from a high school in Texas. In her letter, she said that she had changed her mind, and asked that her application to Duke be withdrawn.

His office wrote back a pro forma letter thanking the young woman for her communication withdrawing her application. Duke was sorry to lose her as an applicant, but wished her all success in her academic career.

A week later, the dean received a frantic call from the college counselor at the applicant's high school. She said, "That young woman never withdrew her application to Duke. Please send us the letter your office received, so we can analyze the handwriting and find out who did."

As you've no doubt guessed, the letter had been written by a classmate who was also applying to Duke.

My editor loved the anecdote and the story. As they say at Stanford, "Q.E.D., baby."

Jailbreak Potatoes

—PRIME CUT—

This became another family favorite. I will sometimes use half grated Gruyère and half grated Parmesan.

4 large russet (baking) potatoes

2 tablespoons unsalted butter

½ cup heavy (whipping) cream

½ teaspoon salt

¼ teaspoon or more white pepper

½ cup freshly grated Parmesan cheese

Makes 4 servings

1. Preheat the oven to 400°F. Scrub and prick each potato 3 or 4 times (in the center of one side) with a fork. Bake the potatoes for 1 hour, or until flaky. Remove from the oven and cool slightly. (Leave the oven on. Butter a rimmed baking sheet.)

2. In a large bowl, with an electric mixer fitted with the whisk attachment, measure in the butter, cream, salt, pepper, and Parmesan. Using a sharp knife, cut the flat top side of each potato (where you pricked it) at a 45-degree angle to remove an oval of skin. (Visualize cutting out the top of a pumpkin.) Using a spoon, scoop most of the potato out of the interior into the bowl with the other ingredients. Leave a thin layer of potato inside the skin. Scrape the potato from the back of the removed ovals of potato skin into the bowl.

3. Whip the potato mixture until smooth. Taste and correct the seasoning.

4. Dividing the whipped potato mixture evenly, spoon it back into the skins. Place the stuffed potatoes on the baking sheet and bake for 15 minutes, or until the filling is thoroughly heated.

Slumber Party Potatoes

—PRIME CUT—

Yes, back in the day I actually used to make these for our kids' slumber parties. (I also asked the kids to do taste tests. They would carefully bite into cookies and vote on 3 x 5 cards for "Cookie A," "Cookie B," or "Cookie C" to see what recipe would go in whatever book I was writing.) To make these potatoes vegetarian, leave out the bacon and use vegetable bouillon.

4 large russet (baking) potatoes

2 tablespoons unsalted butter

3 tablespoons all-purpose flour

1 tablespoon vegetable or chicken bouillon granules

1½ cups milk, preferably whole

1 cup grated Cheddar cheese

1 pound fresh broccoli, stalks discarded, separated into florets, lightly steamed

1 pound thick-sliced bacon, cooked until crisp, drained, and chopped

1. Preheat the oven to 400°F.

2. Scrub and prick the potatoes in 3 or 4 places with a fork. Bake them for about 1 hour, or until flaky.

3. Meanwhile, in a large skillet, melt the butter over low heat. Stir in the flour and cook and stir just until the mixture bubbles, 2 to 3 minutes. Add the bouillon granules, stir, and then gently whisk in the milk. Cook and stir constantly over medium heat until the sauce thickens, about 10 minutes. Add the Cheddar and stir until it melts, 2 to 3 minutes.

4. Split each of the hot potatoes in half lengthwise and place them on a platter. Place the steamed broccoli florets and chopped bacon into bowls. Pour the cheese sauce into a large gravy boat. Diners serve themselves assembly-line style, ending with the cheese sauce.

Makes 4 to 8 servings

Penny-Prick Potato Casserole

—STICKS AND SCONES—

Even though it sounds like an ancient segment from The Tonight Show*—"Sounds Dirty but Isn't"—Penny Prick was a game actually played in Ye Olde Englande. Gamers placed halfpence on sticks, then cast pieces of iron at them. If you knocked off a coin, you got to keep it. A different skill set from winning at Grand Theft Auto, for sure.*

2½ pounds Yukon Gold potatoes (6 medium or 12 small)

1 small garlic bulb or ½ large garlic bulb

1 tablespoon extra-virgin olive oil

2 tablespoons unsalted butter

½ cup milk, preferably whole (or more as needed)

½ cup heavy (whipping) cream

1 cup freshly grated fontina cheese

⅓ cup freshly grated Parmesan cheese

½ teaspoon salt, or to taste

¼ teaspoon white pepper, or to taste

1. Preheat the oven to 350°F. Butter a 9 x 13-inch baking pan.

2. In a large saucepan, bring a large quantity of salted spring water to a boil. Place the potatoes in the boiling water and cook over medium-high heat until fork-tender, about 40 minutes.

3. While the potatoes are cooking, cut a piece of foil into an 8-inch square. Quickly rinse the garlic bulb under cold running water and pat it dry. Place the bulb in the middle of the foil square and carefully pour the olive oil over it. Bring up the corners of the foil and twist to make a closed packet. Place the packet on a pie plate or rimmed baking sheet. Bake for 30 to 40 minutes, or until the garlic cloves are soft but not browned. Using oven mitts, carefully open the packet, remove the garlic bulb with tongs so it can cool, and reserve the olive oil.

4. When the garlic cloves are cool, squeeze them from their skins into a mini food processor. Process the garlic until it is a paste.

5. Drain the potatoes and place them in a large bowl. Add the garlic paste, reserved olive oil, butter, milk, cream, cheeses, salt, and pepper. Using an electric mixer, beat until creamy and well combined. If the mixture seems dry, add a little more milk. Scrape the potato mixture into the baking pan. (If you are not going to bake the casserole immediately, allow it to cool, then cover it with plastic wrap and refrigerate for up to 8 hours.)

6. Bake for 15 to 20 minutes (10 or 15 minutes longer if the casserole has been refrigerated), until hot through and slightly browned on top. Test for doneness by scooping out a small spoonful from the middle of the casserole and tasting it.

Makes 4 servings

Prudent Potatoes au Gratin

—SWEET REVENGE—

Jim is a muscled athlete with an extremely low body mass index. But you wouldn't know it from learning this is his favorite potato dish.

½ tablespoon unsalted butter

1 tablespoon extra-virgin olive oil

2 cups very thinly sliced yellow onions (about 1 large onion)

½ pound Gruyère cheese, grated

½ pound Comté or fontina cheese, grated

½ cup freshly grated Parmesan cheese

4 pounds russet (baking) potatoes, peeled and thinly sliced

1 tablespoon finely chopped fresh sage

1 teaspoon coarse sea salt or kosher salt

½ teaspoon freshly ground black pepper

2 cups heavy (whipping) cream

1. In a large sauté pan, melt the butter with the oil over medium-low heat. Add the onion, reduce the heat to low, and cook, stirring frequently, until the onion is very limp and has caramelized without burning, 15 to 25 minutes. Be sure to cook until the onion has completely changed color. Set the pan aside.

2. Position a rack in the center of the oven and preheat to 375°F. Butter a 9 x 13-inch glass baking dish.

3. In a bowl, toss together the grated cheeses.

4. Place a layer of sliced potatoes in the baking dish, followed by a scattering of the cooked onions. Sprinkle on a layer of cheese, then sprinkle on some of the sage. Continue to layer until you have used up the potatoes, onions, cheese, and sage. End with a layer of cheese.

5. In a bowl, stir the salt and pepper into the heavy cream and pour slowly over the potato mixture so as not to disturb the cheese topping. Bake for 1 to 1½ hours, until the potatoes are very tender and the top is golden brown.

Makes 8 to 12 servings

—DOUBLE SHOT—

These are wonderful on their own, or if you're not going the vegetarian route, they can accompany any kind of pork dish.

- 6 Granny Smith apples
- 8 tablespoons (1 stick) unsalted butter, divided
- ½ cup packed dark brown sugar
- ½ cup Cognac

1. Core, peel, and slice the apples as you would for a pie. In a large skillet or Dutch oven, melt 4 tablespoons of the butter over medium-low heat. Add the apple slices and cook and stir until they begin to soften, 5 to 10 minutes. Remove them to a bowl.

2. Melt the remaining 4 tablespoons butter in the pan over medium-low heat and add the brown sugar, stirring until the sugar dissolves.

3. *Remove the pan from the heat to avoid igniting the Cognac.* Add the Cognac to the butter mixture, stir it in, and return the pan to the stove. Cook this mixture over medium heat until it begins to boil. Boil for 4 minutes, stirring constantly.

4. Reduce the heat to medium. Carefully return the apples to the pan. Keeping the heat on medium, stir frequently until the apples are hot. Either serve immediately or cool and briefly reheat at serving time.

Makes 4 to 6 servings

Goldy's Marvelous Mayonnaise

—CATERING TO NOBODY—

This isn't technically a side dish; it's a sauce. But you can serve it with sliced fresh vegetables, with steamed green beans or broccoli, or in any salad calling for mayonnaise.

- 1 large egg
- 1 tablespoon fresh lemon juice
- 1 tablespoon white wine vinegar
- ½ teaspoon mustard powder
- ½ teaspoon salt
- 1 cup safflower or extra-virgin olive oil

1. In a food processor, combine the egg, lemon juice, vinegar, mustard, and salt and process until well blended, 30 to 40 seconds.

2. Place the oil in a small pitcher. With the processor running, dribble the oil into the egg mixture in a thin stream. When all the oil has been added, turn off the processor and scrape the mayonnaise into a small bowl that can be tightly covered. Keep the mixture chilled. It is best to use homemade mayonnaise within 24 hours.

Makes 1 cup

Wild Man's Rice Salad

—CATERING TO NOBODY—

My brother, Bill Mott, taught me the trick of soaking wild rice overnight before cooking. Thus ended many years of cooking wild rice for hours and still ending up with chewy kernels.

½ cup raw wild rice

Spring water, for soaking

2 cups vegetable or chicken stock

2 tablespoons mayonnaise

1 tablespoon tarragon vinegar

½ teaspoon Dijon mustard, or more to taste

1 tablespoon extra-virgin olive oil

2 scallions, finely chopped (including tops)

3 radishes, diced

1 small tomato, seeded, diced, and drained

⅓ cup peeled diced jicama

1 cup baby spinach, well washed and drained, plus more for lining the platter

Salt and freshly ground black pepper

1. The night before you are to serve the salad, thoroughly rinse the rice, place it in a glass bowl, and completely cover the grains with spring water. Allow the rice to soak overnight. The next morning, carefully drain the rice in a sieve.

2. In a large saucepan, bring the stock to a boil and add the rice. Cover the pan and immediately reduce the heat to the lowest setting. Allow the rice to cook, covered, for 45 minutes at sea level and for 1 hour to 1¼ hours at high altitudes, or until the kernels have puffed and taste done (i.e., they are not chewy or hard). Drain the rice and measure it. You should have between 1¾ and 2 cups cooked rice. Spread the wild rice out on two plates to cool *completely.* For the salad, the grains must be dry and cool. Pat the rice dry with paper towels, if necessary.

3. In a small bowl, combine the mayonnaise, vinegar, and mustard, and whisk well. Add the oil in a thin stream, whisking all the while, until you have a smooth, blended dressing.

4. In a medium bowl, gently combine the cool wild rice with the scallions, radishes, tomato, jicama, and spinach. Pour the dressing over this mixture and mix very gently. Taste and correct the seasoning with the salt and pepper. Chill for at least 2 hours before serving.

5. Turn out onto a small platter that you may line with spinach leaves, if desired. The salad must be consumed the day it is made; it does not keep well.

Makes 4 to 6 servings

New Potato Salad

—DYING FOR CHOCOLATE—

This dish was a particular favorite of my mothers. I would make it when our family would visit Charlottesville, Virginia, in the summer.

- 12 new red potatoes, unpeeled
- About ¾ cup best-quality mayonnaise, preferably homemade (page 78)
- ¼ cup heavy (whipping) cream (or more, if needed)
- 2 garlic cloves, very finely minced
- 2 teaspoons snipped fresh dill
- ½ teaspoon salt
- White pepper

1. In a saucepan of boiling spring water, cook the potatoes just until tender, 15 to 20 minutes. Drain and let cool, then quarter the potatoes.

2. In a small bowl, thin the mayonnaise slightly with cream. Add the garlic, dill, salt, and white pepper to taste. Taste the mixture and correct the seasoning.

3. In a large bowl, toss the potatoes with the mayonnaise mixture. If the potatoes are not completely covered with the mayonnaise mixture, thin another ¼ cup mayonnaise with 1 tablespoon of whipping cream, and mix it in. Cover tightly with plastic wrap. Chill well, preferably overnight in the refrigerator.

Makes 4 servings

Schulz's Guacamole Salad

—DYING FOR CHOCOLATE—

This is a great dish to take to potlucks, especially when you know people are bringing Tex-Mex foods. I invariably end up doubling the recipe. Note that the dressing does indeed have to be made at serving time, and the crushed corn chips sprinkled on just before serving. But it's worth it, and the bowl you took to the potluck will look as if it's been licked clean.

1 head iceberg lettuce

¼ cup grated Cheddar cheese

¼ cup grated Monterey jack cheese

½ cup chopped scallions (including tops)

8 cherry tomatoes, halved

1 avocado, peeled, pitted, and mashed

½ cup regular or light sour cream

⅓ cup corn oil

1 tablespoon fresh lemon juice

1 tablespoon picante sauce

1 cup crushed corn chips

1. Tear the lettuce into small pieces and toss with the cheeses, scallions, and tomatoes. Cover and refrigerate in a salad bowl until serving time.

2. When you are ready to serve the salad, make the dressing. Peel, pit, and scoop the avocado into a small bowl. Mash with the sour cream, oil, lemon juice, and picante sauce and mix well.

3. Toss the salad with the dressing and sprinkle the top with crushed chips.

Makes 4 to 6 servings

Dijon Pasta Salad

—DYING FOR CHOCOLATE—

Back when I was developing this recipe, everyone ran cold water over their pasta to cool it. But these days, that rinsing is frowned upon, as it washes away starch and makes sauces adhere less to the pasta. So I no longer rinse the pasta for this dish. I do let it cool to room temperature, though, because hot pasta will absorb the dressing. So I drain it, put it in a bowl on the counter, and keep an eye on it while I'm doing other things. I give it a stir now and then, and taste-test one piece of pasta every ten minutes or so. Once the pasta is cool, I mix all the ingredients together, then place it in a large, pretty bowl, cover with plastic wrap, and chill several hours before serving. If you're making this vegetarian, leave out the bacon.

1 pound tricolor fusilli or rotini pasta

⅔ cup corn oil

2 tablespoons apple cider vinegar

2 teaspoons Dijon mustard

⅔ cup mayonnaise

2 large celery stalks, chopped

6 slices thick-cut bacon, cooked and chopped

2 large hard-boiled eggs, chopped

2 scallions, chopped (including tops)

½ to 1 teaspoon salt, to taste

Paprika (optional)

1. In a large pot of boiling spring water, cook the pasta until al dente, usually 11 to 13 minutes. Drain and let cool.

2. In a large bowl, whisk together the oil, vinegar, mustard, and mayonnaise. Add the cooled pasta, celery, bacon, eggs, scallions, salt, and paprika (if using). Toss gently and taste for seasoning. Chill thoroughly before serving.

Makes 8 to 10 servings

Sugar Snap Pea and Strawberry Salad

—THE MAIN CORPSE—

People love strawberries in salad, because it makes them think they're not actually eating something that's good for them; they're eating something delicious (which is also good for them). For the edible-pod peas in this dish, you can use either sugar snaps or snow peas.

1 tablespoon extra-virgin olive oil

2 teaspoons raspberry vinegar

¼ teaspoon Dijon mustard

¼ pound (1 cup) sugar snap peas or snow peas, strings removed

1 pound (4 cups) strawberries, thickly sliced

1. In a glass jar with a screw-top lid, combine the oil, vinegar, and mustard. Shake thoroughly.

2. Steam the peas in a small amount of water until bright green but still crunchy, about 30 seconds. Remove them from the heat, drain, then quickly run cold water over them to stop the cooking. Drain again.

3. In a bowl, combine the peapods and sliced strawberries. Shake the dressing again and drizzle over the peapods and strawberries. Serve immediately or chill for no more than 1 hour.

Makes 4 servings

Grilled Slapshot Salad

—THE GRILLING SEASON—

As much of a hassle as it is to grill vegetables (and it is), this salad is worth the trouble. You can make it for a cookout an hour before your guests arrive.

2 tablespooons extra-virgin olive oil

3 large or 4 small garlic cloves, crushed through a press, or 1½ teaspoons finely minced garlic

Salt and freshly ground black pepper

3 medium or 4 small zucchini, cut on the diagonal into ¼-inch-thick slices

8 ounces mushrooms, cleaned, trimmed, and cut crosswise into ¼-inch-thick slices

1 sweet onion, such as Mexican or Peruvian sweet, cut into ¼-inch-thick slices

2 ears of fresh corn, shucked, or frozen ears of corn, thawed

1 tablespoon sherry vinaigrette (page 87), or more to taste

1 to 2 tablespoons chopped fresh basil

1. In a small bowl, whisk together the oil, garlic, and salt and pepper to taste. Divide the mixture between two 9 x 13-inch glass baking dishes.

2. Place the zucchini into one of the baking dishes and mix carefully with your (clean) hands, so that all the zucchini slices are lightly coated with the oil-garlic mixture.

3. Place the mushrooms, onion slices, and corn into the other glass pan and again mix carefully by hand so that all the vegetables are lightly coated with the oil-garlic mixture.

4. Preheat the grill and oil the grates. Preheat the oven to 400°F.

5. Place the zucchini slices on the grill and cook briefly—no longer than 30 seconds—on one side only. Place the zucchini slices back into their glass pan, grilled side up, and put them into the oven while you prepare the rest of the salad (but for no longer than 10 minutes).

6. Briefly grill the mushrooms, onion slices, and corn on all sides, until they have grill marks but are not quite cooked through. This

should only take a few minutes. Remove the onion slices and mushrooms and set them aside to cool. Holding each ear of corn perpendicular to a cutting surface, slice off the kernels.

7. Remove the zucchini from the oven. In a large bowl, combine the zucchini slices, mushrooms, onion slices, and corn kernels. Pour the vinaigrette over the vegetables and carefully stir in the fresh basil. Serve immediately or chill for no more than 1 hour.

Makes 4 servings

Exhibition Salad with Meringue-Baked Pecans

—THE GRILLING SEASON—

I first tasted a salad very similar to this in an upscale New York City restaurant. I resolved to figure out how to do it. I also just make the pecans for the holidays. They freeze well.

Sherry vinaigrette:

1 tablespoon best-quality sherry vinegar

1 teaspoon Dijon mustard

¼ teaspoon sugar

2 tablespoons extra-virgin olive oil

Salt and freshly ground black pepper

Salad:

2 cups fresh arugula (2 ounces)

6 cups mixed greens: fresh radicchio, curly endive, and escarole (6 ounces)

1 cup Meringue-Baked Pecans (recipe follows)

For the sherry vinaigrette:

In a glass jar with a screw-top lid, combine the vinegar, mustard, and sugar. Shake vigorously. Remove the lid, add the oil, and shake vigorously again. Add salt and pepper to taste

For the salad:

Tear the greens into large bite-size pieces and place in a salad bowl. Just before serving, toss with the vinaigrette. Sprinkle the pecans over the top and toss again. Serve immediately.

Makes 4 servings

* * *

Meringue-Baked Pecans

- 1 egg white, from a large egg
- ⅓ cup sugar
- ¼ teaspoon ground cinnamon
- ¼ teaspoon salt
- 4 tablespoons (½ stick) butter, melted
- 2 cups pecan halves (½ pound)

1. Preheat the oven to 325°F. Butter a 10 x 15-inch jelly-roll pan or rimmed baking sheet.

2. In a small bowl, with an electric mixer, beat the egg white until it forms stiff peaks. In another small bowl, stir together the sugar, cinnamon, and salt. Keeping the beaters running, add the sugar mixture 1 tablespoon at a time to the beaten egg white. By hand, fold in the melted butter and pecans. Spread the pecan mixture in the prepared pan and bake for 15 minutes.

3. Remove the pan from the oven. Using a metal spatula, carefully flip the pecan mixture one small section at a time. When all the pecans have been turned over, return the pan to the oven. Bake an additional 15 minutes. Watch them carefully—do not allow them to burn. Cool the pecans on paper towels.

Makes 2 cups

Mediterranean Orzo Salad

—THE GRILLING SEASON—

Orzo is an interesting pasta, because it looks like rice but isn't. This dish looks beautiful on the plate, always a big plus.

1 cup (6 ounces) orzo pasta

1 cup seeded, chopped tomato (about 3 small)

¼ cup chopped celery

3 tablespoons finely chopped red onion

2 tablespoons capers

2 tablespoons finely chopped, pitted Kalamata olives

2 tablespoons chopped fresh basil, or more to taste

1 tablespoon balsamic vinegar

1 teaspoon grainy or regular Dijon mustard

¼ teaspoon sugar

2 tablespoons garlic oil (available in specialty food shops or online)

Salt and freshly ground black pepper

3½ ounces chèvre (French goat cheese), crumbled

1. In a large pot of boiling spring water, cook the pasta according to package directions until al dente. Drain and allow to cool.

2. In a large bowl, toss the pasta with the tomato, celery, onion, capers, olives, and basil.

3. In a glass jar with a screw-top lid, combine the vinegar, mustard, and sugar. Shake vigorously. Remove the lid, add the garlic oil, and shake vigorously again until an emulsion forms.

4. Pour this vinaigrette over the pasta mixture and season with salt and pepper. Chill the salad. When ready to serve, mix in the crumbled goat cheese.

Makes 4 servings

Figgy Salad

—STICKS AND SCONES—

Like the strawberries in Sugar Snap Pea and Strawberry Salad, figs are a welcome salad fruit. People also usually like nuts in a salad: They deliver a crunch unlike that of celery. The chèvre here does double duty, adding protein and a creamy smoothness to the dressing.

4 ounces dried Mission figs

½ cup ruby port

½ teaspoon sugar

1 ounce (about 2 tablespoons) skinned hazelnuts (also called filberts)

2 tablespoons balsamic vinegar

1 large shallot, minced

2 ounces chèvre (French goat cheese), at room temperature, sliced

¼ cup extra-virgin olive oil

¼ teaspoon salt

Freshly ground black pepper

8 cups baby field greens, rinsed, drained, patted dry, wrapped in paper towels, and chilled

1. Cut the stems off the figs, rinse them, and pat dry. Place them in a small saucepan with the port and sugar and bring to a simmer over medium heat. Cover the pan, reduce the heat to the lowest setting, and simmer gently until the figs are soft, about 10 minutes. Reserving the cooking liquid, drain the figs. Allow the figs to cool, then cut them into quarters and set aside.

2. In a large skillet, toast the filberts over medium heat, stirring frequently, until they emit a nutty smell, 5 to 10 minutes. Remove them from the pan to cool, then coarsely chop.

3. Return the fig-cooking liquid to the saucepan and reheat over low heat. Stir in the vinegar, shallot, goat cheese, oil, salt, and pepper to taste. Add the figs and increase the heat to medium-low. Stir the dressing until the cheese is completely melted.

4. Toss the field greens with the warm dressing and sprinkle the nuts on top. Serve immediately.

Makes 6 servings

Wild Girls' Grilled Mushroom Salad

—CHOPPING SPREE—

Cremini mushrooms are small portobellos and are sometimes marketed as "baby bellas." An executive in my publishing house had tasted a dish similar to this at an upscale Denver restaurant (yes, we have them!) and charged me to figure out how to make it. This recipe is the result.

4 ounces fresh portobello or cremini mushrooms

4 ounces fresh shiitake mushrooms

1 ounce fresh oyster mushrooms

3 large garlic cloves, crushed through a press

2 teaspoons Dijon mustard

2 tablespoons best-quality medium-dry sherry, such as Dry Sack

2 tablespoons balsamic vinegar

6 tablespoons extra-virgin olive oil

Cooking spray

6 cups baby field greens

1. To clean the mushrooms, wipe them carefully with damp paper towels. Remove the stems from the mushrooms and discard. Using a sharp knife, lightly trim the gills from the portobello or cremini mushrooms and slice into 1-inch cubes. Cut the shiitake caps in half.

2. In a large glass bowl, whisk together the garlic, mustard, sherry, and vinegar until well combined. Add the oil in a steady stream, whisking all the while. Place the mushrooms into this marinade and toss gently to coat all sides. Set aside to marinate, but not for longer than 10 minutes. Do not overmarinate the mushrooms, or their delicate flavor will be lost.

3. Coat a grill rack with cooking spray and preheat the grill to medium-high to high heat.

4. Grill the mushrooms for 3 to 4 minutes per side, or until cooked through. Serve immediately on a bed of field greens.

Makes 4 servings

Chopping Spree Salad

—CHOPPING SPREE—

When chopped salads were the rage, I tried to get a recipe for one past our family. This one finally succeeded. If you are a vegetarian, leave out the chicken.

1 pound boneless, skinless chicken breasts

¼ cup fresh lime juice

¼ cup extra-virgin olive oil

1 large head romaine lettuce, outer leaves removed

4 canned hearts of palm, well rinsed

Cooking spray

¼ cup pine nuts or slivered almonds

Tangy Lime Dressing (recipe follows)

½ cup diced jicama

1 cup seeded diced tomato (about 2 medium)

½ cup thinly sliced scallions, including tops (about 2 scallions)

1. Place the chicken breasts between sheets of plastic wrap and pound them with a mallet to a ⅓-inch thickness. Slice each breast in half lengthwise.

2. In a 9 x 13-inch glass baking dish, mix the lime juice with the oil and place the chicken in this marinade while you prepare the rest of the ingredients and dressing, 15 to 20 minutes. Do not marinate the chicken for longer than this, or it can turn mushy.

3. Wash the head of romaine very well, then cut off the bottom and slice off an inch from the top (and discard them both). This will give you even edges. Carefully cut the rest of the head crosswise into ½-inch-wide slices. You should have about 8 cups of romaine pieces. Rinse these well, spin them to remove any moisture, and wrap them in paper towels. Chill until you are ready to assemble the salad.

4. Place the rinsed hearts of palm into a bowl of cold spring water and allow them to soak for 5 minutes to remove the brine.

5. Meanwhile, lightly coat a small sauté pan with cooking spray (or use a nonstick pan) and toast the pine nuts over medium-low to medium heat. Stir frequently to prevent burning. When the pine nuts are just beginning to turn golden brown (3 to 4 minutes), remove them from the pan, place on a plate to cool, and set aside until you are ready to assemble the salad.

6. Remove the hearts of palm from the water, pat them dry with paper towels, and cut them crosswise into ¼-inch-thick discs. Wrap the pieces in a paper towel and chill until you are ready to assemble the salad.

7. Coat the grill rack with cooking spray and preheat the grill to medium-high to high while you prepare the Tangy Lime Dressing.

8. Grill the chicken for about 4 minutes per side, or until it is cooked through but not dry. Remove the chicken to a cutting board, cool slightly, and cut into bite-size pieces.

9. When ready to serve, place the lettuce, hearts of palm, jicama, tomatoes, scallions, and chicken in a large, attractive salad bowl. Toss with half of the dressing, then add the dressing by tablespoons until the salad is lightly dressed, not overdressed. (You may have a bit of dressing left over.) Sprinkle the toasted pine nuts on top and serve immediately.

Makes 4 large servings

* * *

Tangy Lime Dressing

½ garlic clove, minced

¼ teaspoon dried fines herbes (available in many supermarkets)

1 teaspoon minced fresh parsley

1½ teaspoons minced fresh cilantro

⅓ cup buttermilk

1½ tablespoons fresh lime juice

⅓ cup best-quality mayonnaise

3 tablespoons heavy (whipping) cream, or more as needed

1 tablespoon finely grated Parmesan cheese

Salt and freshly ground black pepper

In a mini food processor, combine the garlic, fines herbes, parsley, and cilantro and blend until pulverized, less than a minute. In a medium bowl, whisk together the buttermilk, lime juice, and mayonnaise until well combined and smooth. Whisk in the garlic-herb mixture, the cream, and Parmesan, blending until evenly mixed. Taste carefully and add more cream if the dressing seems too tangy. Add salt judiciously, as the mayonnaise and cheese are already salty. Grind in some pepper and taste again. Use immediately.

Primavera Pasta Salad

—DOUBLE SHOT—

This is a great salad to prepare the day of a nighttime cookout. In the Colorado mountains, when the calendar says it's spring (primavera), *we usually can't cook out, because we're still struggling with snow and cold. By the time the Fourth of July rolls around, we're usually okay to grill outside (although it has snowed in Breckenridge in early July).*

8 ounces pasta, in small shapes, such as cavatappi, ditalini, penne, or macaroni

2 cups halved cherry tomatoes

¾ cup grated daikon radish

¾ cup chopped scallions (including tops)

¾ cup finely chopped fresh cilantro

¼ cup Simple Vinaigrette (recipe follows), or more to taste

Salt and freshly ground black pepper

1. In a large pot of boiling spring water, cook the pasta until al dente. Drain it (but do not rinse it) and allow it to cool to room temperature, stirring gently from time to time to keep it from sticking.

2. In a large serving bowl, mix the pasta with the tomatoes, daikon, scallions, and cilantro. Add enough vinaigrette to lightly dress (but not slather) every ingredient. Season with salt and pepper to taste. Chill. This salad is best served within 4 to 6 hours of being prepared.

Makes 4 servings

* * *

Simple Vinaigrette

- ¼ cup best-quality red wine vinegar
- 1 tablespoon Dijon mustard
- ¾ to 1 teaspoon sugar
- ½ teaspoon salt
- ½ teaspoon freshly ground black pepper
- 1 cup extra-virgin olive oil

In a glass jar with a screw-top lid, combine the vinegar, mustard, ¾ teaspoon sugar, salt, and pepper. Put on the lid and shake vigorously. Remove the lid, add the oil, screw the lid back on, and shake vigorously again to make an emulsion. Taste, and if you wish, whisk in the extra ¼ teaspoon sugar. Keep refrigerated. If the dressing congeals while in the refrigerator, allow it to come to room temperature before shaking the jar again before using.

Stylish Strawberry Salad

—SWEET REVENGE—

Who can say no to strawberries with avocado slices?

1 head baby romaine

3 tablespoons best-quality sherry vinegar

1½ teaspoons Dijon mustard

1½ teaspoons shallots, peeled and minced

2 tablespoons sugar

¼ to ½ teaspoon kosher salt to taste, plus more for sprinkling

¼ teaspoon freshly ground black pepper, plus more for sprinkling

6 tablespoons extra-virgin olive oil

2 avocados

2 cups halved strawberries

1. Carefully separate the lettuce into leaves, wash, and pat or spin dry. Wrap it in a kitchen towel. Refrigerate until serving time.

2. In a glass jar with a screw-top lid, combine the vinegar, mustard, shallots, sugar, ¼ teaspoon salt, and pepper. Put on the lid and shake vigorously. Remove the lid, add the oil, screw the lid back on, and shake vigorously again until the mixture emulsifies. Taste and add the additional salt if desired. Set the vinaigrette aside.

3. Just before serving time, peel, pit, and slice the avocados.

4. To serve, divide the lettuce among 4 plates. Arrange the strawberries and avocado slices (each person gets ½ avocado's worth of slices) on top of the leaves. Shake or whisk the vinaigrette and ladle a few spoonfuls onto each salad. If desired, sprinkle a tiny amount of salt onto each salad, then follow with a few grinds of black pepper. Serve immediately.

Makes 4 servings

Heirloom Tomato Salad

—FATALLY FLAKY—

When Jim and I were newlyweds, one of the first salads I made that wasn't iceberg lettuce dabbed with mayonnaise was Tomatoes Vinaigrette. We both loved it, although I learned the hard way not to mix it and allow it to marinate in a metal pan. If you are having company (or even if you aren't), prepare and serve this salad in a pretty glass or crystal bowl. The Camembert gives the dish a certain cachet, and if your kids will eat any cheese with a rind, you're in luck.

1 pound fresh heirloom or vine-ripened tomatoes

2 tablespoons chopped fresh basil plus 4 large leaves, divided

2 teaspoons fresh garlic crushed through a press (2 to 3 cloves)

½ pound Camembert cheese

½ cup pear vinegar (available online) or red wine vinegar

1 tablespoon Dijon mustard

½ teaspoon sugar

Sea salt and freshly ground black pepper

1 cup extra-virgin olive oil

1. Cut the stems and cores out of the tomatoes. Holding them, one at a time, over the sink, gently squeeze until most of the seeds come out. Place them on a cutting board and cut each tomato into fourths if they are small, or eighths if they are large. Place in a large glass bowl.

2. Sprinkle the tomatoes with the chopped basil. Sprinkle the pressed garlic on top of the basil. Using a sharp serrated knife, trim most of the rind from the cheese. Slice it into 16 equal wedges, and place these on top of the garlic.

3. In a glass screw-top jar with a lid, combine the vinegar, mustard, sugar, and salt and pepper to taste. Screw the lid onto the jar and shake well. Remove the lid, add the olive oil, screw the lid back on, and shake vigorously, or until the dressing is completely emulsified.

4. Pour the dressing over the ingredients in the bowl and gently toss the salad. Cover the bowl with plastic wrap and chill the salad for at least 4 hours and up to 24 hours.

5. When you are ready to serve the salad, place it in a pretty bowl, sprinkle lightly with a bit more salt and a grating of black pepper. Garnish with the whole basil leaves.

Makes 8 servings

Chilled Curried Chicken Salad

—FATALLY FLAKY—

Clearly, there is no way you can make this dish vegetarian. But I've included it here becasue it is, after all, a salad, and it is good to make ahead as a main dish for a ladies' luncheon (or a gentlemen and ladies' luncheon!). It also works for a cold summer dinner. I developed this recipe because so many people order curried chicken salad in restaurants.

3 large or 4 medium bone-in, skin-on chicken breast halves

Extra-virgin olive oil

Sea salt or kosher salt and freshly ground black pepper

Contents of three 15-ounce cans mandarin oranges, drained

Contents of one 20-ounce can pineapple tidbits, drained

½ cup raisins, or more to taste

¾ cup finely chopped red onion

1½ cups mayonnaise

1 tablespoon curry powder, or more to taste

2 tablespoons chutney, plus more for serving

1. Preheat the oven to 400°F. Line a large rimmed baking sheet with a silicone baking mat.

2. Place the chicken breasts on the baking sheet and rub oil onto the pieces. Sprinkle them with salt and pepper.

3. Bake the chicken for 25 to 40 minutes, or until it is thoroughly cooked and a meat thermometer inserted in the chicken reads 160°F. Check for doneness by slicing into one of the pieces, all the way to the bone. All the meat should have turned completely white, with no trace of pink. *Do not overcook the chicken.* Remove the pan from the oven and allow the chicken to cool completely.

4. When the chicken is cool, remove the skin and bones and discard them. Tear the meat into bite-size pieces. Measure it; you should have 4 cups. Reserve any remainder for another use.

2 tablespoons regular or light sour cream

2 tablespoons fresh lime juice

Whole salted peanuts, for serving

5. In a large glass serving bowl, combine the chicken, oranges, pineapple, raisins, and red onion.

6. In a food processor, combine the mayonnaise, curry powder, chutney, ¾ teaspoon salt, sour cream, and lime juice and process until almost completely smooth. You may have to turn the processor off and scrape down the sides one or two times with a spatula. This should not take more than 2 minutes. Taste and add more curry powder if desired.

7. Pour the dressing over the ingredients in the serving bowl and stir gently but well, until all the ingredients are evenly distributed. Cover the bowl with plastic wrap and chill the salad for at least 24 hours.

8. Serve with a large bowl of peanuts and another bowl of chutney, if desired, for people to use to garnish their own salads.

Makes 4 to 6 servings

Goldy's Caprese Salad

—CRUNCH TIME—

This recipe is living proof that two palates can be better than one. Once again, I developed this recipe after having something similar in a restaurant. Before tasting this particular one, I'd steered clear of caprese salads, because they usually consisted of wedges of tasteless tomato alternating with thick, chalky slices of equally tasteless mozzarella. Then a longtime friend, Carole Kornreich, and I had lunch in Denver. She ordered a dish similar to this and offered me a bite. I thought I'd gone to heaven. Ciliegine *are manageable bites of mozzarella that are creamy rather than chalky. With organic tomatoes, they are luscious. My only problem was that the restaurant menu said the dressing was made with "extra-virgin olive oil." No matter how hard I tried, I could not replicate the results at home. So Carole and I trekked back to the restaurant, where we both ordered the dish. This is when I discovered that those folks who write menus sometimes lie. Before we went inside, I insisted to Carole that the dressing on the restaurant's caprese was not olive oil and vinegar, as the menu claimed. Carole took a couple of tiny bites, and suggested that the restaurant might be using* basil oil. *Right away, I suspected she was correct. After lunch, I raced home and ordered basil-infused oil from Boyajian. When it came, I whisked together the dressing and realized we were home. So I want to give full credit to my fellow foodie for figuring this out. (Carole and I went to sixth and seventh grades together back in Chevy Chase, Maryland; we were in the same Girl Scout troop. I always maintained that she was the smartest kid in the entire Montgomery County School District. And guess what? I was right. She became an M.D. I was ecstatic when we rediscovered each other in Denver.)*

1½ pounds organic heirloom tomatoes, chopped if large, or you can use organic grape or cherry tomatoes, halved

½ pound *ciliegine* (cherry-size fresh mozzarella balls), drained

12 fresh basil leaves, finely chopped

3 cups baby field greens (mesclun or mâche), gently rinsed and spun dry

Dressing:

¼ cup best-quality white wine vinegar

2 teaspoons Dijon mustard

¼ teaspoon sugar

½ teaspoon kosher salt

¼ teaspoon freshly ground black pepper

⅔ cup best-quality basil oil (infused with basil, not with dried basil leaves in it)

In a medium glass bowl, combine the tomatoes, *ciliegine,* and basil. Place the dry greens in an attractive glass or crystal salad bowl. Set aside.

For the dressing:

1. In a glass screw-top jar with a lid, combine the vinegar, mustard, sugar, salt, and pepper. Screw the lid on tightly and shake to combine well. Take off the lid, pour in the basil oil, screw the lid back on tightly, and shake very well to combine.

2. Place the tomato mixture on top of the greens. Shake the dressing again, and pour on ¼ to ½ cup dressing. Taste carefully. Depending on the sweetness of the tomatoes, you may need a bit more sugar. (Do not use too much dressing. Store the remainder, still in its covered jar, in the refrigerator.)

3. Toss the salad and serve immediately.

Makes 4 to 6 servings

Love Potion Salad

—CRUNCH TIME—

I no longer remember where Jim and I tasted a salad that we both adored. I only remember that it contained mayonnaise in the vinaigrette. But since Jim's default dressing is bottled ranch (insert heartfelt sigh here), I resolved to figure out how to make one he would like. He thought it was marvelous, and came up with the title for the recipe.

1 ounce pine nuts (¼ cup)

4 cups baby field greens (mesclun or mâche), gently rinsed and spun dry

1 pound grape tomatoes, halved

About ¼ cup Love Potion Salad Dressing (recipe follows)

½ cup blue cheese crumbles, or to taste

1. In a large skillet, toast the pine nuts over low heat, stirring constantly, until they are lightly browned and emitting a nutty scent, about 4 minutes. Turn out on a paper towel to cool.

2. Place the greens and tomatoes in an attractive salad bowl. Toss with about ¼ cup dressing and taste. (You may need to add more dressing, but do not overdress the salad.) Sprinkle the blue cheese crumbles and pine nuts on top of the salad and toss again. Serve immediately.

Makes 4 servings

* * *

Love Potion Salad Dressing

- 3 tablespoons best-quality aged balsamic vinegar
- 2 tablespoons freshly grated Parmesan cheese
- 1 tablespoon mayonnaise
- 1 tablespoon Dijon mustard
- 1 tablespoon finely chopped fresh basil
- 2 teaspoons minced shallot
- 1 teaspoon minced garlic
- Kosher salt and freshly ground black pepper, to taste
- 1 cup extra-virgin olive oil

1. In a blender jar, combine everything but the oil and blend to purée. Stop the blender twice to scrape down the sides of the jar. When the mixture is a uniform color, remove the small filler cap, and with the blender running, very slowly drizzle in the olive oil. (With your free hand, you may want to hold a paper towel over the filler cap opening between drizzling operations, to prevent spattering.) When the mixture is completely emulsified (less than a minute), stop the blender and pour the dressing into a pint jar or pitcher.

2. Use right away or cover the jar or pitcher tightly and refrigerate. Bring the dressing to room temperature before using. When it is at room temperature, use a whisk and quickly stir the dressing, so it can re-emulsify.

Chapter 4

Meat, Poultry, and Fish *or* The Heart of the Matter

Sometimes you are just driving merrily along, minding your own business—or running carpool—and you hear a report on the radio that almost lands you in a ditch. But it doesn't, and you think, *Wow, that's what my next book is about.* This has actually only happened to me twice, with *Dying for Chocolate* and *Crunch Time*. With the latter, it was my friend Jasmine Cresswell who heard an episode of *The Diane Rehm Show* and told me I needed to write about stalking, which ended up being central to *Crunch Time*.

But long before that, with *Dying for Chocolate,* I was driving to pick up one of our children on Valentine's Day, which turned out to be important, because an author was talking on the radio about her book on aphrodisiac foods. *Hm,* thought I, *could Goldy ever be asked to provide an aphrodisiac feast?*

I'd sat in on enough booking appointments with my catering instructors to know that eccentric clients asked for all kinds of foods, and didn't think twice

about paying for them. Or maybe they did think twice about paying for them, but something else was going on.

There was the bride who wanted her wedding reception buffet, which featured prime rib and lots of other expensive foods, to include frisée salad drenched with—wait for it—bottled ranch dressing, for which you have probably guessed I have no affection. Supposedly, the dressing had sentimental value for her and the groom. The caterer gently tried to persuade her to choose a lemon vinaigrette, but she was adamant, so that was what the catering team served.

Another time, one of my instructors invited me to sit in on a meeting with a prospective groom and his parents. He warned me ahead of time, "Say nothing." (It's amazing how often people feel they have to tell me that.) As is traditional, these parents-of-the-groom wanted to pay for the rehearsal dinner. But they were only willing to shell out fifteen dollars per guest. They, too, asked for prime rib, to which the caterer said, "No problem." The parents also wondered if they could have . . . lobster tail . . . and three vegetables . . . and dessert, within the fifteen-bucks-per-person ceiling. "Absolutely," the caterer replied. Okay, then, the parents asked, how about some wine? The caterer said, "Sure, we can do two kinds of wine for fifteen dollars per person."

I took a deep breath. I'd mentally totaled the tab at a hundred dollars-plus per person . . . and this was over thirty years ago. Today, with set-up, servers, and gratuity, you'd be looking north of that.

After the meeting, the caterer told me that the parents had grown up during the Depression and despite "having money," did not want to spend it on so frivolous an event as a rehearsal dinner. The son was a recent arrival in our small town. He drove a Porsche and was a full-fledged participant in the go-go eighties. *He* was picking up the tab for whatever was in excess of the fifteen bucks per person, but the parents were not to have a glimmer of this fact. And to my knowledge, they never did.

But to get back to the Valentine's Day radio story: In the Goldy books, people in Aspen Meadow seem to know each other, or at least, they're aware of people within their social, ecclesiastical, athletic, or parental circle. Country club members know each other, as do members of different religious communities, as do mothers whose kids are the same age, and so on. Everyone knows everyone, or knows somebody who knows that person.

The same used to be true in our town, as I learned when I began work on my second novel, *Dying for Chocolate*. Background: After *Catering to Nobody* sold in 1989, I decided to write a book featuring Goldy preparing aphrodisiac foods, which I'd heard about on the radio. I went to our wonderful local library to order books on the subject, available through interlibrary loan.

I received the notice that my books had come in and hightailed it to the library. The librarian, who had known me well for years as the borrower of many Dr. Seuss books, slid the large pile across the counter. Here were titles like *How to Get Your Man Back with Food, A to Z of Aphrodisia, Food and Love,* and *Food and Sex*. The librarian lifted an eyebrow and asked, "How's Jim?"

(We will pause here as we imagine yours truly blushing furiously, checking out the books, and slithering out of the library.)

So sometimes you get your idea from NPR. Other times, life gives you the idea, and it has mileage either because of the emotional energy or just because something happened that really, really pissed you off. This has also happened to me.

Once our youngest son was three and could take skiing lessons, Jim and I used to take all three boys for a day on the slopes. When Jim had to work overtime on Saturdays, I would take the boys up to ski. (If you were a Colorado resident and bought coupon books sold by the Cub Scouts, skiing *used* to be cheap.) The Ski Patrol was omnipresent and performed well at maintaining order and helping skiers. This included everything from reviving someone having a heart attack to bringing a special stretcher for skiers who'd hurt themselves. The Patrol would also clip the lift ticket of skiers who skied too fast, got into fistfights (usually after having too many beers at lunch), did not yield to the downhill skier and caused an accident, or otherwise disobeyed the rules. (Our youngest son, once he graduated from ski school—still three years old—promptly tucked himself into the cool racing position he'd seen on TV, and skied away. No matter how many times I cajoled or scolded him, he did this. He had his ticket clipped more than once.)

One time, I had agreed to meet the boys for lunch at the base of Copper Mountain. From behind, I heard a loud *whoosh whoosh whoosh* and a hollered "Look out! Look out! Look out!" Then I was hit from behind, *from higher on the hill,* by a snowboarder.

I went airborne, then down hard. I couldn't move.

Remember that rule, *Yield to the downhill skier*? This fellow hadn't done that.

Skiers gathered around me, concerned. My skis had popped off my boots. This was before cell phones, so someone said they were going for the Ski Patrol. I was embarrassed and slowly rolled over. Two skiers had released their skis and were kneeling next to me. One looked into my eyes and asked if I was okay. I was sort of seeing double, my knee was killing me, and I gagged on an answer.

The snowboarder, meanwhile, leaned over me and said, "Get up, bitch."

This is when you know you have another book.

And what does the mystery writer say to that snowboarder?

You are so dead.

Snowboarders' Pork Tenderloin

—TOUGH COOKIE—

This is our family's favorite pork recipe. All of our sons, now old enough to cook as well as ski, make it. My brother Bill came up with the idea to grill the tenderloin, and that's a great way to make it, too. Be sure to use a meat thermometer. Tenting all pork, chicken, or beef with foil after it comes out of the oven or off the grill allows the juices to reabsorb. We like this pork with cinnamon-flavored applesauce.

2½ pounds pork tenderloin (2 tenderloins)

½ cup Dijon mustard

¼ cup best-quality dry red wine

¼ cup extra-virgin olive oil

1 tablespoon pressed garlic (4 large or 6 small cloves crushed through a press)

1 tablespoon dried thyme, crushed

½ bay leaf

½ teaspoon sugar

¼ teaspoon freshly ground black pepper

Makes 6 to 8 servings

1. Trim fat and silver skin from tenderloins. Pat dry and set aside. Place all the other ingredients in a glass baking dish and whisk together well. Place tenderloins in the dish, turn them to coat with the marinade, cover the pan with plastic wrap, and place in the refrigerator for at least 6 hours or up to overnight.

2. Thirty minutes before you plan to roast the pork, remove the tenderloins from the refrigerator to come to room temperature.

3. Preheat the oven to 400°F. Using a roasting pan with a rack, line the bottom of the pan with foil (this makes cleanup easier) and place the tenderloins on the rack. Roast the tenderloins for 20 to 25 minutes, or until a meat thermometer inserted in one of them registers 140°F. *Do not overcook the pork.* Remove from the oven, tent the pork with foil, and let sit 10 to 15 minutes before slicing. The center should still be pink when served.

Party Pork Chops

—DOUBLE SHOT—

I'm aware that osmosis *and* diffusion *may be words you haven't heard since high school science, but they're important for cooking pork (and poultry, but we'll get to that). During the whole low-fat craze, pigs were bred to be lower in fat. And guess what? That meant that you could no longer fry a pork chop, much less roast a porkloin, without brining it first. With no fat in the meat to moisturize it as it cooked, you got shoe leather. But by brining using salt and spring water, the pork absorbs moisture (osmosis), which penetrates the meat (diffusion). My preference is away from adding herbs and spices to a brine, because I think they just make the meat taste vaguely seasoned. Very vaguely. But sugar in the brine gives the finished dish a lovely, delicious crust. Serve the chops with Party Apples (page 77) or (our kids' favorite) cinnamon applesauce.*

4 pork chops, preferably bone-in, 1 inch thick

Brine:

5 cups spring water

¼ cup kosher salt

¼ cup sugar

Pat the chops dry with paper towels.

For the brine:

1. In a large bowl, whisk together the water, salt, and sugar until the sugar and salt are dissolved. Place the pork chops in the brine, cover, and brine overnight in the refrigerator.

2. Drain the brine and discard.

3. Rinse the chops in cold water and let them stand in more fresh cold water for 10 minutes, to remove excess saltiness. Remove from the water and pat dry.

Marinade:

2 tablespoons balsamic vinegar

1 teaspoon dried thyme, crumbled

1 teaspoon dried rosemary, crushed

2 garlic cloves, crushed through a press

2 tablespoons extra-virgin olive oil

2 additional tablespoons extra-virgin olive oil, for sautéing

For the marinade:

1. Whisk together the vinegar, thyme, rosemary, garlic, and oil. Place the pork chops in the marinade and allow them to marinate for 1 hour. (You are marinating for flavor here, not tenderizing.)

2. Preheat the oven to 375°F.

3. Heat a large sauté pan over medium-high heat, then pour in the additional oil and let it heat until it shimmers. Sear the chops for about 2 minutes (until well caramelized), then flip and do the other side of each chop for 2 minutes.

4. You can either remove them from the pan and place them in a roasting pan, or, if your skillet can be placed in the oven, roast them directly in the pan. Insert a meat thermometer into the middle of one of the chops, without allowing it to touch the bone or the bottom of the pan.

5. Roast the chops until the meat thermometer reads 140° to 145°F. Remove them from the oven and tent them with foil for 10 minutes. Serve hot.

Makes 4 servings

Figgy Piggy

—FATALLY FLAKY—

I gave credit in the acknowledgments section of Fatally Flaky *to my former publicist, Dee Dee DeBartlo, for coming up with this recipe. When she described the pork stuffed with figs that she had made for her family the evening before, I begged her for the recipe. I tested it out, and added a marinade in order to make the pork extra flavorful. This is a great favorite of our children.*

Two 2-pound whole pork tenderloins

Dijon marinade:

½ cup Dijon mustard

2 tablespoons pressed or minced garlic

½ cup dry red wine

2 tablespoons dried thyme, crushed

1 teaspoon freshly ground black pepper

1 teaspoon sugar

½ cup extra-virgin olive oil

1 bay leaf

Figgy stuffing:

1 tablespoon extra-virgin olive oil

2 shallots, peeled and chopped

Using a sharp knife, remove the fat and silver skin from the tenderloins.

For the Dijon marinade:

1. In a 9 x 13-inch glass baking dish, whisk together the mustard, garlic, red wine, thyme, pepper, and sugar. Whisking constantly, mix in the olive oil until the mixture emulsifies. Slip the bay leaf under the surface of the mixture.

2. Pat the pork dry, then place the tenderloins in the marinade. Turn them to make sure they are evenly coated. Cover the pan tightly with plastic wrap and place in the refrigerator to marinate overnight.

For the figgy stuffing:

In a large ovenproof skillet, heat the olive oil over medium-low heat. Add the shallots and cook until they are limp and translucent, about 5 minutes. Add the figs, stock, and sage, increase the heat, and bring the mixture to a boil. Reduce the heat to low, cover the pan, and simmer the

½ pound fresh figs, stems removed, chopped

¼ cup chicken stock, homemade (page 30) or canned

2 tablespoons chopped fresh sage

Roasting:

2 teaspoons kosher salt

2 teaspoons freshly ground black pepper

⅓ pound sliced prosciutto

2 tablespoons extra-virgin olive oil

½ cup dry white vermouth

mixture until the figs are tender and the liquid is absorbed, 5 to 10 minutes. Set the mixture aside in a bowl to cool slightly while you prepare the tenderloins.

For roasting:

1. Position a rack in the center of the oven and preheat to 375°F.

2. Remove the tenderloins from the marinade (discard the marinade), wipe dry with paper towels, and place them side by side on a cutting board, with the thick end of one next to the thin end of the other. Using the flat side of a mallet or the palm of your hand, pound the tenderloins until they are an even 1-inch thickness. (This will make them able to hold the stuffing.) Sprinkle them with the salt and pepper.

3. Spread the fig stuffing down the length of one of the tenderloins. Carefully place the other tenderloin on top. Place the prosciutto slices crosswise down the length of the tenderloin "sandwich."

4. Cut 4 feet of kitchen twine into four 12-inch lengths. Carefully slide the kitchen strings crosswise, evenly spaced apart, *underneath* the tenderloin "sandwich." Tie the strings around the "sandwich" and cut off any excess string.

5. Wipe out the ovenproof skillet the figs were cooked in and heat the olive oil over medium-high heat, just until the oil ripples. Add the

tenderloin "sandwich," curving it to fit the pan. Cook for 3 minutes. Then, using tongs, very carefully turn the tenderloin "sandwich" over to cook for another 3 minutes.

6. Remove the skillet from the stove and add the vermouth to the skillet. Insert a meat thermometer into the pork and place it in the oven. Roast the pork until the thermometer reads 140°F, about 15 minutes.

7. Carefully remove the tenderloin "sandwich" to a platter, cover it with foil, and let rest for 10 minutes.

8. To serve, slice the pork crosswise into ¾-inch-thick slices. (You can pass a bowl with the pan drippings, if there are any.)

Makes about 8 servings

Puerco Cubano

—CRUNCH TIME—

Crunch Time *has two Cuban-American characters, so I wanted to introduce the flavor of Cuban-style pork (with garlic, lime juice, and orange juice). Alas, Jim and the kids vetoed all my experiments. I was at wit's end when I finally thought of using ground pork. (This is* not *an authentic Cuban dish! So please don't write and tell me;* I know.) *But it didn't dry out, it gives some of the flavors of Cuban cuisine, and it passed muster with the family. This dish goes well with rice.*

- 4 tablespoons (½ stick) unsalted butter
- 1 pound ground pork
- 2 tablespoons minced or pressed garlic
- 2 teaspoons chicken or veal demi-glace (available in specialty food shops)
- ¼ cup all-purpose flour
- ½ teaspoon dried oregano
- ¼ teaspoon kosher salt
- ¼ teaspoon freshly ground black pepper
- 2 cups fresh-squeezed orange juice
- ¼ cup fresh-squeezed lime juice
- 2 teaspoons sugar, or more to taste
- 1 cup chopped fresh cilantro

1. In a 12-inch sauté pan that is *not* nonstick, melt the butter over medium-low heat. Add the pork and garlic and cook, stirring and breaking up the pork, until the meat is just cooked. Add the demi-glace and stir well. Add the flour, oregano, salt, and pepper and cook, stirring, until the flour is cooked and the mixture bubbles.

2. Stir in the orange juice, lime juice, and sugar and increase the heat to medium. Stir constantly until the mixture bubbles and is thickened. Taste and correct the seasoning.

3. Spoon the pork onto a large platter and sprinkle with the chopped cilantro. Serve immediately.

Makes 4 to 6 servings

Chinese Beef Stir-Fry with Vegetables

—THE CEREAL MURDERS—

The forebears of my family of origin, Adam and Jacob Mott, settled in New York during the seventeenth century. I love the fact that Mott Street in New York City is now located in Chinatown. You can cut up any type of high-quality, tender beef for this dish, but I would recommend buying a whole tenderloin (prime, if possible) from Costco (usually 4 to 5 pounds), trimming it, and weighing out a pound to slice up for this dish. Then you can cook the rest of the tenderloin for a family meal, and not have too many leftovers.

1 tablespoon dry sherry

1 tablespoon soy sauce

3 teaspoons cornstarch, divided

½ teaspoon sugar

2 tablespoons plus ½ teaspoon peanut oil or vegetable oil

⅛ teaspoon freshly ground black pepper, or more to taste

2 garlic cloves, crushed through a press

1 pound good-quality tenderloin or sirloin beef, cut into 1-inch cubes

1 tablespoon oyster sauce (found in the Asian foods aisle at your grocery)

2 large stalks broccoli, stems removed and discarded, cut into florets

2 carrots, sliced on the diagonal

½ cup beef broth

8 ears water-packed baby corn (contents of about half of a 15-ounce can), drained

20 fresh snow peas, strings removed

1 scallion, chopped (including tops)

1. In a large bowl, mix together the sherry, soy sauce, 1 teaspoon of the cornstarch, the sugar, ½ teaspoon of the oil, the pepper, and garlic until smooth. Place the beef in this mixture and marinate in the refrigerator for 1 to 2 hours. When you are ready to prepare the dish, remove the beef from the refrigerator and allow it to come to room temperature.

2. In a wok, heat 1 tablespoon of the oil over high heat. Add the beef and its marinade and stir-fry quickly, until the meat is browned on the outside and pink inside. Remove to a plate and set aside.

3. In a small bowl, mix the remaining 2 teaspoons cornstarch with the oyster sauce, set aside. Reheat the wok with the remaining 1 tablespoon oil. Add the broccoli and carrots and stir-fry for 30 seconds. Add the broth, cover the wok, and steam until the vegetables are tender but retain their crunch, about 1 minute. Add the corn, snow peas, scallion, beef, and oyster sauce–cornstarch mixture. Heat quickly, until the sauce is clear and thickened. Serve immediately.

Makes 4 servings

Shakespeare's Steak Pie

—STICKS AND SCONES—

Even though steak-and-kidney pie is the traditional English dish, members of our family vehemently vetoed the kidneys. An all-steak pie was the result. Alas, this ended up being an expensive recipe. Because tenderloin cooks so quickly and is easily overcooked, it is imperative that you purchase a good meat thermometer so that the beef is cooked to an ideal medium-rare temperature.

2 tablespoons unsalted butter

1 medium or ½ large onion, chopped

1 medium carrot, chopped

2 garlic cloves, crushed through a press

2 tablespoons minced fresh parsley

6 tablespoons all-purpose flour

½ teaspoon crumbled dried thyme

½ teaspoon crumbled dried oregano

½ teaspoon crumbled dried sage

1½ teaspoons salt

¼ teaspoon freshly ground black pepper

1. In a large sauté pan, melt the butter over medium-low heat. Add the onion, carrot, garlic, and parsley and gently sauté for a moment, stirring until the vegetables are well mixed. Cover the pan and cook over medium-low heat, stirring occasionally, until the onion is limp and translucent and the carrot has lost some of its crunch, about 10 minutes. Uncover the pan and set aside to cool.

2. Place the flour, thyme, oregano, sage, salt, and pepper in a large, heavy-duty zippered plastic bag and mix well. Add the beef to the bag, zip the top closed, and shake until all the cubes are evenly covered with the dry mixture.

3. Butter a 9 x 12-inch oval gratin dish. Place the floured cubes into the pan along with the sautéed vegetables, mixing very lightly with your hands, just until the vegetables and meat are evenly distributed. Place the filled pan in the refrigerator while you prepare the crust. (Or you

2½ pounds beef tenderloin, trimmed (about 2 pounds after trimming), cut into 1½-inch cubes

Upper Crust Pastry (recipe follows)

¼ cup best-quality dry red wine

can cover the filled pan with plastic wrap, place it in the refrigerator, and chill until you are ready to prepare the crust and cook the pie. If you do this, bring the meat and vegetables to room temperature before proceeding. It is best not to prepare the crust in advance.)

4. Preheat the oven to 350°F.

5. Pour the wine into the pan of meat and vegetables. Gently fit the dough over the pan as directed in the pastry recipe. Carefully insert a meat thermometer through a slash in the crust, making sure it spears a piece of beef.

6. Bake for about 25 minutes, or until the meat thermometer reads 125°F for medium rare. Serve immediately.

Makes 4 large servings

* * *

Upper-Crust Pastry

1 large egg, beaten

1 tablespoon milk, preferably whole

1¼ cups all-purpose flour

½ teaspoon salt

6 tablespoons (¾ stick) cold unsalted butter, cut into 6 pieces

1. Measure out 1 tablespoon of the beaten egg and set aside. Beat the milk into the egg remaining.

2. In a food processor, combine the flour and salt and process for 5 seconds. With the motor running, drop in the butter, one piece at a time. Add the egg-milk mixture to the processor and process for a few moments, just until the dough pulls into a ball. Gently flatten the dough and place it into a rectangular jumbo-size (2-gallon) zippered plastic bag. Using a rolling pin, roll the pastry to the edges of the bag, or until it will fit over your pan.

3. Open the bag at the zipper and, using scissors, carefully cut down the sides of the bag. Remove one whole side of the bag and place the pastry side down over the filling in the pie pan. Gently peel off the top of the bag. Flute the edges of the pastry and slash the center in 3 places to vent. Using a pastry brush, paint the reserved tablespoon of beaten egg on top of the pastry.

Love-Me-Tenderloin Grilled Steaks

—THE WHOLE ENCHILADA—

During the blizzard of 2003, when we received a remarkable sixty inches of snow over a three-day period in March, *a nearby power line went down. We had no heat, no power, and no water for five days. The axe for splitting logs for the fireplace broke on Day Four. Our youngest son, in high school at the time, proclaimed that as soon as our electricity was restored, he was never again eating peanut butter or canned ravioli (which we heated in a pan over the fire). Jim laboriously shoveled a path out to the unplowed street. Each morning, we had to take our dogs out on leashes, because otherwise they would merrily run over the tops of our snow-buried fences. And in the morning, the scent of bacon cooking on our neighbors' propane grills was agonizing. So for Father's Day that year, Jim received a propane grill. But in the meantime, once we had the power back, I bought a grill pan to make these steaks, as a special treat. Allowing the beef to come to room temperature before grilling is key, as is allowing them to rest after they come out of the oven.* You must have a meat thermometer that has an oven-safe probe and cord to make this recipe. *(The cord is plugged into the read-out, which is outside of the oven.) I actually use two probes with cords attached, one in each of the two steaks, to make sure the meat is cooking properly.*

- 4 filet mignon steaks (6 ounces each), 1½ to 2 inches thick (prime grade, if at all possible)
- ¼ cup garlic oil (available at specialty food shops or online)
- Kosher salt and freshly ground black pepper

1. Allow the beef to come to room temperature.

2. Preheat the oven to 350°F. Have your meat thermometer(s) ready.

3. Pat the steaks on both sides with paper towels until they are thoroughly dry.

4. Heat an ovenproof grill pan on the stovetop over high heat. (If the steaks will not fit in the

pan without crowding, you might have to use 2 pans. Alternatively, you could use a large ovenproof skillet.) When the pan is hot, add the oil. Heat for about 5 seconds, or until the oil shimmers (you do not want to burn the oil).

5. Lay the steaks in the pan. Reduce the heat to medium-high, sprinkle the steaks lightly with salt and pepper, and cook for 1 minute only. Turn off the heat.

6. Using tongs, flip the steaks and remove the pan from the heat. Insert a meat thermometer into one steak, place the grill pan in the oven, and cook until the thermometer reads 125°F (for medium-rare). Remove the pan from the oven, loosely cover the steaks with foil, and let sit for 5 to 10 minutes before serving.

Makes 4 servings

Sweethearts' Swedish Meatballs in Burgundy Sauce

—CHOPPING SPREE—

This oldie-but-goodie recipe for Swedish meatballs was given to me by a dear church friend, Barb Coulter. While I was making variations and testing it (fifteen years ago), one of our sons was living in Boulder and coming for dinner. So I asked him to stop by a famous wine store to pick up a bottle of dry red Burgundy, and I would reimburse him. I told him to tell the famous wine store people I was just using the wine for Swedish meatballs. The bottle he purchased cost fifty dollars. (Remember, this was fifteen *years ago. That bottle would probably be triple that now, at least.) Aghast, I said to our son, "Did you remember to tell them it was just for cooking?" He replied that he had.* This *was the bottle they'd recommended* for cooking. *I paid our son, made the dish, and was absolutely blown away by the resulting flavor. These days, all the major chefs recommend using the best wine possible for whatever dish you are making. So buy the best dry red Burgundy you can afford, and have the rest of the bottle with dinner. If the dish is to be served as an appetizer, provide small bowls or dishes and spoons. If the dish is to be served as a main course, serve over hot egg noodles.*

Meatballs:

⅔ cup cornflake crumbs

1 teaspoon cornstarch

1 tablespoon dried minced onion

⅛ teaspoon freshly grated nutmeg

1¼ teaspoons salt

For the meatballs:

1. Preheat the oven to 300°F. Line a rimmed baking sheet with a silicone baking mat (or grease the pan with butter).

2. In a large bowl, mix the cornflake crumbs, cornstarch, onion, nutmeg, salt, and pepper to taste. In another bowl, mix together the cream and egg. Pour the egg mixture over the crumb

Freshly ground black pepper

⅔ cup heavy (whipping) cream or Crème Fraîche (see Note)

1 large egg, well beaten

1 pound lean ground beef

4 tablespoons extra-virgin olive oil

Burgundy sauce:

Melted unsalted butter (see first step of sauce below)

¼ cup all-purpose flour

1½ teaspoons sugar, or to taste

Freshly ground black pepper

2 cups homemade beef stock or 1 tablespoon beef bouillon granules dissolved in 2 cups hot spring water

1 cup best-quality dry red Burgundy wine

mixture and stir gently. Allow this mixture to sit until the liquid is absorbed.

3. Gently mix in the ground beef until thoroughly combined. Using a 1-tablespoon (or slightly larger) ice-cream scoop, measure out the beef mixture into 36 scoops onto 2 plates covered with wax paper. Gently roll the scoops between your fingers to form balls.

4. In a large skillet, heat 2 tablespoons of the oil over medium-high heat until the oil shimmers. Carefully place the balls into the hot oil and sauté, turning once, until the outside is browned. (Do not cook the meatballs all the way through; they will be finished in the oven.) Using tongs, place the browned meatballs on the baking sheet. (Set the skillet with drippings aside to use for the Burgundy sauce.) Bake the meatballs for 10 minutes. Test the doneness of the meatballs by slicing one in half. The interior should no longer be pink. *Do not overbake the meatballs.* Set the meatballs aside until you are ready to reheat them in the sauce, which should not be until shortly before serving: The meatballs are delicate and will fall apart if cooked too long in the sauce. (If making the meatballs ahead, cool them and place them in a container that can be covered.)

For the Burgundy sauce:

1. Pour the fat from the meatball skillet (reserve the browned bits) into a glass measuring cup. Add melted unsalted butter to make ¼ cup.

2. Return the fat to the pan and set over low heat. Whisk in the flour, and keeping the heat between low and medium-low, whisk and cook this mixture until it bubbles. (This should not take more than a couple of minutes.) Whisk in the sugar and pepper to taste, then slowly add the stock, whisking constantly to avoid lumps. Finally, whisk in the wine.

3. Allow the mixture to come to a slow simmer and cook for about 5 minutes. Taste and correct the seasoning. If the sauce tastes bitter, add a bit more sugar and allow the sauce to simmer another 10 minutes. (If the dish is not to be served immediately, cool the sauce and chill, covered, until ready to heat and serve. Then gently reheat.)

4. With the sauce at a simmer, lower the meatballs into the hot sauce and bring the mixture back to a simmer. Check a meatball with sauce to be sure the dish is heated all the way through.

Makes 36 meatballs in sauce

Note: If you choose to use crème fraîche instead of heavy cream in the meatball recipe, note that you have to start it 2 days ahead.

* * *

Crème Fraîche

- ¼ cup active-culture buttermilk (do not use buttermilk powder)
- 2 cups heavy (whipping) cream

In a glass container, mix the buttermilk into the cream, cover with plastic wrap, and allow to sit at room temperature until the mixture is the thickness of commercial sour cream, usually about 2 days. It can be refrigerated, covered, for up to 3 days. Use the crème fraîche in sauce recipes (like the Swedish Meatballs) or dips.

Ad Guys' Roast Beef and Gravy

—CHOPPING SPREE—

When the same son who'd bought the expensive Burgundy had a bad ski accident requiring surgery, my husband (retired from a job that had required long hours) took care of him at home while I went to our son's classes at the University of Colorado, ostensibly to take notes. ("Don't say anything, Mom" was our son's whispered warning from the couch. As if!) There was another reason I needed to go to the classes, though. As any of you who have attended—or whose children have attended—state universities in the past twenty-plus years know, they are oversubscribed. What this means in practice is that if you finally do *get into the courses you requested, they will be the popular ones, and there will likely be waiting lists for that class. Our son was in the second semester of his senior year. He'd finally made it into the classes he wanted. But then he took that fall at Copper Mountain. If someone named "Davidson" did not say "Here!" on the first day of class, he feared he would be bumped from the course. Since we were paying the tuition, I was willing to ask each professor if I could be the placeholder and note-taker for our son. (In fact, roll was never taken. I also told each of the professors before class why I was there. They said it was fine, and they wished our son a speedy recovery.)*

So . . . I went to class, took notes, and kept my mouth (mostly) shut. One of our son's Film Studies professors invited me to a lecture being given by a visiting instructor from a Los Angeles studio. I thought the class was terrific, so I signed our son up for it. (Our son needed *that course, I reasoned.) To make room for the extra class, I dropped a class our son had signed up for. (I told our son, but not the professor, that the class was not worth his time.) So I didn't interfere too much and I hardly said a word. Plus, I did take good notes.*

In the meantime, I didn't want to commute to Boulder every day, so a lovely friend, the writer Julie Kaewert, invited me to stay with her family for one night. I volunteered to make dinner, and went back to the wine store where our son had bought the fifty-dollar bottle. I splurged and bought the same wine, then was lucky enough to find a prime-grade standing rib roast at a fancy grocery store. I made this dish, and Julie recommended I put it into the book.

4- to 5-pound standing rib roast, prime grade

½ teaspoon salt

½ teaspoon freshly ground black pepper

Melted unsalted butter, if necessary

¼ cup best-quality dry red Burgundy

¼ cup all-purpose flour

3½ cups homemade beef stock or 2 tablespoons beef bouillon granules dissolved in 3½ cups boiling spring water

1. Allow the roast to come to room temperature.

2. Preheat the oven to 450°F.

3. Take out a roasting pan with a rack and line the bottom (underneath the rack) with either a very large piece of foil that completely covers the bottom of the pan and can be folded up over the sides, or two pieces of foil that have been rolled tightly in the middle to form one large piece. The bottom of the pan should be completely covered with a leakproof piece of foil.

4. Use a paper towel to pat the roast dry, then season the roast with the salt and pepper. Place the roast, bone side down, on the rack. Insert a meat thermometer into the roast so that the sensor is in the middle of the roast.

5. Place the roast in the oven and immediately reduce the oven temperature to 325°F. Roast until the meat thermometer reads 115°F. (At this point the beef is quite rare, and the cooking is not done yet.) Transfer the roast to another pan (even a large pie plate will do) and return it, along with the meat thermometer, to the oven. (To obtain medium-rare, the roast should be removed when the thermometer reaches 125° to 130°F; for medium, 135° to 145°F.) When the

thermometer reaches the desired temperature, transfer the roast to a serving platter and tent it with foil.

6. Pour the fat from the bottom of the foil-covered pan into a glass measuring cup. You should have ¼ cup. If you have more, discard it. If you have less, add melted butter until you have ¼ cup. Pour the Burgundy directly into the bottom of the foil-covered roasting pan and let it sit while you start on the gravy.

7. Pour the fat into a sauté pan over low heat. Increase the heat under the sauté pan to medium-low and whisk the flour into the fat. Whisking constantly, cook the flour in the fat until the mixture just begins to bubble and turn color, less than 5 minutes.

8. Using a silicone spatula, scrape up the flavorful browned bits adhering to the foil in the first pan, so that they mix with the wine. Pour the wine mixture into the flour mixture. Whisking constantly, add the beef stock in a slow stream. When all the stock has been added, taste the gravy and correct the seasoning.

9. Over medium-low to medium-high heat, whisk and cook the gravy until it thickens and bubbles. Serve hot with the roast beef.

Makes 4 to 6 servings

Anniversary Burgers

—DYING FOR CHOCOLATE—

In Dying for Chocolate, *Goldy makes this for the cookout celebrating the wedding anniversary of General and Mrs. Farquhar. But you don't have to be celebrating to make them; they're our family's favorite burger for summer barbecues. Be sure to use real butter in the sauce, and serve the burgers right off the grill, when they're very hot and at their best.*

2 large eggs, beaten

2 tablespoons heavy (whipping) cream

2 tablespoons milk, preferably whole

2 slices bread, torn up

1 tablespoon dried minced onion

2 teaspoons prepared horseradish

1½ teaspoons salt

½ teaspoon mustard powder

¼ teaspoon dried thyme

¼ teaspoon freshly ground black pepper

2 pounds lean ground beef

8 tablespoons (1 stick) unsalted butter

½ cup ketchup

1. In a bowl, mix the eggs with the cream and milk. Add the torn-up bread, onion, horseradish, salt, mustard powder, thyme, and pepper. Stir well and let stand for 10 minutes. Stir well again, until all the ingredients are well moistened and the bread is no longer in pieces. Add the ground beef and mix gently with your hands, just until thoroughly combined. Measure out the beef in ½-cup increments and form patties.

2. In a small saucepan, melt the butter with the ketchup and keep warm.

3. Preheat a gas grill to high or prepare a charcoal fire and allow it to become very hot. Grill over hot coals for 3 minutes on one side. Flip and brush with the butter-ketchup mixture. Grill the other side, until center is done to your liking, about another 3 minutes for medium, and brush other side with mixture. Serve hot.

Makes about 9 patties

The Whole Enchilada Pie

—DOUBLE SHOT—

This is a family favorite, and much easier than actual enchiladas.

1 pound ground beef

1 medium onion, chopped

2 garlic cloves, crushed through a press

⅓ cup picante sauce

Contents of one 16-ounce can refried beans

Contents of one 10-ounce can enchilada sauce

1 cup sliced, pitted black California olives

1 teaspoon salt

6 cups crushed corn chips

6 cups grated Cheddar cheese

Garnishes:

Sour cream

Chopped fresh tomatoes

Sliced iceberg lettuce

Chopped scallions (including tops)

Avocado slices or prepared guacamole

1. Preheat the oven to 375°F. Grease a 9 x 13-inch glass baking dish.

2. In a large, deep skillet set over medium heat, brown the ground beef with the onion and garlic until the beef is browned and the onion is soft, about 5 to 8 minutes. Stir constantly for even browning.

3. Reduce the heat and add the picante sauce, refried beans, enchilada sauce, olives, and salt. Stir and cook until well combined and bubbling. Remove from the heat.

4. Place 1 cup of the crushed corn chips in the bottom of the baking dish. Put half the beef mixture on top. Top with another cup of the chips and 2 cups Cheddar. Put in the rest of the beef mixture, then the rest of the chips, then top with the remaining 4 cups cheese.

5. Bake the pie for 30 to 40 minutes, or until the center is hot and bubbling. Serve immediately with bowls filled with the garnishes. (If you bake the pie and reheat it later, cover it with a piece of buttered foil to keep it from drying out.)

Makes 8 servings

Unorthodox Shepherd's Pie

—SWEET REVENGE—

This recipe has "unorthodox" in the title because it is not made with lamb. But in this country, most of what we call "shepherd's pie" is made with ground beef. Our Denver Costco used to sell a version of this dish (made with ground beef), and the family loved it. There were many groans from the family when Costco stopped carrying the dish. Jim asked if I could try to duplicate it, and this recipe is the result. This dish is made truly amazing if you use homemade chicken stock. The pie goes well with a fruit salad.

2 tablespoons extra-virgin olive oil

2 pounds lean ground beef

2 cups chopped yellow onions

2 cups chopped celery

¼ cup plus 1 tablespoon all-purpose flour

2 cups chicken stock, preferably homemade (page 30)

2 teaspoons dried thyme, crumbled

½ teaspoon dried rosemary, crushed

1 teaspoon kosher salt, plus more for seasoning the potatoes

1. Bring a large saucepan of salted spring water to a boil. Peel the potatoes and lower them into the water. Cook until tender, 40 to 45 minutes.

2. In a very large sauté pan, heat the oil over medium heat until it shimmers. Add the ground beef, onions, and celery and cook until the beef is browned and the vegetables are limp. Add the flour and stir until the mixture begins to bubble, 2 to 3 minutes. Slowly add the chicken stock. Stir until completely combined, then stir in the thyme, rosemary, salt, and pepper. Cook and stir until the mixture is bubbling and thickened. Stir in the peas and corn and set aside.

3. Meanwhile, in a small saucepan, heat the half-and-half until it is steaming, but not boiling.

4. Preheat the oven to 350°F. Butter two 9-inch deep-dish pie plates. Grease a large baking sheet

¼ to ½ teaspoon freshly ground black pepper, plus more for seasoning the potatoes

1 cup frozen baby peas

1 cup frozen baby corn kernels

4½ pounds russet (baking) potatoes

1½ cups half-and-half

1 cup grated Gruyère cheese

½ cup freshly grated Parmesan cheese

4 tablespoons (½ stick) unsalted butter, cut into bits

Paprika

or line it with a silicone baking mat. (This makes for easier clean-up.)

5. Drain the potatoes and place them in a large bowl. With an electric mixer, beat the potatoes on low speed, slowly adding the hot half-and-half, the cheeses, and salt and pepper to taste, until the ingredients are well mixed.

6. Place half the beef mixture in each of the two pie plates. Dividing evenly, top the beef mixture with the mashed potatoes. Scatter the butter bits on top of each potato mixture. Sprinkle generously with paprika.

7. Place the pies on the baking sheet and put them in the oven. Bake for about 45 minutes, or until the potatoes are browned and the pies are completely heated through.

Makes 8 large servings

Goldy's Garlic Lamb Chops

—CRUNCH TIME—

I've worked on preparing lamb chops numerous ways over the years, and finally came up with this dish that the family liked best. Since it's somewhat mild, it's also the one that I take to neighbors who've had surgery, are sick, or just need cheering up. I always serve these with mint jelly.

2 racks baby lamb rib chops (about 1¾ pounds each)

2 tablespoons pressed garlic

Extra-virgin olive oil

½ teaspoon kosher salt, or to taste

½ teaspoon freshly ground black pepper, or to taste

1. Allow the lamb chops to come to room temperature before beginning to prepare the dish.

2. Preheat the oven to 425°F. Lightly oil the rack on a roasting pan.

3. Pat the chops dry and place them on a cutting board. Using a very sharp knife, carefully trim a ¼-inch layer of fat from the area above the meat. Set this fat aside.

4. Still using the sharp knife, cut 7 evenly spaced, deep pockets in the meat of each rack, between the chops. Stuff the pockets with the garlic. If you have garlic left over, spread it across the top of the meat.

5. Pour enough olive oil over the lamb racks to evenly coat. Sprinkle the racks with the salt and pepper, then place the reserved layers of fat lengthwise, over the chops and the pockets of garlic. Place the chops on the prepared rack of

the roasting pan. Carefully insert a meat thermometer into the meat, so as not to touch the bone.

6. Roast until the meat thermometer reads 145°F. Remove the lamb from the oven and tent a piece of foil over the racks. Allow to sit for 10 to 15 minutes. Remove and discard the extra pieces of fat that you placed lengthwise over the meat. Serve carved into 2 to 3 chops per person.

Makes 6 to 8 servings

Grilled Chicken à l'Orange

—THE GRILLING SEASON—

One of the tricks I learned in the catering business is to pound boneless, skinless chicken breasts to an even thickness between sheets of plastic wrap. This makes for easier stovetop cooking and grilling, because the chicken can cook through without becoming overcooked. Jim and I had enjoyed my own version of "Orange Chicken" for years before I decided to see if it would work as a grilled dish. We were all pleased with the results.

Marinade:

Grated zest and juice (about ⅓ cup) of 1 medium orange

1 teaspoon mustard powder

Tiny pinch of ground cumin (optional)

2 tablespoons red wine vinegar

⅓ cup extra-virgin olive oil

4 boneless, skinless chicken breast halves (about 6 ounces each)

For the marinade:

1. In a 9 x 13-inch glass baking dish, make the marinade by combining the orange zest, juice, mustard, cumin (if using), and vinegar. Whisk in the olive oil.

2. Place the chicken breasts on a sheet of plastic wrap. Cover with a second sheet of plastic wrap. Using the flat side of a meat mallet, gently pound the chicken breasts to an even ½-inch thickness. Remove the plastic wrap and place the chicken breasts in the marinade. Cover, place in the refrigerator, and allow to marinate for at least 30 minutes and up to 1 hour.

3. When you are ready to cook the chicken, preheat the grill.

Sauce:

2 tablespoons butter

2 tablespoons all-purpose flour

1½ tablespoons sugar

¼ teaspoon ground cinnamon

¼ teaspoon mustard powder

2 tablespoons red wine vinegar

1½ cups orange juice

For the sauce:

1. In a large skillet, melt the butter over low heat and stir in the flour. Cook over low heat until it bubbles, a minute or two. Add the sugar, cinnamon, mustard powder, and vinegar and stir until well combined. Whisk in the orange juice, increase the heat to medium, and stir until thickened. Reduce the heat and cover the pan to keep the sauce hot while you grill the chicken.

2. Discard the marinade and pat the chicken dry. Grill the chicken just until cooked through, 3 to 5 minutes per side. *Do not overcook the chicken.*

3. To serve, place the grilled chicken on a heated platter, pour some of the sauce over it, and pass the rest of the sauce at the table.

Makes 4 servings

André's Coq au Vin

—PRIME CUT—

Before working on this dish, I'd followed cookbook recipes for coq au vin, only to be disappointed that the chicken would overcook before the sauce was done. The solution was to flip the order of preparation. This sauce is made and simmered first; then the chicken is quickly sautéed and added to the sauce.

3 tablespoons butter

1 carrot, diced

1 medium onion, chopped

2 garlic cloves, crushed through a press

3 tablespoons chopped fresh parsley

1 cup best-quality dry red wine

½ cup beef stock or bouillon

1 tablespoon tomato paste or ketchup

1 tablespoon cornstarch

4 skinless, boneless chicken breast halves (about 6 ounces each)

1 tablespoon all-purpose flour

½ teaspoon salt

¼ teaspoon freshly ground black pepper

1 tablespoon extra-virgin olive oil

1. In a large skillet, melt the butter over low heat. Add the carrot, onion, garlic, and parsley and cook slowly, stirring often, until the onion is soft and translucent, 10 to 20 minutes. Add the wine, stock, and tomato paste or ketchup. Simmer, covered, over low heat for 20 minutes. Stir 2 tablespoons spring water into the cornstarch until smooth. Mix into the wine mixture and stir until the sauce is thick and clear. Set aside, covered, over very low heat, while you prepare the chicken.

2. Place the chicken breasts on a sheet of plastic wrap. Cover with a second sheet of plastic wrap. Using the flat side of a meat mallet, gently pound the chicken breasts to an even ½-inch thickness. In a shallow bowl, mix together the flour, salt, and pepper, and dredge the chicken breasts in this mixture.

3. In a large heavy skillet, heat the oil over medium-high heat. Add the chicken breasts and cook until almost cooked through, about 1½ minutes per side.

4. Transfer the chicken breasts to the skillet with the wine mixture, cover, and cook over medium-low heat until the chicken is just cooked through and no pink remains in the center, another 6 to 10 minutes. Serve immediately.

Makes 4 servings

Trudy's Mediterranean Chicken

—DOUBLE SHOT—

Since Trudy, Goldy's next-door neighbor, had managed to stay alive and unheralded through all of the books up to Double Shot, *I decided to name a recipe after her. As with André's Coq au Vin (page 139), I realized that preparing the sauce first, then sautéing the chicken, was the way to go.*

Sauce:

¼ cup extra-virgin olive oil

3 medium onions, thinly sliced

6 garlic cloves, crushed through a press

2 cups tomato juice

½ cup dry sherry

½ teaspoon salt

½ teaspoon best-quality paprika, preferably imported

Chicken:

4 boneless, skinless chicken breasts (about 6 ounces each)

½ cup all-purpose flour

½ teaspoon salt

¼ teaspoon best-quality paprika

¼ cup extra-virgin olive oil

For the sauce:

In a large skillet, heat the oil over medium heat until it shimmers. Add the onions and immediately reduce the heat to low. Stir and cook the onions for 1 minute, then add the garlic. Stir and cook over low heat until the onions are soft and translucent, about 10 minutes. Add the tomato juice, sherry, salt, and paprika. Stir and cook until the mixture bubbles. Cover and keep over low heat while you prepare the chicken breasts.

For the chicken:

1. Preheat the oven to 350°F. Grease a 9 x 13-inch glass baking dish.

2. Pat the chicken breasts dry with paper towels. Place the chicken breasts on a sheet of plastic wrap. Cover with a second sheet of plastic wrap. Using the flat side of a meat mallet, gently pound the chicken breasts to an even ½-inch thickness. Remove the plastic wrap.

3. On a large plate, whisk together the flour, salt, and paprika. Dip the chicken breasts one at a time into the mixture, until they are completely dusted.

4. In a large skillet, heat the olive oil over medium heat, just until it shimmers. Place the chicken in the pan and cook until seared on each side, about 1½ minutes per side. Place the chicken in the baking dish. Pour the hot sauce over it. Place in the oven and cook *just* until the chicken is done, about 20 minutes, or until a meat thermometer inserted into one of the pieces of chicken reads 160°F. Serve immediately.

Makes 4 servings

Chicken Piccata Supreme

—DARK TORT—

Assuming you pound the chicken in advance and assemble all your ingredients, chicken piccata is a delicious dish that works well for company. For reasons I have never understood, recipes including pressed, chopped, or minced garlic often say you should sauté it. Sauter *literally means "to jump," and if the oil in your sauté pan is hot enough to make the garlic jump, you're just going to end up with burnt garlic. In my opinion, garlic should never be sautéed, but should be cooked gently and thoroughly without browning (the technical term is "sweated") over low heat. Again, the most important aspect of this or any other chicken dish is not to overcook it. Finally, traditional chicken piccata usually calls for lemon juice, but repeated testings made the family say they liked lime better. Up to you.*

4 boneless, skinless chicken breast halves (about 6 ounces each)

½ cup all-purpose flour, for dredging

½ teaspoon salt

¼ teaspoon freshly ground black pepper

3 tablespoons extra-virgin olive oil, divided

2 teaspoons pressed garlic (crushed through a press)

½ cup finely chopped scallions (including tops)

1 tablespoon fresh lime or lemon juice

¼ cup dry white vermouth

6 tablespoons (¾ stick) unsalted butter

1. Place the chicken breasts on a sheet of plastic wrap. Cover with a second sheet of plastic wrap. Using the flat side of a meat mallet, gently pound the chicken breasts to an even ½-inch thickness. In a shallow plate, whisk together the flour, salt, and pepper. Dredge the pounded chicken breasts in the seasoned flour and set aside.

2. In a large sauté pan, heat 1 tablespoon of the oil over medium-high heat. When the oil shimmers, put in two of the chicken breasts and sauté for about 1½ minutes per side, until the

outside is nicely browned but the interior of the chicken is still very slightly pink. Remove the pieces to a plate and repeat with the other two chicken breasts and another tablespoon of oil. Set aside.

3. Reduce the heat under the sauté pan to low. When the heat is low, add the remaining 1 tablespoon oil and the garlic. Cook the garlic very gently ("sweating" it) for several minutes, until it is very soft and cooked through. *Do not burn the garlic.*

4. Add the scallions, lime juice, vermouth, and butter to the pan. Increase the heat to medium, stirring constantly. Once the butter is melted, continue to cook and stir for a bit longer to reduce the sauce slightly. Keeping the heat up, return the chicken to the pan and cook until the chicken has *just* cooked through (check that there is no pink, uncooked center by cutting into one piece), 2 or 3 more minutes.

5. Place the chicken on a heated serving platter. Pour the sauce over the chicken and serve immediately.

Makes 4 servings

Portobello Mushroom Stuffed with Grilled Chicken, Pesto, and Sun-Dried Tomatoes

—THE LAST SUPPERS—

Like Chilean sea bass and balsamic vinegar, portobello mushrooms are an ingredient that swept into this country about twenty years ago, a fabulous blessing.

Chicken and marinade:

1 pound boneless, skinless chicken breast halves, cut into 8 equal pieces

½ cup extra-virgin olive oil

2 tablespoons balsamic vinegar

1 teaspoon Dijon mustard

1 garlic clove, crushed through a press

For marinating the chicken:

Place the chicken in a 9 x 13-inch glass pan. Mix together the olive oil, balsamic vinegar, mustard, and garlic and pour over the chicken pieces. Cover and set aside to marinate in the refrigerator for 1 to 2 hours. When you are ready to prepare the dish, remove the chicken from the refrigerator.

Mushrooms and marinade:

4 large portobello mushrooms (about 4 ounces each)

5 tablespoons extra-virgin olive oil

5 tablespoons best-quality dry sherry

4 tablespoons prepared pesto

2 tablespoons finely chopped oil-packed sun-dried tomatoes, drained and blotted with paper towels

For marinating the mushrooms:

1. Carefully clean the mushrooms with a damp paper towel and trim the ends of the stems. Remove and chop the stems. Place the mushroom caps, tops *down,* as well as the chopped stems, in another 9 x 13-inch glass baking dish. Pour 1 tablespoon of the olive oil and 1 tablespoon of the sherry over the gill side of each mushroom cap. Pour the remaining 4 tablespoons each olive oil and sherry over the stems. Cover and set aside to marinate at room temperature for 1 hour.

2. Preheat a grill. Grill the chicken quickly, 1 to 2 minutes per side (they will be cooked further).

3. Preheat the oven to 400°F. Butter a 9 x 13-inch baking pan.

4. Carefully spread 1 tablespoon pesto over the gill side of each mushroom cap. Sprinkle 1½ teaspoons sun-dried tomatoes on top of the pesto. Evenly distribute the marinated mushroom stems on top of the sun-dried tomatoes. Place 2 slices of chicken on top.

5. Place the stuffed mushrooms in the baking pan and bake for 20 to 25 minutes, or until the chicken is done and the mushrooms are heated through. Serve immediately.

Makes 4 servings

Stir-Fry Chicken with Asparagus

—THE MAIN CORPSE—

It was a great day when I discovered the magic of fermented black beans, used here in the form of black bean sauce.

1 egg white, from a large egg

1 tablespoon cornstarch

1 tablespoon dry sherry

1 tablespoon soy sauce

1 small onion (6 ounces), halved and thinly sliced

1 garlic clove, crushed through a press

1½ pounds boneless, skinless chicken breasts, cut into ½-inch-thick, bite-size pieces

2 tablespoons peanut, canola, or other vegetable oil

1 pound fresh asparagus, tough ends trimmed, cut on the diagonal into 2-inch pieces

½ cup canned water chestnuts, drained and sliced

½ cup black bean sauce (see Note)

Freshly ground black pepper

About 4 cups freshly cooked medium-grain rice

1. In a glass pie plate, thoroughly mix the egg white, cornstarch, sherry, soy sauce, onion, and garlic. Place the chicken pieces in this mixture, cover, and place in the refrigerator for at least 30 minutes and up to 1 hour. When you are ready to prepare the dish, remove the chicken from the refrigerator.

2. In a large skillet or wok, heat the oil over moderately high heat. Add the marinated chicken and stir-fry for several minutes, until it is just done. *Do not overcook the chicken.* Remove the chicken from the pan and set aside.

3. Reheat the pan over high heat and add ½ cup spring water. Quickly stir up the browned bits from the bottom of the pan, then add the asparagus, water chestnuts, and black bean sauce. Cover the pan and cook over medium heat until the asparagus is bright green but

still crunchy, 2 to 5 minutes. Return the chicken to the pan and stir over medium-high heat until the mixture is heated through. Season to taste with pepper. Serve immediately over hot rice.

Makes 4 servings

Note: If you cannot find black bean sauce in the Asian foods section of your local grocery store, the grocery manager should be able to order it for you. The brand I use is Ka-Me. I ceased being frustrated by its frequent unavailability at my local store once I started ordering it by the case. Order forms are usually available at the customer service desk; the order generally takes about two weeks to a month to fill. Ordering by the case usually means you will receive a discount.

Chicken Divine

—SWEET REVENGE—

Like pork, chickens have been bred to be lower in fat, and the dish usually offered to the poor dieter is—alas—dry, leathery chicken breast. But white chicken can be lovely, if it is brined and roasted, skin on, and not overcooked. I was just playing around with brines when I came up with this dish, and Jim insisted it go into a book. Originally I had the chicken topped with dried tarragon, but we also like it with thyme.

2 cups buttermilk

1 cup heavy (whipping) cream

1 tablespoon kosher salt, plus more for sprinkling

1 tablespoon sugar

4 pounds (about 5 pieces) bone-in, skin-on chicken breast halves

Freshly ground black pepper

¼ cup dried thyme or tarragon

1. In a large nonreactive or glass bowl, mix together the buttermilk, cream, salt, and sugar and stir until dissolved. Pat the chicken dry, then place it in the buttermilk mixture. Make sure all the pieces are completely submerged. Cover the bowl with plastic wrap and place the bowl in the refrigerator overnight.

2. When you are ready to start on the chicken, take it out of the refigerator and allow it to come to room termperature.

3. Preheat the oven to 400°F. Butter a 9 x 13-inch glass baking dish.

4. Remove the chicken from the marinade (discard the buttermilk mixture), rinse under running water, and pat dry with paper towels. Place the chicken, skin side up, in the baking dish, being careful not to crowd the pieces.

Sprinkle with salt and pepper to taste. Crush the thyme or tarragon between your fingers and sprinkle it evenly over the chicken.

5. Bake for 35 to 40 minutes, or until a meat thermometer inserted into the thickest part of the chicken, not touching the bone, reads 160°F. Bring the chicken out of the oven, tent with foil for 5 to 10 minutes to allow the juices to reabsorb, and serve.

Makes 4 to 5 servings

Enchiladas Suizas

—THE WHOLE ENCHILADA—

Goldy gives Arch the background on why people in Mexico would eat "Swiss" enchiladas: It is because of the presence of the Sanborn coffee shops in Mexico, which serve dairy-rich dishes favored by the frequent Swiss tourists. Our daughter-in-law, Rosa, gave me her mother's recipe for tortillas, and I tried making them for this dish. The tortillas were delicious, but I simply couldn't get them thin enough to roll around the filling. So I repeatedly put the filling between the tortillas, and ended up with what looked like a very tall stack of pancakes. I thought it tasted delicious, but the family said that slices from the stack were too hard to eat. So with the veto, I went back to grocery-bought corn tortillas, which the family proclaimed superior to my thick creations. Oh, well. This dish is now such a family favorite that our (grown) children ask for it, if they're coming over for their birthday.

12 corn tortillas

⅓ cup extra-virgin olive oil

Filling:

2 cups shredded rotisserie chicken, dark and light meat, skin and bones removed

2¼ cups crema (Mexican-style sour cream), Crème Fraîche (page 127), or commercial sour cream, plus more for serving

1. Preheat the oven to 350°F. Have ready a large plate and 13 absorbent paper towels. Fold the paper towels into quarters.

2. Overlap the tortillas in two large (9 x 13 inches or larger) pans, so that as much of the surfaces of the tortillas is showing as possible. Drizzle the olive oil evenly over the tortillas in both pans. (You may have to use your hands or a pastry brush to spread the oil evenly over the tortillas.) Place the pans in the oven and allow the tortillas to soften for about 5 minutes. Remove the pans from the oven and check that the tortillas are softened by using tongs to lift up one of them. (You want them soft and pliable. If they are

2 cups grated mild or medium-sharp Cheddar cheese

1 teaspoon kosher salt

Sauce:

2 tablespoons extra-virgin olive oil

2 cups chopped yellow onions

2 tablespoons minced garlic

1¾ cups (14.5 ounces) canned diced Italian-style (with garlic, basil, and oregano) tomatoes (see Note)

Contents of two 4.5-ounce cans chopped fire-roasted mild chiles

½ teaspoon dried leaf oregano

Canned Italian-style tomato sauce, if necessary

not yet soft, put the pans back in the oven for a couple of minutes. You do not want to cook the tortillas through, which will harden them.) When the tortillas are just cool enough to touch, place one of the folded towels on a plate. Using tongs, place one tortilla on the folded towel. Place another folded towel on top of the tortilla and press lightly to absorb excess oil. Continue with remaining tortillas. Set aside. (Leave the oven on.)

For the filling:
In a large bowl, stir together the chicken, crema or sour cream, Cheddar, and salt until blended. Set aside.

For the sauce:
In a large skillet, heat the oil over low heat. Add the onions and cook for a minute, stirring. Add the garlic and stir. Continue to cook and stir over low heat until the onion is translucent, about 10 minutes. Add the tomatoes, chiles, and oregano. Simmer this mixture over low heat for 5 to 8 minutes. Remove from the heat, allow to cool slightly, and spoon into a 4-cup measuring cup. You should have 3 cups of sauce. If you do not have 3 full cups, add the canned tomato sauce to make 3 cups.

Assemble the dish:

1. Butter a 9 x 13-inch glass baking dish.

2. To fill the enchiladas, place each tortilla on a flat surface and scoop ¼ cup of the chicken-cheese filling into the center. Using your fingers or a spoon, shape the filling into a cylinder in the center of the tortilla. Roll up the tortilla and place it, seam side down, in the baking dish. Continue until all the tortillas are rolled up.

3. Spoon the sauce over the enchiladas. Bake for 20 to 25 minutes, or until the center of the enchiladas is steaming hot. (Check with a spoon to make sure the center enchilada is very hot.) Serve with sour cream on the side, if desired.

Makes 12 enchiladas

Note: Measure the actual contents of the can of diced tomatoes. Depending on the brand, you may need more than one can in order to get 1¾ cups.

Sonora Chicken Strudel

—TOUGH COOKIE—

Our family used to visit a restaurant (now shuttered) that served chicken strudel. I tried to duplicate the flavors here. For ease of preparation, remove the skin and bones from a grocery-store rotisserie chicken, and shred the cooked meat into bite-size pieces.

2 tablespoons vegetable oil

3 cups seeded and chopped tomatoes

2 garlic cloves, crushed through a press

Contents of two 4-ounce cans chopped green chiles

1½ cups chopped onions

⅛ teaspoon ground cumin

2 cups cooked, shredded chicken

1¼ cups grated Cheddar cheese

1 cup regular or light sour cream

1 teaspoon salt

½ pound frozen phyllo dough, thawed

8 tablespoons (1 stick) unsalted butter, melted

Makes 9 large servings

1. In a large skillet, heat the oil over medium-low heat until it shimmers. Reduce the heat to low and add the tomatoes, garlic, chiles, onions, and cumin. Cook, uncovered, stirring occasionally, until the mixture is thick, about 30 minutes. Set aside to cool slightly.

2. Preheat the oven to 400°F. Butter a 9 x 13-inch glass baking dish.

3. In a large bowl, combine the chicken, Cheddar, sour cream, and salt. Stir in the tomato mixture. Pour this mixture into the pan.

4. Working quickly with the phyllo, lay one sheet at a time over the chicken-tomato mixture and brush lightly but thoroughly with the melted butter. Continue until you are almost out of butter, then lay on a last piece of phyllo and brush it with the last of the melted butter. With a sharp knife, cut down through the layers of phyllo to make 9 evenly spaced rectangular servings.

5. Bake for 20 to 30 minutes, or until the filling is hot and the phyllo is puffed and golden brown. Serve immediately.

Turkey Curry with Raisin Rice

—KILLER PANCAKE—

I deeply regret having fallen for the fad—and that's what it was, a fad—for low-fat cooking. But I had readers repeatedly demanding low-fat food, so I did my best. (These days, people ask me for gluten-free dishes. I encourage them to use a gluten-free cookbook.) When making the turkey curry now, instead of the dry milk powder and skim milk, I use 2 cups of half-and-half or (horrors!) heavy cream.

1 pound ground turkey

Cooking spray or 2 tablespoons unsalted butter

1 cup chopped unpeeled apple

1 cup chopped onion

2 tablespoons extra-virgin olive oil or unsalted butter

2 tablespoon all-purpose flour

1 tablespoon curry powder

1 tablespoon beef bouillon granules

2 cups half-and-half or heavy (whipping) cream

Raisin rice:

1 cup long-grain white rice

½ cup raisins

2¼ cups chicken stock, preferably homemade (page 30)

1. In a large sauté pan, sauté the turkey over medium-high heat, stirring frequently, until browned evenly, about 10 minutes. Turn out onto a plate, set aside, and wipe out the pan with a paper towl.

2. Melt 2 tablespoons of the butter in the pan. Increase the heat to medium and sauté the apple and onion, stirring frequently, until the onion is translucent, about 4 to 5 minutes. Turn out onto another plate, set aside, and wipe out the pan again.

3. In the pan, heat the olive oil or butter over low heat just until it is warm. Stir in the flour and curry powder. Heat and stir over medium-low heat until the flour begins to bubble. Combine the bouillon with the half-and-half or cream, and whisk until combined. (The bouillon granules will dissolve when they are heated in the sauce.) Gradually add the half-and-half or cream mixture to the curry sauce, continuing to

stir over medium-low heat until the mixture is thick. Add the turkey and the apple-onion mixture. Stir well and heat through.

For the raisin rice:

1. In a large nonstick skillet, toast the rice over medium heat, stirring frequently, until most of the rice is browned. (Appearance may be mottled; this is desirable.) Add the raisins and the chicken stock and bring the mixture to a boil. Reduce the heat to low, cover the pan, and cook until the liquid is absorbed, about 25 minutes.

2. Serve the curry with the raisin rice.

Makes 4 servings

Shrimp on Wheels

—THE LAST SUPPERS—

I tried so many versions of this dish, I thought the family was going to rise up in revolt, the way they had with the manicotti. But they were patient, mainly because they enjoy the combination of shrimp, pasta, and any kind of cheese sauce.

Salt

5 ounces wagon-wheel pasta (ruote)

¼ lemon

1 tablespoon crab boil (crab-and-shrimp seasoning)

¾ pound large deveined easy-peel shrimp

2 tablespoons unsalted butter

2 tablespoons minced shallot

2 tablespoons all-purpose flour

1 tablespoon chicken bouillon granules dissolved in ¼ cup boiling spring water

1 cup milk, preferably whole

½ cup dry white vermouth

2 tablespoons best-quality mayonnaise

1 teaspoon Dijon mustard

1 cup shredded sharp Cheddar cheese

1 cup frozen baby peas

1. Preheat the oven to 350°F. Butter a 2-quart casserole dish with a lid.

2. In a large pot of boiling salted spring water, cook the pasta until al dente, 10 to 12 minutes. Drain and set aside.

3. In a large sauté pan, bring 4 cups spring water to a boil and add the lemon quarter and crab boil. Add the shrimp, cook until *just pink* (about 1 minute) and *immediately* transfer with a slotted spoon (leaving the seasonings behind) to a colander to drain. *Do not overcook the shrimp.* Peel and set aside. (Discard the cooking water and seasonings.)

4. In another large sauté pan, melt the butter over low heat. Add the shallot and sauté until limp but not browned, several minutes. Sprinkle the flour over the shallot and cook over low heat, until the mixture bubbles, 1 to 2 minutes. Stirring constantly, slowly add the chicken bouillon liquid, milk, and vermouth, stirring until thickened.

5. In a small bowl, stir together the mayonnaise and mustard. Add a small amount of the warm sauce to the mayonnaise mixture and stir until smooth, then add that mixture to the rest of the sauce in the skillet. Stir until heated through. Add the Cheddar, stirring until melted. Add the pasta, shrimp, and peas and stir until well combined.

6. Transfer the mixture to the buttered dish, cover, and bake for 15 to 25 minutes, or until heated through.

Makes 4 servings

Shrimp Risotto with Portobello Mushrooms

—KILLER PANCAKE—

There's no getting around it: Risotto is a time-consuming, labor-intensive dish. You're standing over the stove stirring in the chicken stock, a little bit at a time, until each measure of it is absorbed . . . then you start with the next bit. Yet a properly made risotto is so creamy and hearty, you wish you could enjoy it more often. So turn on your favorite music or radio show, and have at it.

1 tablespoon dry sherry

1½ cups cubed (½ inch) trimmed portobello mushrooms

4 to 4½ cups chicken stock, preferably homemade (page 30)

1 teaspoon Old Bay seasoning

¾ pound (20 to 22) large easy-peel shrimp

3 teaspoons extra-virgin olive oil

½ cup finely chopped onion

1 garlic clove, crushed through a press

1¼ cups Arborio rice

4 cups broccoli florets

1 teaspoon finely chopped fresh thyme

1. Pour the sherry over the chopped mushrooms, stir, and set aside to marinate while you prepare the risotto.

2. In a large saucepan, bring 1 cup of the chicken stock, 1 cup spring water, and the Old Bay to a boil. Add the shrimp and poach until *just pink*, 3 to 5 minutes. *Do not overcook.* Remove from the heat and drain, discarding the cooking water. Peel the shrimp and set aside.

3. In a heavy-bottomed saucepan, heat 2 teaspoons of the olive oil. Add the onion and sauté over medium heat until it is limp, 2 to 5 minutes. Add the garlic and rice. Cook and stir for 1 minute or until the rice just begins to change color. Continuing to stir over medium-low heat, add the chicken stock ⅓ cup at a time, each time stirring until the liquid is absorbed before adding more. Continue the

process until the rice is tender and the mixture is creamy (this can take up to 30 minutes).

4. In a small sauté pan, heat the remaining 1 teaspoon olive oil over medium-high heat and briefly sauté the marinated mushroom pieces until they release their liquid. Remove from the heat.

5. Over high heat, bring an inch of water to boil in a saucepan that has a lid. Add the broccoli, put on the lid, and reduce the heat to low. Cook the broccoli until it is bright green and tender, 5 to 6 minutes. Drain and set aside.

6. Stir the cooked shrimp, thyme, and mushrooms into the cooked risotto and stir over medium-low heat until heated through. Place the broccoli around the edge of a large platter. Fill the center with the risotto.

Makes 4 to 6 servings

Shuttlecock Shrimp Curry

—STICKS AND SCONES—

The most important thing to keep in mind with this dish is that you need to get the sauce piping hot before adding the shrimp. Then watch carefully so you don't overcook the shrimp. Serve with several of the side dishes, as well as cooked rice. Beer is the traditional beverage.

3 tablespoons unsalted butter

2 cups cored, unpeeled chopped Granny Smith apples

2 cups chopped yellow onions

3 large garlic cloves, crushed through a press

1 tablespoon plus 1 teaspoon curry powder, or more to taste

3 tablespoons all-purpose flour

½ teaspoon mustard powder

½ teaspoon salt, or more to taste

¼ teaspoon paprika

¼ teaspoon crumbled dried thyme

¼ teaspoon freshly ground black pepper, or more to taste

2 cups chicken stock, preferably homemade (page 30)

1 pound (39 to 40) large peeled cooked shrimp, deveined, shells and tails removed and reserved

1 tablespoon ketchup

¼ cup dry white vermouth

½ cup heavy (whipping) cream

Possible side dishes (choose 4 or 5): chutney, dry-roasted peanuts, chopped hard-boiled egg, sweet pickle relish, crushed pineapple, flaked coconut, mandarin oranges, chopped scallions, chopped crisp-cooked bacon, chopped olives, raisins, yogurt, and orange marmalade

1. In a large skillet, melt the butter over low heat. Increase the heat to medium-low, add the apples, onions, and garlic and cook gently, stirring frequently, until the onions start to become translucent, a few minutes. Stir in the curry powder, flour, mustard powder, salt, paprika, thyme, and pepper. Reduce the heat to low, cook and stir occasionally for a few more minutes, while you prepare the stock.

2. In a large saucepan, combine the chicken stock and reserved shrimp shells and tails. Bring to a boil, then turn off the heat. Strain the stock and discard the shells and tails.

3. Keeping the heat low, add the shrimp-flavored stock to the apple mixture, stirring well. When all the stock has been added, increase the heat to medium-high, stirring constantly, and add the ketchup and vermouth. Stir and cook until the mixture is thickened. Reduce the heat and add the cream, stirring well, until the mixture has heated through. Add the shrimp and stir and cook until the shrimp are heated through but *not overcooked.*

Makes 4 servings

Plantation Pilaf with Shrimp

—THE MAIN CORPSE—

3 tablespoons extra-virgin olive oil, divided

½ pound yellow onions, halved and very thinly sliced (you should have 1¼ cups sliced onion)

3 garlic cloves, crushed through a press

1¼ cups long-grain rice

2 cups vegetable or chicken stock, store-bought or homemade

¾ cup tomato juice

¼ cup dry sherry

¾ teaspoon paprika

½ teaspoon salt

1 tablespoon Old Bay seasoning

24 medium or large easy-peel shrimp, fresh or frozen

1 cup canned pineapple chunks, thoroughly drained and patted dry with paper towels

1 cup frozen baby peas

1. In a large nonstick skillet, heat 1 tablespoon of the olive oil over medium heat. Add the onions, and cook and stir until they are translucent, about 10 minutes. Reduce the heat to low, stir in the garlic, and cook very briefly, only until the garlic is also translucent. Do not brown the onions or the garlic.

2. In another large skillet, heat the remaining 2 tablespoons olive oil over medium heat. Add the rice and cook, stirring, until golden brown. Add the cooked onions and garlic, stock, tomato juice, sherry, paprika, and salt. Cover and cook until the rice has absorbed the liquids, 20 to 30 minutes.

3. Meanwhile, in a saucepan, bring 4 cups spring water to a boil. Add the Old Bay and shrimp and cook until the shrimp are *just pink. Do not overcook.* Drain immediately and discard the cooking water. Peel, devein, and set the shrimp aside until the rice is cooked.

4. Remove the cover from the rice and add the shrimp, pineapple, and peas. Increase the heat to medium and cook, stirring, until the peas are just cooked and the mixture is heated through. Serve immediately.

Makes 4 servings

Chesapeake Crab Cakes with Sauce Gribiche

—TOUGH COOKIE—

My sister Lucy and I are both allergic to bell peppers, which is a very unfortunate allergy to have, I assure you. Restaurants and caterers add bell peppers to dishes with abandon, primarily for color, I'm told. Worse, 99 percent of the crab cakes out there contain bell peppers. So I challenged myself to develop a crab cake recipe without them. The sauce gribiche *is somewhat labor-intensive, but the strong flavors are well worth the effort. (There is another version of* sauce gribiche *on page 317. We love them both.)*

Crab cakes:

3 tablespoons vegetable oil, divided, plus more for the baking pan

½ cup finely chopped celery

½ cup finely chopped onion

2 garlic cloves, crushed through a press

⅔ cup mayonnaise

1 teaspoon salt

¾ teaspoon mustard powder

½ teaspoon paprika

⅛ to ¼ teaspoon cayenne pepper, to taste

1. In a sauté pan, heat 1 tablespoon of the oil over medium heat. Add the celery and onion, reduce the heat to low, and add the garlic. Cook, stirring frequently, or until translucent but not browned, 3 to 5 minutes. Remove from the heat.

2. In a large bowl, combine the mayonnaise, salt, mustard powder, paprika, and cayenne. Add the crab, ⅔ cup of the cracker crumbs, and the celery mixture. Stir until well combined. Using a ½-cup measure, scoop out crab mixture and form into 6 cakes, 4 to 5 inches in diameter.

3. Spread the remaining ⅔ cup cracker crumbs on a plate. Dredge the cakes in the crumbs.

4. Preheat the oven to 300°F. Lightly oil a 9 x 13-inch baking pan.

1 pound pasteurized crabmeat, flaked and picked over to remove any stray bits of shell and cartilage

1⅓ cups club crackers crumbs

Sauce gribiche:

1½ teaspoons shallots, peeled and finely chopped

2 gherkins or cornichons, minced

1½ teaspoons capers, drained and chopped

1 tablespoon finely chopped fresh parsley

1½ teaspoons finely chopped fresh tarragon

1 teaspoon fresh lemon juice

½ teaspoon Worcestershire sauce

¼ teaspoon mustard powder

½ teaspoon salt

¼ teaspoon sugar

Freshly ground black pepper

1 cup mayonnaise

1 large egg, hard-boiled and finely chopped

5. In a large sauté pan, heat 1 tablespoon of the oil over medium heat until it shimmers. Place 3 crab cakes in the pan and cook until golden brown, about 4 minutes per side. Place the cooked crab cakes in the baking pan and put them in the oven while you cook the rest of the crab cakes. Add the remaining 1 tablespoon oil to the hot sauté pan and cook the last 3 crab cakes, about 4 minutes per side, until golden brown. Place in the baking pan in the heated oven while preparing the sauce.

For the sauce gribiche:

1. In a mini food processor or coffee grinder (that you do not use for coffee), combine the shallots, gherkins, capers, parsley, and tarragon. Pulse for about 5 seconds, or until thoroughly combined and well minced.

2. In a bowl, stir together the lemon juice, Worcestershire sauce, mustard powder, salt, sugar, and black pepper. Stir in the mayonnaise along with the egg and minced shallot mixture.

3. Serve with crab cakes.

Makes 6 crab cakes

Chilean Sea Bass with Garlic, Basil, and Vegetables

—THE LAST SUPPERS—

The first time I tasted buttery, meaty Chilean sea bass, I swooned. I guess the rest of the world swooned, too, because it became overfished. Restrictions were put in place until the ocean could recover, which we are now told it did. So it's back to being my favorite fish. This preparation, although expensive, is a marvelous entrée for company. And by the way, a joke in the food service industry is that people will order fish, then feel they've earned their chocolate cake. Apparently, people think consuming seafood cancels out a rich dessert. So with that unconscious expectation in mind, my advice is to follow this with the flourless chocolate cake on page 260.

4 tablespoons (½ stick) unsalted butter, at room temperature

4 teaspoons finely chopped fresh basil

2 garlic cloves, crushed through a press

2 tablespoons fresh lemon juice

4 red-skinned new potatoes

8 baby carrots

1½ pounds fresh (not frozen) Chilean sea bass fillets

8 fresh asparagus spears

Makes 4 servings

1. Preheat the oven to 425°F. In a small bowl, beat the butter, basil, garlic, and lemon juice until well combined. Set aside.

2. In a medium saucepan of boiling spring water, parboil the potatoes and baby carrots for 5 minutes. Drain.

3. Divide the fillets into 4 equal portions. Place them in a buttered 9 x 13-inch baking pan (or an attractive gratin dish with the same volume). Arrange the vegetables over the fish in an appealing pattern. Top each fish portion with one-fourth of the butter-garlic mixture.

4. Cover tightly with foil and bake for 20 to 30 minutes, or until the fish flakes easily when tested with a fork. Serve immediately.

Power Play Potatoes and Fish

—THE GRILLING SEASON—

Our boys are avid ice hockey fans, so in The Grilling Season, *Goldy is dealing with competitive guys squaring off in a "pretend" ice hockey game, only they were wearing Rollerblades. (Ever notice how men never play a game that is "just pretend"? Neither have I, and neither has Goldy.) No matter who's playing in the Stanley Cup finals, though, this potato and fish dish is a winner.*

4 large russet (baking) potatoes

4 Chilean sea bass fillets (6 to 8 ounces each)

½ cup all-purpose flour

2 large eggs

2 tablespoons extra-virgin olive oil

Salt and freshly ground black pepper

Makes 4 servings

1. Preheat the oven to 400°F. Butter a 9 x 13-inch glass baking dish.

2. Peel the potatoes and grate them onto a large kitchen towel that can be stained. Roll the potatoes up in the towel and squeeze to remove moisture. (It is best to do this over the sink.) Divide the potatoes into four equal piles.

3. Pat the fillets dry with paper towels. Sprinkle the flour on a plate. Beat the eggs in a shallow bowl.

4. In a large skillet, heat the olive oil. Working quickly, dip each fillet first in the flour, then in the egg. Pat the potato shreds in each potato pile on the top and bottom of each fillet (the equivalent of one grated potato per fillet). Bring the skillet up to medium-high heat. Place the potato-covered fillets in the hot oil, season with salt and pepper, and brown quickly on each side. When all the fillets are browned, transfer them to the buttered baking dish and bake about 10 minutes, or until they are cooked through. *Do not overcook the fish.*

Goalies' Grilled Tuna

—THE GRILLING SEASON—

For The Grilling Season, *I had to come up with a number of grilled dishes. People tend to be intimidated by the idea of grilled fish, but this is very easy.*

4 tuna steaks (6 to 8 ounces each)

Salt and freshly ground black pepper

¼ cup sherry vinaigrette (page 87)

1. Using paper towels, pat the tuna steaks dry. Place them in a glass pan, season with salt and pepper, and pour the vinaigrette over them. Cover with plastic wrap, place in the refrigerator, and marinate for at least 30 minutes and up to 1 hour. When you are ready to grill the fish, remove the pan from the refrigerator.

2. Oil the grill grates and preheat the grill. Grill the steaks for 2 to 3 minutes per side for rare, 5 minutes per side for well done. Serve immediately.

Makes 4 servings

Chapter 5
Breads *or* This Is Not Your Low-Carb Chapter

Since my father worked off stress by making bread, the lovely scent of baking loaves curled through our home most weekends. Every time I went back to boarding school, what I most enjoyed taking with me was not cookies, so favored by my classmates. No, it was a serrated knife and a loaf of Dad's Bread.

And just to show you what kind of imagination I had at age twelve, I was convinced that one of the housemothers was angling to kill me. In the early morning hours, as I shivered in bed, an ominous *clank clank clank* filled the hallway. I would grip that knife's handle and wait, muscles tensed. It took me a while to realize that I was shivering because the dorm was cold, that the *clank clank clank* was the radiators coming on, and that the housemother was not a killer, she was just a bitch.

I saw how much joy our father's bread brought to people. He always followed the ancient biblical tradition of bringing homemade bread and a twist of salt to new neighbors. Everyone loved "Dad's Bread." So I knew I wanted to learn how to make it some day. Before I went away to boarding school, I would watch our father proof the yeast (in those days, yeast only came in refrigerated, compressed blocks), add oats, liquids, and flour, stir and knead, let the mixture rise, punch it down, knead it again, allow it to rise again, carefully place the dough in loaf pans, allow the dough to rise a final time, then put the bread into the oven. He used large pans that always made two loaves. We kids invariably wanted to tear into the first of these while it was still warm. Sometimes he let us, athough this compresses the baked bread and is a no-no these days. (Yet Jim still insists on cutting into warm, fresh-baked bread. He loves it slathered with butter, so I reluctantly give my consent. The key to avoiding this problem is to make bread and allow cooling time when your spouse and kids are out of the house.)

Back before I received the scholarship to go to boarding school, our family even unwittingly participated in a sacrilege: Since my mother was from the School of Margarine, that was what we spread on Dad's luscious homemade bread. So it was a great day when I was introduced to real butter at St. Anne's in Charlottesville. I learned that in the South, one had rolls (called "bread") with dinner each evening. They were also served at the Sunday midday meal (called "dinner"). Those rolls were fantastic, and spread with real butter, they were amazing.

Still, the bread dish I remember most clearly from St. Anne's was my favorite breakfast: Cinnamon Toast with Applesauce. I worked hard trying to re-create that hot, crunchy, buttery, sugary dish, finally succeeded (I hope), and put it into *The Whole Enchilada.*

I also wanted to teach myself to make good cinnamon rolls. And in fact I made them quite a bit, but they always lacked a certain *je ne sais quoi*. Our kids loved Cinnabon, and no visit to Cherry Creek Mall in Denver was complete without a stop there. Watching those bakers making their signature creations, I realized what I was doing wrong: Mine were too small! And I placed them too close together!

Enter the Monster Cinnamon Roll, which is one of the recipes people mention to me often as "something our family loves."

Now, how does all this relate to Goldy? Catering clients do not just want dinner parties. They arrange for staff breakfasts, lunches, and picnics. And to distinguish their affairs from those that serve store-bought food, they invariably ask for homemade yeast breads and rolls. They will also order all manner of muffins, scones, and sweet breads, the only problem is that the scones must be consumed within an hour of baking, or they will go stale.

Usually, one person in the caterer's kitchen is tasked with both bread-baking and making desserts. Goldy and Julian do both, of course. But since bread can be made in chunks of time, the proofing, kneading, rising, and so on provide extended periods when Goldy can think about whatever crime has her attention.

This is actually a trick I learned from reading Robert B. Parker's Spenser novels. Spenser loves to cook, and working at the stove allows him time to reflect on the crime. Ha, I thought, that's what Goldy needs to do.

Her job demands that she cook. But someone has asked for her help or someone she knows has died mysteriously or been poisoned at a party she catered, or some other circumstance—like her nosiness—has gotten her involved in crime-solving. So she cooks and she thinks.

She also listens. One of the most startling things I learned while catering is that the guests at a party think the caterers are *deaf.*

We are not. In fact, we hear everything you say, including how much you hate your mother-in-law (who is seated two tables away, and is telling everyone there that you are an *overgrown brat).* We also hear you brag about screwing up a business deal and not getting caught, and who at your office is having sex with whom. You'd be amazed at how many party guests think the caterers have done van Gogh one better, and cut off both ears.

Even though our kids scolded me for talking too much, learning to listen was a skill that helped me become a writer. I was pleased to learn on the research trip to England for *Sticks and Scones* that overhearing what you perhaps should not goes back at least as far as theaters like Shakespeare's Globe. For light and fresh air, the central sections were open to the sky. Whenever it rained, the groundlings, or those too poor to pay for seats, would scoot as far back as possible, where they were under the eaves of the covered seats. There, they would overhear bits of conversation. Hence: *eavesdropping.*

I didn't mean to eavesdrop when I was little; it just seemed to come naturally. Whenever our family was driving somewhere, my father enjoyed entertaining my mother with stories about the neighbors, or conjectures about people at church. Or he would tell a long, funny, probably exaggerated story about anyone he thought needed his take on their situation.

I found all this very interesting. My mother could detect when I was perking up, and would warn my father, "You know you've got the *Washington Post* taking notes in the backseat."

And of course this was several decades before Watergate.

Note on the recipes: The yeast breads are listed first; the quick breads and Crunchy Cinnamon Toast (page 199) second. The Bread Dough Enhancer (page 173) is for yeast breads. Since Julia Child encourages bread-bakers to allow their dough to rise three times for the best texture, this is what I recommend for yeast breads, except in the case of Yolanda's Cuban Bread (page 188), which is meant to rise quickly. But if you do not have time to allow the bread to rise a third time, no one will judge you, least of all me.

Bread Dough Enhancer for Yeast Breads

—THE WHOLE ENCHILADA—

One used to be able to buy Lora Brody's wonderful bread dough enhancer at Williams-Sonoma. But when I could no longer find it there, I worked with different recipes until I came up with one that worked. The general rule is to use 1 tablespoon of enhancer per cup of flour in yeast bread recipes.

1 cup vital wheat gluten (available at Whole Foods and other natural grocers)

½ cup nonfat dry milk

2 tablespoons unflavored gelatin powder

2 tablespoons lecithin (available at Whole Foods and other natural grocers)

1 teaspoon ground ginger

1 teaspoon powdered pectin

In a large bowl, mix all the ingredients. Place the mixture in a heavy-duty zippered plastic bag and keep in the refrigerator. The mixture will last 6 months.

Dad's Bread

—THE WHOLE ENCHILADA—

This recipe did indeed come down from my father—he'd cut it out of a newspaper, taped it to a card, and placed it as a marker inside a gift I'd given him: Beard on Bread, by the incomparable James Beard. But by the time we were cleaning out my parents' house, the tape holding the recipe to the card was brown and curling. For years thereafter, the recipe on the card bedeviled me; I never could get it to work. The dough was too sticky. It wouldn't come together in kneading. It neither looked nor tasted like my father's feathery loaves. Agh! Finally I realized the disintegrating tape had taken off some crucial words in the middle of the recipe. Just as Goldy does in The Whole Enchilada, *I finally pressed down hard on that accursed tape, and saw that I needed to add more flour. Dad's Bread finally came out right.*

- ½ cup plus 1 tablespoon packed dark brown sugar, divided
- 1 cup old-fashioned rolled oats
- 2 teaspoons kosher salt
- 2 tablespoons unsalted butter
- 1¾ cups spring water
- 1 tablespoon plus 2 teaspoons instant (also called rapid-rise) yeast
- 2 large eggs
- ¼ cup dough enhancer (page 173)
- 5 to 6 cups bread flour

1. In the large bowl of a stand mixer, combine ½ cup of the brown sugar, the oats, salt, and butter. In a small saucepan, heat 1½ cups of the spring water just until it is hot (125°F) and pour over the oat mixture. Stir to mix and allow to cool to about 110°F. (A thermometer is handy for this. You do not want the mixture so hot that it destroys the yeast or cooks the eggs.)

2. In a glass bowl, stir the remaining 1 tablespoon brown sugar into the remaining ¼ cup spring water. Stir the yeast into this mixture and set in a warm spot (no hotter than 150°F) for 10 minutes to proof. It should be foamy.

3. In a small bowl, beat the eggs well. Measure out 2 tablespoons of the beaten egg and set aside. Add

the remaining beaten eggs and the yeast mixture to the oat mixture. Attach the dough hook to the mixer and stir to combine.

4. In a large bowl, stir the dough enhancer into the first cup of the flour.

5. Turn the mixer to "stir" and add the flour, 1 cup at a time, until you have used 5 cups of flour. The dough should come together. If the dough does not come together, add the additional cup of flour, ¼ cup at a time, until it does. Increase the speed slightly and knead on low speed for at least 5 minutes, until the dough comes together into a ball and cleans the bowl.

6. Butter a large, hard plastic container with a lid and butter the lid. Place the dough in the container and, using a measuring tape and a marker, measure on the *outside* of the container the volume of the dough. Mark the container (still on the outside) where double that amount would be. Place the lid on the container.

7. Allow the dough to rise at room temperature until it is doubled in bulk, 45 minutes to 1 hour. Remove the lid and gently punch the dough down and knead it to roughly its original size. Replace the lid. Allow the dough to rise again until doubled in bulk, about 40 minutes. Punch down again.

8. Butter three 8½ x 4½-inch glass loaf pans. Divide the dough evenly into thirds. (You can use a kitchen scale to make sure the loaves all weigh the same.) Shape the dough pieces into loaves and place them in the pans. Butter a large piece of plastic and place it loosely over the pans. Allow the dough to rise at room temperature until it is again doubled in bulk, 40 minutes to 1 hour. Remove the plastic.

9. Preheat the oven to 350°F.

10. Whisk the reserved 2 tablespoons beaten egg and brush it over the tops of the risen loaves. Place the pans in the oven and bake for 30 to 40 minutes, or until the internal temperature reads 180°F and the loaves sound hollow when thumped.

11. Place the pans on racks, allow to cool for 5 minutes, then turn out onto the racks to cool completely, covered with a clean kitchen towel.

Makes 3 loaves

Galaxy Doughnuts

—THE CEREAL MURDERS—

These doughnuts are baked, not fried. And they are not in a traditional doughnut shape. But whenever I have had to serve a breakfast that has some protein in the baked offering, this recipe and the one for Chicky Bread (page 186) are what I use.

Two ¼-ounce envelopes active dry yeast (4½ teaspoons)

⅓ cup warm spring water

2¼ cups plus ½ teaspoon sugar

⅓ cup solid vegetable shortening, melted

1½ cups milk, preferably whole, scalded and cooled to lukewarm

2 teaspoons salt

2 teaspoons vanilla extract

2 large eggs

¼ cup wheat germ

¼ cup soy flour

¼ cup oat bran

4¼ cups all-purpose or bread flour

2 teaspoons ground cinnamon

2 sticks (½ pound) unsalted butter

1. In a large bowl, sprinkle the yeast on top of the warm water. Allow the yeast to soften for 5 minutes, then mix the yeast into the water and stir in ½ teaspoon of the sugar. Set the mixture aside in a warm, draft-free place, to proof for 10 minutes. It should be foamy.

2. Mix the melted shortening into the warm milk, then add the liquid to the yeast mixture along with ¼ cup of the sugar, the salt, vanilla, eggs, wheat germ, soy flour, oat bran, and 1½ cups of the flour. Beat vigorously until very well blended. Stir in the remaining flour and beat until smooth. (You can do this by hand or in a stand mixer with a dough hook.)

3. Cover the bowl with plastic wrap and put it in a warm, draft-free place until the dough is doubled in bulk, about 1 hour.

4. Punch the dough down, turn it onto a well-floured board, and pat it out so that the dough is about ½ inch thick. Using a 3-inch star cookie cutter, cut out the dough and place the

doughnuts 2 inches apart on buttered baking sheets. Allow the doughnuts to rise uncovered for another 20 to 30 minutes or until they are doubled.

5. Preheat the oven to 400°F.

6. Bake the doughnuts for 10 to 15 minutes, or just until they are golden brown.

7. Meanwhile, in a medium bowl, mix the remaining 2 cups sugar with the cinnamon. Melt the butter and place it in a second bowl.

8. When the doughnuts come out of the oven, dip them quickly into the melted butter and roll them in the cinnamon sugar. Serve immediately.

Makes about 3 dozen

Monster Cinnamon Rolls

—THE LAST SUPPERS—

We love these. Do not frost until just before serving.

Dough:

1½ sticks (6 ounces) unsalted butter

1 cup milk, preferably whole

¾ cup plus 1 teaspoon sugar

1¼ teaspoons salt

Three ¼-ounce envelopes active dry yeast (6¾ teaspoons)

½ cup warm spring water

5 large eggs

2 tablespoons dough enhancer (page 173)

8½ to 9½ cups all-purpose or bread flour

For the dough:

1. In a small saucepan, heat the butter with the milk, ¾ cup of the sugar, and the salt until the butter is melted. Set aside to cool.

2. In a large bowl, sprinkle the yeast over the warm water, add the remaining 1 teaspoon sugar, stir, and set aside in a warm place for 10 minutes to proof, until the mixture is foamy. Add the lukewarm milk mixture and the eggs and beat until well combined. Add the dough enhancer and then the flour 1 cup at a time, stirring and using enough flour to form a stiff dough. Turn out on a floured board and knead until smooth and satiny, about 10 minutes. (Or place in the bowl of a stand mixer and knead with a dough hook until the dough cleans the sides of the bowl, about 5 minutes.) Place the dough in a very large buttered bowl, turn to butter the top, and allow to rise, covered loosely with a kitchen towel, in a warm place until doubled in bulk, about 1 hour.

Filling:

5 cups packed dark brown sugar

20 tablespoons (2½ sticks) unsalted butter

3 tablespoons ground cinnamon

Frosting:

8 ounces cream cheese, at room temperature

About ¼ cup heavy (whipping) cream

1 teaspoon vanilla extract

3 to 4 cups powdered sugar

Meanwhile, for the filling:

1. In a bowl, beat together the brown sugar, butter, and cinnamon until well combined.

2. Punch the dough down and roll out to a large rectangle, 24 x 36 inches. Butter two 9 x 13-inch glass baking dishes.

3. Spread the filling evenly over the surface of the dough. Starting on a short side, roll the dough up into a log, then cut the log crosswise at 2-inch intervals to make 12 rolls. Place 6 rolls, evenly spaced, in each buttered dish. Cover loosely with a kitchen towel and allow to rise until doubled in bulk, about 1 hour.

4. Preheat the oven to 350°F.

5. Bake the rolls for 20 to 30 minutes, or until puffed and browned. Cool to room temperature in the pans on racks.

For the frosting:

In a bowl, with an electric mixer, beat the cream cheese, cream, and vanilla until well combined. Add the powdered sugar and beat until smooth. You want a soft, not stiff frosting, so add either more cream or sugar to obtain the right consistency. Frost the rolls in the pans and serve immediately.

Makes 12 large rolls

What-to-Do-with-All-the-Egg-Yolks Bread

—KILLER PANCAKE—

Back when low-fat cooking was all the rage and people were throwing away egg yolks with abandon, the waste upset me. So I developed this recipe. It is very similar to brioche.

One ¼-ounce envelope active dry yeast (2¼ teaspoons)

¼ cup sugar

¼ cup warm spring water

¾ cup milk, whole or skim

4 tablespoons (½ stick) butter, melted

½ cup canola oil

1 tablespoon minced orange zest

1 teaspoon salt

4 egg yolks, from large eggs, lightly beaten

3½ to 4 cups all-purpose flour

¾ cup dried cranberries

1 cup chopped pecans

1. Butter a 10-inch tube pan and set aside.

2. In a large bowl, combine the yeast, 1 teaspoon of the sugar, and the warm water. Set aside in a warm place for 10 minutes to proof, until the mixture is foamy. Add the milk, butter, oil, orange zest, salt, and remaining sugar and stir into the yeast mixture. Add the egg yolks, stirring well. Add the flour ½ cup at a time, stirring well after each addition to incorporate the flour thoroughly. Knead 5 to 10 minutes (or use the dough hook and a stand mixer to do this), until the dough is smooth, elastic, and satiny. Knead in the cranberries and pecans.

3. Butter a large bowl. Put the dough into the bowl, cover it, and let the dough rise at room temperature until it is doubled in bulk. Using a wooden spoon, beat down the risen dough for about a minute.

4. Place the dough into the buttered tube pan and allow it to rise at room temperature until it is doubled in bulk, about 2 hours.

5. Preheat the oven to 375°F.

6. Bake the bread for 45 to 50 minutes, or until it is dark golden brown and sounds hollow when tapped. Ease the bread out of the pan and place on a rack to cool. The bread is wonderful as is and is also excellent sliced and toasted.

Makes 1 large loaf

Julian's Five-Grain Bread

—TOUGH COOKIE—

Whole wheat flour tends to produce heavy, dense loaves. With the help of the dough enhancer, you can make a healthful bread that does not have the texture of opus caementicum *(ancient Roman concrete).*

- 2 cups five-grain cereal (available either in the cereal or the health-food section of the grocery store) or old-fashioned rolled oats
- 2⅓ cups spring water
- 2 tablespoons unsalted butter
- ¾ cup dark molasses
- 1 teaspoon salt
- ¾ cup whole milk
- 1 teaspoon dark brown sugar
- Two ¼-ounce envelopes active dry yeast (4½ teaspoons)
- 2 tablespoons dough enhancer (page 173)
- 4 cups bread or all-purpose flour, plus up to 1 cup more flour for kneading (if required)
- 2 cups whole wheat flour

1. Butter two 9 x 5-inch loaf pans.

2. Place the cereal in a large bowl. In a small saucepan, bring the water, butter, molasses, and salt to a boil. Pour this mixture over the cereal and set aside to cool to 100°F. (It is helpful to have a digital-probe thermometer for this.)

3. In another small saucepan, heat the milk and brown sugar to 100°F. Pour into a large bowl and stir in the yeast. Allow to proof for 10 to 15 minutes, at which point the mixture should be foamy.

4. Mix the cooled grain mixture into the yeast mixture. Combine the dough enhancer with 1 cup of bread flour and stir that into the yeast mixture. Beat the remaining 3 cups bread flour and all the whole wheat flour into the mixture, beating well to combine. Place the dough in an oiled bowl, turn the dough to oil the top, cover with a clean kitchen towel, and let rise in a draft-free spot, at room temperature, until doubled in bulk, about 1 hour.

5. Stir as much of the additional bread flour into the dough as needed to make a dough that is not too sticky to knead. Knead on a floured surface until the dough is smooth and satiny, about 10 minutes (or use a stand mixer with a dough hook to do this).

6. Divide the dough into 2 pieces and place them in the pans. Cover with a towel and allow to rise until almost doubled in bulk, about 1 hour.

7. Preheat the oven to 375°F.

8. Bake for 50 to 60 minutes, or until the loaves are deep brown and sound hollow when thumped. Remove the loaves from the pans and allow them to cool completely on racks.

Makes 2 loaves

Got-a-Hunch Brunch Rolls

—DOUBLE SHOT—

When you love to cook, people are always giving you fabulous bittersweet orange marmalade. Luckily, these rolls became a way to incorporate them into a fancy yeast roll, good for brunch. (Caterers are called upon to work an unimaginable number of brunches, usually corporate events.)

1 teaspoon sugar

¼ cup warm spring water

One ¼-ounce envelope (2¼ teaspoons) active dry yeast

8 tablespoons (1 stick) unsalted butter, at room temperature

½ cup honey

1 tablespoon grated lemon zest, finely minced after grating

1 tablespoon grated orange zest, finely minced after grating

2 teaspoons orange extract

½ teaspoon salt

1 tablespoon fresh lemon juice

6 large eggs—3 whole, 3 separated

½ cup milk, preferably whole, warmed to 110°F

2 tablespoons dough enhancer (page 173)

5 to 6 cups bread flour

½ cup best-quality bittersweet orange marmalade

1. In a large bowl, stir together the sugar, water, and yeast. Set aside in a warm, draft-free place and allow to proof for 10 minutes, at which point the mixture should be foamy.

2. In another large bowl, with an electric mixer, beat the butter until creamy, about 5 minutes. Blend in the honey and beat until thoroughly combined. Add the zests, extract, salt, and lemon juice. Beat until well combined. (The mixture will look curdled.)

3. Refrigerate the 3 egg whites, covered, until you are ready to bake the rolls. Add the 3 egg yolks and 3 whole eggs one at a time to the butter mixture, and beat in thoroughly. Add the yeast mixture and the milk and beat on low speed until thoroughly combined. Set aside.

4. Mix the dough enhancer into 1 cup of the 5 cups of flour. Add the flour mixture 1 cup at a time to the yeast mixture, beating thoroughly after each addition. If the dough is very sticky, add the additional cup flour, ¼ cup at a time, until the dough is only slightly sticky. Switch to a wooden spoon or dough hook when the dough becomes too stiff to beat. When the dough is pliable and only very slightly sticky, turn it out onto a floured surface and knead vigorously for 10 minutes. (Alternatively, you can knead using the dough hook for 10 minutes.)

5. Place the dough into a large oiled bowl, turn to oil the top, cover with a clean kitchen towel, and set it in a warm, draft-free place to rise until doubled in bulk, 1 to 1½ hours.

6. Punch the dough down, turn it out onto a board, and allow it to rest for 10 minutes. Divide it into 24 equal pieces. Butter two 12-cup muffin tins.

7. Keep the dough you are not working with covered with a kitchen towel. Take each piece of dough, flatten it into a 4-inch round, and spread 1 teaspoon marmalade from the center out, leaving a ½-inch border around the edges. Carefully roll the dough into a cylinder, pinch the edges of the roll together, and pull the pinched-together edges underneath, to make a round roll. Carefully place each roll into a muffin cup. When you have made all the rolls, cover the muffin tins with a kitchen towel and allow the rolls to rise until doubled in bulk, about 1 hour.

8. Preheat the oven to 350°F.

9. Remove the egg whites from the refrigerator and whisk them until frothy. Using a pastry brush, paint the top of each roll. (You will have egg white left over.)

10. Working with one muffin tin at a time, bake for 15 minutes, or until the rolls are puffed and golden brown and sound hollow when tapped. Cool on racks for 10 minutes, then use tongs to remove the rolls from the pans to cool completely on the racks.

Makes 2 dozen rolls

Chicky Bread

—DARK TORT—

This is another high-protein bread, one you make in a bread machine. It makes a large loaf. Note, though: It does not keep well.

Contents of one 15-ounce can chickpeas (garbanzo beans), drained

½ cup plus 1 tablespoon molasses, divided

¼ cup lukewarm spring water

1 tablespoon active dry yeast

1 tablespoon dough enhancer (page 173)

1 cup whole wheat flour

2 cups bread flour or all-purpose flour, plus more if needed

2 teaspoons salt

⅓ cup old-fashioned rolled oats

⅔ cup spring water, plus more if needed

¼ cup nonfat dry milk

¼ cup safflower oil

1 large egg, beaten

1. Rinse the chickpeas well and pat them dry. Pour them into a blender along with ½ cup of the molasses. Blend until the mixture is smooth (no chickpeas visible). Measure out 1 cup of this mixture; discard remainder.

2. Mix the remaining 1 tablespoon molasses into the ¼ cup lukewarm spring water and sprinkle the yeast over the top. Let this sit for 3 to 5 minutes, until the yeast is completely moistened. Stir the yeast down into the water and place in a warm, draft-free spot for 10 minutes to proof. The mixture will be foamy.

3. In a bowl, combine the dough enhancer, whole wheat flour, and bread flour (or all-purpose flour). Place this mixture into a bread machine, followed by the chickpea puree, the salt, oats, ⅔ cup spring water, nonfat dry milk, safflower oil, and egg. Pour the yeast mixture in on top. Program for white bread (about 3 hours and 10 minutes) and press Start.

4. After the first few minutes of mixing, lift the lid of the machine and check that the dough is neither too sticky and wet nor so dry that it cannot incorporate all the ingredients. Do not touch the blade or the dough. If the mixture looks too wet, add up to 2 more tablespoons bread flour. If the mixture looks dry, add up to 2 more tablespoons spring water. What you are aiming for here is a smooth, supple dough that holds together and that the machine's blade can knead easily. Once a smooth, supple dough is obtained, close the lid of the bread machine and let the bread-making process continue.

5. Once the bread is done, remove it from the machine and allow it to cool on a rack before slicing.

Makes 1 large loaf

Yolanda's Cuban Bread

—FATALLY FLAKY—

Unlike most yeast breads, this one rises and bakes quickly. Even if you start in the late afternoon, it can be served with dinner.

2 cups spring water

2 tablespoons dark brown sugar

Two ¼-ounce envelopes active dry yeast (4½ teaspoons)

2 tablespoons dough enhancer (page 173)

5½ cups bread flour

¼ cup soy flour

¼ cup nonfat dry milk

2 tablespoons wheat germ

1 tablespoon kosher salt

About 2 tablespoons poppy seeds

1. In a small saucepan, heat the spring water to 110° to 115°F. Pour the water into a warm bowl and stir in the brown sugar and yeast. Place in a warm, draft-free spot to proof, about 15 minutes. The mixture will be foamy.

2. In a bowl, mix together the dough enhancer, bread flour, soy flour, dry milk, wheat germ, and salt. Place this mixture into the bowl of a stand mixer fitted with the dough hook. Add the proofed yeast mixture and stir until well combined. Knead for 10 minutes.

3. Place the kneaded dough into a buttered bowl, cover with buttered plastic wrap, and set aside to rise until doubled in bulk, about 30 minutes.

4. Remove the plastic wrap, punch the dough down, and divide it into 2 equal pieces. Shape the pieces into 2 round loaves and place them on a baking sheet lined with a silicone baking mat. Using a sharp knife, cut a 1-inch deep cross into the tops of the loaves. Brush the loaves with spring water and sprinkle the poppy seeds on top.

Note: Do not preheat the oven.

5. Place a cake pan filled with hot spring water on the bottom rack of the *cold* oven. Place the baking sheet with the loaves on the middle rack of the oven. Close the oven door and turn the oven to 400°F. Bake for 30 to 40 minutes, until the loaves are golden brown. (They will open up and look like flowers; this is normal.) Serve warm or cool.

Note: This bread does not keep well. If you are not going to serve both loaves immediately, allow the second loaf to cool completely, then freeze it in a zippered plastic freezer bag.

Makes 2 loaves

Almond Poppy Seed Muffins

—THE LAST SUPPERS—

Yes, your grocery store and local coffee shop will offer almond poppy seed muffins. But when our middle son (a poppy seed muffin hound) and I were visiting colleges in New York and California, we ordered poppy seed muffins wherever we went. This recipe was the result. Although this recipe calls for almond extract, we also tasted outstanding lemon poppy seed muffins in Greenwich Village and San Francisco. If you want to make lemon poppy seed muffins, omit the almond extract, add ½ teaspoon lemon extract and 1 teaspoon of grated lemon zest. To gild that particular lily, you can moisten powdered sugar with fresh lemon juice and drizzle it over the muffins.

4 large eggs

2 cups sugar

1½ cups evaporated milk (contents of one 12-ounce can)

½ cup whole milk

2 cups vegetable oil

3½ teaspoons baking powder

½ teaspoon salt

4 cups all-purpose flour

1 teaspoon vanilla extract

1 teaspoon almond extract

½ cup poppy seeds

1. Preheat the oven to 325°F. Line 30 muffin cups with paper liners.

2. In a large bowl, beat together the eggs, sugar, evaporated milk, milk, and vegetable oil. Sift together the baking powder, salt, and flour. Gradually add the flour mixture to the egg mixture, beating until well combined. Add the extracts and poppy seeds, stirring only until well combined. Using a ⅓-cup measure, measure out the batter evenly into the muffin cups. Bake for 25 to 30 minutes, or until a toothpick inserted into the center of a muffin comes out clean.

Makes 30 muffins

Irish Soda Bread

—THE CEREAL MURDERS—

Every now and then you will be invited to a St. Patrick's Day party and be asked to bring something. Or maybe you are Irish and will want to remind your relatives of a dish from the home country. Then again, you could just have a hankering to make this for yourself.

2½ cups all-purpose flour

½ cup sugar

1½ teaspoons baking powder

¾ teaspoon salt

½ teaspoon baking soda

8 tablespoons (1 stick) unsalted butter, chilled and cut into 8 equal pieces

1 cup raisins

1 tablespoon caraway seeds

1 large egg

1¼ cups buttermilk

¼ cup regular or light sour cream

1. Preheat the oven to 350°F. Butter a 9-inch round cake pan.

2. Sift together the dry ingredients. Using a food processor or a pastry cutter, cut the butter into the flour mixture only until it resembles small peas. Place in a large bowl. Blend in the raisins and caraway seeds.

3. In a separate bowl, beat together the egg, buttermilk, and sour cream until blended.

4. Stir the egg mixture into the dry mixture *just* until blended.

5. Transfer the batter to the pan and bake for 50 to 55 minutes, or until a toothpick inserted in the center comes out clean.

Makes 1 round loaf

Piña Colada Muffins

—SWEET REVENGE—

Our family loves dried pineapple, so I was duty-bound to come up with a muffin recipe that contained it.

- 1 cup dried diced pineapple, plus 12 pieces of dried diced pineapple for garnish before baking (about 6½ ounces pineapple, total)
- 1 cup dark Jamaican rum or 1 cup spring water
- 2 cups all-purpose flour (high altitude: add 1 tablespoon)
- 1 teaspoon baking powder
- ½ teaspoon baking soda
- ¼ teaspoon salt
- 1½ sticks (6 ounces) unsalted butter, at room temperature
- 1 cup sugar
- 2 large eggs, at room temperature
- 1 cup regular or light sour cream
- 1 teaspoon vanilla extract
- ¾ teaspoon finely minced orange zest
- ¾ cup sweetened flaked coconut

1. Place all the pineapple in a small saucepan and pour the rum or water over it. Bring to a boil, then allow the pineapple to cool in the liquid for about 30 minutes. Drain the pineapple. (If you are using rum, either discard it or reserve it for another use.) Pat the pineapple dry with paper towels and reserve 12 pieces. Roughly chop the remainder and set aside.

2. Preheat the oven to 350°F. Thoroughly butter the *top* of a 12-cup muffin tin. (This is to ensure easy release of the muffins after baking.) Place paper liners in the 12 muffin cups.

3. Sift together the flour, baking powder, baking soda, and salt. Set aside.

4. In a large bowl, with an electric mixer, beat the butter on medium speed until it is very creamy. Gradually beat in the sugar until the mixture turns light. Add the eggs, one at a time, and beat until the mixture is well combined. On low speed, mix in the sour cream, vanilla, and orange zest until completely combined. (The mixture will look curdled.) Gently stir the

flour mixture, pineapple, and coconut into the butter mixture, stirring only until completely combined. (The batter will be thick.)

5. Using a ½-cup measure, measure a scant ½ cup batter into each paper liner. Top each muffin with a reserved piece of pineapple. Bake for 15 to 20 minutes, or until the muffins are puffed, golden brown, and a toothpick inserted in the center of a muffin comes out clean. Gently remove the muffins from the pan. Serve hot or at room temperature.

Makes 12 muffins

Banana-Pecan Muffins

—THE MAIN CORPSE—

I'm of the opinion that banana bread is overdone in this country, but that's me. It still sells out at Starbucks and everywhere else. But our family does love these muffins, and this easy, inexpensive recipe will help you use up ripe bananas. Moreover, I think any recipe with whole pecan halves is worth making.

4½ cups all-purpose flour

1¾ cups sugar

5 teaspoons baking powder (high altitude: 4½ teaspoons)

1¾ teaspoons salt

1¾ cups mashed ripe banana

¼ cup canola or other vegetable oil

2 large eggs

1⅓ cups milk, preferably whole

1¾ cups pecan halves (do not chop)

1. Preheat the oven to 350°F. Line 24 cups of 2 muffin tins with paper liners.

2. In a large bowl, mix together the flour, sugar, baking powder, and salt. In another large bowl, mix together the banana, oil, and eggs. Alternating with the milk, gradually add the flour mixture to the banana mixture, beginning and ending with the flour mixture. Stir in the pecans.

3. Divide the batter evenly among the muffin cups, filling the cups just shy of full. Bake for 25 minutes, or until the muffins are puffed and golden brown, and a toothpick inserted into the center of one comes out clean.

4. Serve warm, or cool the muffins on racks. Freeze in zippered plastic freezer bags for longer storage.

Makes 24 muffins

Cinnamon Griddle Scones

—THE MAIN CORPSE—

Scottish scones were originally made on a griddle, and fresh ones are divine. The problem with most of the scones sold in this country is that they are not served fresh and therefore have the consistency of sawdust. Serve these scones right off the griddle. They do not keep.

1 cup all-purpose flour

2 tablespoons buttermilk powder (available in the baking aisle in the grocery store)

1 teaspoon sugar

½ teaspoon baking soda

½ teaspoon cream of tartar

½ teaspoon ground cinnamon

¼ teaspoon salt

½ cup spring water

2 tablespoons solid vegetable shortening

Butter and apple butter, for serving

1. Preheat a griddle over medium-high heat.

2. In a bowl, stir together the flour, buttermilk powder, sugar, baking soda, cream of tartar, cinnamon, and salt. Add the water and stir until well combined. Turn the batter out on a very well-floured surface, knead a few turns, and pat into a round about 6½ inches in diameter. With a sharp knife, cut the dough into 8 wedges.

3. Melt the shortening on the griddle or in a large, heavy-bottomed skillet. When the shortening is *hot,* reduce the heat to medium and place the scones on the griddle. Cook until the first side is golden brown, about 2 minutes. Turn and cook the other side, about another 2 minutes. Test for doneness by splitting one scone. It should not be doughy, but should look like a biscuit. Remove the scones from the griddle and serve immediately with butter and apple butter.

Makes 8 small scones

Castle Scones

—STICKS & SCONES—

¼ cup currants

2 cups spring water

2 cups all-purpose flour

2 tablespoons sugar

1 tablespoon baking powder

½ teaspoon salt

4 tablespoons (½ stick) well-chilled unsalted butter, cut into 4 equal pieces and chilled again

1 large egg

¼ cup heavy (whipping) cream

¼ cup milk, preferably whole

2 teaspoons sugar (optional)

Butter, whipped cream, jams, lemon curd, or marmalades, for serving

1. Place the currants in a medium bowl. Bring the spring water to a boil and pour it over the currants. Allow to stand for 10 minutes. Drain the currants and discard the water. Pat the currants dry with paper towels and set aside.

2. Preheat the oven to 400°F. Butter a baking sheet. In a food processor, mix the flour, sugar, baking powder, and salt. With the machine running, add the butter, one piece at a time, and process only until the mixture looks like cornmeal.

3. In a separate bowl, beat the egg slightly with the cream and milk. Turn the food processor back on and pour the egg mixture in a thin stream into the flour mixture just until the dough holds together in a ball. Fold in the currants.

4. On a floured surface, lightly pat the dough into 2 rounds, each about 7 inches in diameter. Cut each round into 6 even wedges. Place the scones on the baking sheet 2 inches apart. If desired, sprinkle them with the sugar.

5. Bake for about 15 minutes, or until the scones are puffed, golden, and cooked through. Serve immediately with butter or whipped cream, and jams, curds, or marmalades.

Makes 12 scones

Grand Marnier Cranberry Muffins

—KILLER PANCAKE—

Oranges and cranberries are soulmates. Playing around with those ingredients led to this recipe.

1¼ cups orange juice

¼ cup Grand Marnier liqueur

¾ cup canola or other vegetable oil

2½ cups all-purpose flour

1 cup whole wheat flour

1½ cups sugar

2 tablespoons baking powder

½ teaspoon salt

1½ tablespoons minced orange zest

4 egg whites, from large eggs

2 cups chopped fresh cranberries

1. Preheat the oven to 400°F. Line 24 cups of 2 muffin tins with paper liners.

2. In a bowl, combine the orange juice, Grand Marnier, and oil and set aside.

3. In a large bowl, combine the all-purpose flour, whole wheat flour, sugar, baking powder, salt, and orange zest.

4. In another large bowl, beat the egg whites until frothy with soft peaks. Combine the juice mixture with the beaten egg whites. Add the egg mixture and the cranberries to the flour mixture, stirring just until moist.

5. Using a ¼-cup measure, divide the batter among the muffin cups. Bake for 25 minutes, or until golden brown and puffed, and a toothpick inserted into one muffin comes out clean.

Makes 24 muffins

Stained-Glass Sweet Bread

—STICKS AND SCONES—

This is our family's favorite sweet bread. How it came about was a happy accident. Jim, tired of hunting for peanuts through all the packages of dried fruits on our pantry shelf, vowed he was going to throw them all out. Horrors! I promised to put something together that would use them. This recipe was the result. Now I end up having to quadruple the recipe, just so I have enough of the bread for the holidays.

1½ cups dried tart cherries

½ cup chopped dried pineapple

4 cups spring water

4 tablespoons (½ stick) unsalted butter, at room temperature

1½ cups sugar

2 large eggs

4 cups all-purpose flour (high altitude: add 2 tablespoons)

4 teaspoons baking powder (high altitude: 1 tablespoon)

½ teaspoon baking soda

2 teaspoons salt

1½ cups orange juice

Makes 2 loaves

1. Place the cherries and chopped pineapple in a large bowl. Bring the spring water to a boil and pour it over the fruit. Let stand 15 minutes, then drain (discard the water). Pat the fruit dry with paper towels. Set aside.

2. Butter and flour two 8½ x 4½-inch loaf pans.

3. In a bowl, with an electric mixer, cream the butter with the sugar until well blended. (The mixture will look like wet sand.) Add the eggs and beat well. Sift the dry ingredients together twice. Alternating with the orange juice, add the flour mixture to the creamed mixture, beginning and ending with the flour mixture. Stir in the fruits, blending well. Divide the batter evenly between the pans. Allow to stand for 20 minutes. Meanwhile, preheat the oven to 350°F.

4. Bake the breads for 45 to 55 minutes, or until toothpicks inserted in the loaves come out clean. Cool in the pans for 10 minutes, then transfer to racks to cool completely.

Crunchy Cinnamon Toast

—THE WHOLE ENCHILADA—

If you're really into cooking, you could make your own applesauce, or you could just serve it with fresh apples. What I do now for a big family breakfast is to serve it with sliced fresh apples or cups of applesauce, and a baked ham.

1 teaspoon ground cinnamon

1 cup sugar

8 thick slices best quality bread, preferably brioche

About 8 tablespoons (1 stick) unsalted butter, melted

Apples or applesauce, for serving

1. Preheat the oven to 350°F. Butter 1 or 2 large baking sheets or line with silicone baking mats.

2. In a small bowl, mix together the cinnamon and sugar.

3. Lay the bread slices on the baking sheets so that they are not touching. Place them in the oven and toast the bread for about 5 minutes. Remove the sheets from the oven, but do not turn the oven off.

4. Using tongs, flip the bread slices so that the untoasted side is facing up. Using a pastry brush, completely brush each slice of bread with melted butter. Carefully sprinkle each piece of bread generously with the cinnamon sugar. You want a thick layer of cinnamon sugar on each slice.

5. Return the sheets to the oven and watch carefully. In 10 to 20 minutes, the cinnamon sugar layer will begin to bubble. Remove the sheets from the oven.

6. Serve immediately with apples or applesauce on the side.

Makes 8 servings

Goldy's Guava Coffee Cake

—CRUNCH TIME—

This coffee cake recipe is very sturdy, because you can make all kinds of changes to it and still have a wonderful result. Sometimes I omit the guava preserves and substitute cherry, strawberry, or raspberry jam. You can even get by without the zests, although they do add marvelous flavor. And if you are charged with bringing the coffee cake for the dreaded morning meeting, this cake can be made the evening before, cooled, and securely wrapped. Cakes made with sour cream actually are better the next day.

8 tablespoons (1 stick) unsalted butter, at room temperature

1 cup sugar

2 large eggs

1 cup regular or light sour cream

2 teaspoons vanilla extract (see Note)

1 tablespoon finely minced orange zest (about 1 large navel orange)

2 teaspoons finely minced lemon zest (about 1 large lemon)

½ cup best-quality guava preserves, such as Queensberry, well stirred

1. Preheat the oven to 350°F. Butter and lightly flour two 9-inch round cake pans or two 8-inch square pans.

2. In a large bowl, with an electric mixer, beat the butter with the sugar until very light and fluffy. Add the eggs one at a time and beat well, until very well combined. Add the sour cream and stir in thoroughly.

3. Add the vanilla. Mince the zests together (or whirl them in a coffee grinder dedicated to mincing zests). Stir in along with the preserves. Stir thoroughly.

4. Sift together the flour, baking powder, baking soda, and salt. Add the dry ingredients to the butter mixture and stir carefully until thoroughly combined. Do not overmix. The batter will be stiff.

2 cups all-purpose flour (high altitude: add 2 tablespoons)

1 teaspoon baking powder

1 teaspoon baking soda

¼ teaspoon salt

Powdered sugar, for sprinkling on top of the cakes (optional)

5. Divide the batter evenly between the two pans. Spread the batter to the edges of the pan.

6. Bake for 20 to 30 minutes, or just until the cakes pull away from the sides of the pans, and a toothpick inserted in the center comes out clean.

7. Cool the cakes in the pans on racks for 10 minutes. Then remove the cakes from the pans and cool completely.

8. When you are ready to serve the cakes, if you'd like, sift powdered sugar over the tops.

Makes 2 cakes

Note: If possible, use Mexican vanilla. You may also substitute 1 teaspoon vanilla extract and 1 teaspoon vanilla bean paste.

Chapter 6

Desserts *or* This Is Not Your Low-Carb Chapter, Either

People love desserts. Caterers know this; restaurauters know this; *children* know this. The only people who don't know it—or who pretend not to—are the women's magazine writers, who announce (on their fall covers) *Lose 30 pounds by Christmas!* And of course the photo next to that headline is of a holiday dessert: a three-tier chocolate cake. So maybe the magazine writers do know you can't, nor should you try, to lose thirty pounds by Christmas. (And by the way, I checked the calorie count on a piece of that particular cover cake. It was northward of 1,500 calories *for one slice,* with enough carbohydrates to keep one going to New Year's.)

So in the interest of full disclosure, let me say that I know people should *not* overindulge in desserts. People with diabetes need sugar-free sweets, as do any

folks who are limiting their intake of simple carbohydrates, which is just about everyone. But limiting is not prohibiting. We all need to be careful, and there's the rub.

The tales of people fooling themselves are legion. I once helped cater a very high-end dinner for forty. The host had had a heart attack, and—I learned later—his doctor had sternly warned him to lower his intake of sugar and fat. For dessert, our host had been told to have berries. He ordered the following from us for dinner: tossed salad, rolls with butter, grilled shrimp, new potatoes, and a green vegetable medley, followed by . . . brownies topped with Häagen-Dazs frozen vanilla yogurt, with a few strawberries and blueberries strewn on top. Like the customer in the restaurant who orders fish followed by chocolate cake, the berries don't cancel out the brownies and—*spare me*—frozen vanilla yogurt.

Now for the good news. (You already know it.) Dessert is special because it's fun. You don't have to have a whole lot of pie for indulging in it to be joyful. Children love birthday cakes and holiday cookies. If we parents and grandparents take the time to teach them how to make them, as Mrs. Jones did for me, that's even better.

Since Jim and I live part of the year at 8,000 feet above sea level, where baking can be *challenging*, I developed all of the recipes at that altitude. Then I tested them at sea level, often at one of my siblings' homes in Maryland and New Jersey. At that point I *wrote* the recipes for sea level, as is the custom in the food business, but put the high-altitude directions, if necessary, in parentheses. Some recipes needed no alteration, thank goodness.

I've learned a thing or two in the years since 1982, when I started on the Goldy books. Now don't panic when I say this, but as with any other adventure in the kitchen, *science* is involved. For example, just as osmosis and diffusion are important in brining, diffusion is important in the making of cookies. In order for cookies to bake up with the best flavor, the dough should be refrigerated overnight, to allow the liquids to diffuse through the dry ingredients. Thus, with the cookie recipes that do better with chilling, I have altered them or suggested that you put the dough into the refrigerator overnight. Some cookie recipes *require* overnight chilling, which is indicated in the recipe.

And before you ask how a flourless chocolate cake can be a cake without flour, it is because technically, it is not really a cake: It is a (baked) confection.

It was with desserts that I have had the most fun experimenting over the years. For Dungeon Bars, I thought, I like vanilla; why is it bar recipes never call for more than a teaspoon of the stuff? I wanted to put in more, so I did. The idea for Scout's Brownies came to me in 1990, as I was falling asleep one night. (Neuroscientists tell us that just as you're drifting off is one of the times the right side of the brain is most active. The left, critical side goes to sleep first, we're told, so the right brain is free to take off.)

What I thought as I hit the pillow was: Why do chocolate cake recipes always use dry cocoa powder, and brownie recipes call for melted unsweetened, or sometimes bittersweet, chocolate? What if I combined cocoa powder and melted bittersweet chocolate?

So I did, and Scout's Brownies were born. The combination, and the recipe, have been widely copied and republished (with no credit given to yours truly, but never mind).

What does this have to do with writing? Remember that right-brain thing? I once heard Sue Grafton say that it behooves all writers to keep a scribble pad by the bed. As you're on your way to Dreamland and an idea hits, please don't think, *Oh, I'll remember that,* because you probably won't, which is another thing the neuroscientists tell us.

This is how I come up with titles. I have learned to trust the process. The original title for the book that became *Dying for Chocolate* was so long and complicated that I don't even remember it. Then just as I was going to sleep one night, it came to me: *Dying for Chocolate*. I had my title. The book was published in 1992, and before I went on the road, I had buttons made up that said:

I am
DYING FOR CHOCOLATE

When I went to conventions and bookstores, I gave them out.

I couldn't believe no one had used the title *The Cereal Murders,* so I snagged it. For a mystery set in the church (where Goldy is catering board meetings), *The Last Suppers* was a natural. Our youngest son contributed *Killer Pancake*; my agent came up with *The Grilling Season*. I had characters who were *Fatally Flaky* and one who was *The Main Corpse*. I began to keep an entire file called Possible Titles.

Another thing that is important for both bakers and artists to remember is that we have permission to make mistakes, to start over, to come at material, or ingredients, or titles, in different ways.

Now, a personal rant: I'd say that the very worst thing that writers and other artists do to themselves is to take themselves too seriously. Once they announce (you have no idea how many times I've heard this), "I'm going to write the Great American Novel," they're sunk. They can't figure out why they're blocked, why they can't get anything down on paper.

Guess what? *There are many great American novels.*

So please: Start with a class, then a critique group with regular deadlines. Write your complete novel. If it doesn't sell, write another.

If you have (lots of) money and are desperate to have your story published, hire a ghost writer.

I think writing is fun. That's what has kept me at the computer since 1982. You do not have to be published to enjoy yourself while writing.

With cooking: I started from scratch, gaining proficiency in this area, then acquiring the skills to cater. I took cooking classes from caterers and even took that very eye- and palate-opening course at the California Culinary Academy.

In writing, I joined writers' organizations and attended writers' conferences. A key hint that I learned early on was: Whatever it is you really love to *read* is what you should be writing. If you want to become a professional writer, there are excellent writers' organizations that can help. If your taste runs to commercial fiction, there are Romance Writers of America, Mystery Writers of America, Science Fiction and Fantasy Writers of America, and so on. Sisters in Crime is an outstanding organization dedicated to helping female writers of mystery fiction. The Society of Children's Book Writers and Illustrators is also superb. In addition to these, there are classes and organizations for poets, memoir-writers, essayists, and literary novelists.

In the Denver area, I belonged for many years to Rocky Mountain Fiction Writers, dedicated to helping writers of commercial fiction. Another excellent, relatively new group in Denver is Lighthouse Writers. I have attended a number of outstanding workshops given by both groups. In addition, these organizations usually run critique groups where you can take your material.

I also need to put in a plug here for your local independent bookstore. The people who own and run these wonderful shops are readers. (Trust me, they're not in it for the money.) They can give the person who wants to write recommendations for reading, as well as point him or her in the direction of good local writing groups.

So get writing, or baking, or both. Just don't be too serious about it.

Note: Because I took cookies, bars, and brownies to bookstores and other events, this is a very long chapter. Those cookie and bar recipes are listed first, followed by the other dessert recipes. When measuring any type of flour, I fold a large piece of wax paper in half, put the measuring cups on the paper, then lightly spoon the flour into the cups. I level off the cups with a kitchen knife. Following the crease in the paper, the leftover flour is easily dumped back into the bag. When making cookies, I bake them one sheet at a time. Except for Goldy's Nuthouse Cookies, I do not rotate the sheet. Instead, I keep an eye on the cookies as the time ticks down.

Honey-I'm-Home Gingersnaps

—CATERING TO NOBODY—

Gingersnaps that actually "snap" (i.e., crack apart when you break them in two) means people will sometimes complain that they are too hard. If you like a "snappy" cookie, overbake these slightly. If you prefer a softer one, bake them less. No matter what, if your cookies turn out too hard (or become too hard when stored), the trick my husband's mother used still works: Place the cookies in a plastic container with a lid, allowing some room on top; put a piece of fresh bread on the cookies. Put the lid on the container. In the morning, your cookies will be soft, and the piece of bread will be hard. Osmosis and diffusion again. Go figure.

2 cups all-purpose flour (high altitude: add 1 tablespoon)

2 teaspoons baking soda

1½ teaspoons ground ginger

1 teaspoon ground cinnamon

½ teaspoon ground cloves

¼ teaspoon freshly grated nutmeg

¼ teaspoon salt

¼ cup solid vegetable shortening

8 tablespoons (1 stick) unsalted butter, at room temperature

1. Sift together the flour, baking soda, ginger, cinnamon, cloves, nutmeg, and salt. Set aside.

2. In a large bowl, with an electric mixer, cream the shortening, butter, and sugar until light and fluffy. Beat in the egg and the honey or molasses until well combined. Stir in the flour mixture and the lemon zest, stirring until well combined, with no traces of flour visible. (If you have time, cover the bowl with plastic wrap and refrigerate overnight. When you are ready to make the cookies, let the dough come to room temperature.)

3. Preheat the oven to 350°F. (High altitude: 375°F.) Butter 2 baking sheets or line them with silicone baking mats.

- 1 cup sugar
- 1 large egg
- ¼ cup honey or molasses
- ¼ teaspoon finely minced lemon zest

4. Using a 1-tablespoon scoop, place the dough about 2 inches apart on the baking sheets. Do not attempt to fit more than one dozen per sheet. Baking one batch at a time, bake for 10 to 12 minutes, or until the cookies have puffed and flattened and have a crinkly surface.

5. Cool the cookies completely on racks.

Makes 32 cookies

Ice-Capped Gingersnaps

—TOUGH COOKIE—

While researching Tough Cookie, *I learned many ways a killer could hide in a kitchen on the ski slopes—and make a clean getaway. In keeping with the skiing theme of* Tough Cookie, *these cookies are "iced."*

2 sticks (½ pound) unsalted butter, at room temperature

1½ cups packed dark brown sugar

2 large eggs

½ cup dark molasses

2 teaspoons apple cider vinegar

4 cups all-purpose flour

1 tablespoon plus 1 teaspoon ground ginger

1 teaspoon ground cinnamon

1 teaspoon baking powder

½ teaspoon baking soda

½ teaspoon salt

¼ teaspoon ground allspice

¼ teaspoon ground cloves

¼ teaspoon freshly grated nutmeg

Icing (recipe follows)

1. In a large bowl, with an electric mixer, beat the butter until creamy. Add the brown sugar and eggs and beat until well combined, then add the molasses and vinegar and beat thoroughly. Sift together the flour, ginger, cinnamon, baking powder, baking soda, salt, allspice, cloves, and nutmeg. Add the flour mixture gradually to the butter mixture. (If you have time, cover the bowl with plastic wrap and refrigerate overnight. When you are ready to make the cookies, let the dough come to room temperature.)

2. Preheat the oven to 350°F. Butter 2 baking sheets or line them with silicone baking mats.

3. Using a 1½-tablespoon scoop, measure out dough and place the cookies 2 inches apart on the baking sheets. Bake, 1 sheet at a time, for 8 to 10 minutes, or until the cookies have puffed. (After you have made the first dozen, allow the cookies to cool on the baking sheet for 1 minute, then on a rack for 10 minutes, then taste one. If it is very dark brown on the

bottom and is dry, they are overcooked and you should bake the next sheet for a bit less time. If they are not quite baked through, bake the second sheet for a bit longer.) Allow the cookies to cool on the baking sheet for 1 minute, then transfer to racks to cool completely.

4. Holding the cooled cookies upside down by the edges, dip the tops into the icing. Allow to cool, icing side up on racks, until the icing hardens. Store between layers of wax paper in an airtight container.

Makes about 4 dozen cookies

* * *

Icing

1½ cups powdered sugar

2 tablespoons heavy (whipping) cream

¼ teaspoon vanilla extract

1 to 2 tablespoons whole milk

In a shallow bowl, whisk together the powdered sugar, cream, vanilla, and 1 tablespoon of the milk. If the icing seems too thick, add up to 1 tablespoon more milk. Strain the mixture through a sieve into another bowl.

Chocolate-Dipped Biscotti

—THE CEREAL MURDERS—

I decided to develop this recipe after seeing the high prices charged for chocolate-dipped, usually desert-dry biscotti in upscale coffee shops. Biscotti are easy to make; they just require time: *first to bake the "loaves," then to slice the loaves into cookies, then to bake again to make the biscotti, which you cool before dipping in chocolate. And for those of you interested in the origins of words,* biscotti *and* biscuits *come from the same roots,* bis *means "twice" and* cocere *means "to cook." So biscotti are literally twice-cooked, and they are a great deal of fun to make, especially with children (who may or may not be receptive to the etymology lesson).*

1 cup sugar

8 tablespoons (1 stick) unsalted butter, melted and cooled

2 tablespoons anise-flavored liqueur

1½ tablespoons sour mash whiskey, such as Jack Daniel's

2 tablespoons anise seeds

3 large eggs

1 cup coarsely chopped almonds

2¾ cups all-purpose flour

1½ teaspoons baking powder

One 12-ounce package semisweet chocolate chips

2 tablespoons solid vegetable shortening

1. In a large bowl, stir together the sugar and melted butter. Add the liqueur, whiskey, and anise seeds. Beat in the eggs, then stir in the nuts. Sift the flour and baking powder together. Gently stir in the flour mixture until well incorporated. Cover with plastic wrap and chill at least 3 hours.

2. Preheat the oven to 375°F. Butter 2 baking sheets or line them with silicone baking mats.

3. Shape the dough on the baking sheets into 3 loaves, well spaced apart. Each loaf should be

about 2 inches wide and ½ inch thick. Bake for 20 minutes, or until the loaves are puffed and browned. Cool on a rack. Leave the oven on.

4. When the loaves are cool enough to touch, use a serrated knife to slice each loaf on the diagonal into slices about ½ inch thick. Lay the slices on their cut sides and return them to the oven for an additional 15 minutes, or until lightly browned. Cool completely.

5. Dip the biscotti in chocolate the day they are to be served. In the top of a double boiler, over simmering water, melt the chocolate chips with the shortening, stirring frequently. Turn off the heat, remove the double boiler top, and stir the chocolate mixture until a candy thermometer reads 85°F.

6. Holding each cookie by one end, gently dip the tops into the chocolate mixture. Turn immediately and lift from the chocolate mixture. Allow to dry, uncoated side down, on wax paper. Continue until all the biscotti are topped with chocolate.

Makes about 4 dozen biscotti

Red 'n' Whites

—THE CEREAL MURDERS—

We absolutely adore the combination of cream cheese with . . . anything, but especially—as you will see with other dessert recipes here—fresh or cooked strawberries. When Goldy is tasked with making cookies in Stanford colors (Cardinal red and white), this is what she comes up with. (Yes, caterers are often asked to make food in school or team colors.)

There is good news and bad with these cookies. The bad: They do not hold up to humidity, so if you live in a humid climate, wrap them tightly in plastic as soon as they finish cooling and place that package in a zippered plastic bag. Once unwrapped, serve them as soon as possible. The good news: If by any chance you ever have to be on TV—say you've been given two minutes to promote the school book fair—make these cookies in advance and serve them up to the person interviewing you. The camera will zoom in on you offering the cookies to the interviewer (who probably has not had lunch), and while she's munching on one, you can say to the camera, "And I'm sending a tray of these back to the station, too!" The people back at the station, who probably have had neither breakfast nor lunch, will not be able to stop talking about your cookies and your fund-raising event *for the rest of the hour, with veiled threats of what they will do to the interviewer and the cameraman if they return empty-handed.*

Maybe this is dirty pool, but publicity for charity events is hard to get.

2 sticks (½ pound) unsalted butter, at room temperature

3 ounces cream cheese, at room temperature

½ cup sugar

1 teaspoon vanilla extract

2 cups all-purpose flour

36 small ripe strawberries, hulled and halved

1. In a bowl, with an electric mixer, beat the butter with the cream cheese until well blended. Beat in the sugar and vanilla, then stir in the flour until well mixed. (If you have time, cover the bowl with plastic wrap and refrigerate overnight. When you are ready to make the cookies, let the dough come to room temperature.)

2. Preheat the oven to 350°F.

3. Using a ½-tablespoon measure, shape the mixture into small balls and place 2 inches apart on ungreased baking sheets. Make a small indentation in the top of each cookie with your thumb. Carefully place a strawberry half, cut side down, in each indentation. Bake, one sheet at a time, for 12 to 18 minutes, or until very lightly browned. Cool on racks.

Makes 5 dozen cookies

Cereal Killer Cookies

—THE CEREAL MURDERS—

While visiting family in Charlottesville in the 1990s, I used to walk several miles into town in the morning to have a cappuccino at the one *place that served it. (This was before Starbucks swept across America.) Sometimes I would try a cookie, too (walks can be so exhausting), and one with bits of toffee in it got me to thinking. I came home and started experimenting, but nothing quite duplicated the cookie from that coffeehouse. Jim had never developed a recipe—and never has since—but he seemed to know what I was aiming for, and took over the development of the recipe. And am I glad he did! The cookie he came up with was buttery and crunchy, with just enough toffee made from Heath Bits 'O Brickle toffee bits.*

And then, horrors! Bits 'O Brickle stopped being made. They were literally nowhere to be found.

I had been in this predicament before, when I was developing the recipe for Scout's Brownies. I'd had my epiphany about combining cocoa with melted bittersweet chocolate, then experimented with different cocoa powders. The cocoa that baked up into the best brownies was made by Hershey, and it was called "Hershey's Premium European-Style Cocoa." Just as the book was coming out, there was no more of that cocoa on the shelves. I mean, it was nowhere. *I called the Hershey company in a panic, and was told that Evergreen, Colorado, had been a test market! Clearly, I had not bought enough of the stuff. Now there is Hershey's Special Dark Cocoa, and it is very good. I also use Droste, Ghirardelli, and Guittard cocoa.*

So: Back to the Bits 'O Brickle. Eventually, I found bags of toffee bits in my grocery store. Thank goodness.

Of all the cookies Goldy has ever served, Cereal Killer Cookies seem to be the favorite. It was even published—and I remain very thankful for this—in Ladies' Home Journal. *Despite that lovely publicity, people never seem to remember the name of the cookie. They just say, "We love that one with the toffee chips in it."*

- 2¼ cups old-fashioned rolled oats
- Two 6-ounce packages toffee chips (aka almond brickle chips)
- 1⅔ cups all-purpose flour
- 1 teaspoon baking soda
- 1 teaspoon baking powder
- ½ teaspoon salt
- 1 cup packed dark brown sugar
- ¾ cup granulated sugar
- 2 sticks (½ pound) unsalted butter
- 2 large eggs
- 1 tablespoon vanilla extract

1. In a large bowl, mix the oats with the toffee bits.

2. Sift the flour, baking soda, baking powder, and salt together.

3. In a food processor, mix the sugars until blended, then gradually add the butter. Continue to process until creamy and smooth. Add the eggs and vanilla and process until blended. Add the flour mixture and process just until combined. Pour this mixture over the oats and toffee bits and stir until well combined. (If you have time, cover the bowl with plastic wrap and refrigerate overnight. When you are ready to make the cookies, let the dough come to room temperature.)

4. Preheat the oven to 375°F.

5. Using a 2-tablespoon scoop, place scoops of dough at least 2 inches apart on 2 ungreased baking sheets. Bake, 1 sheet at a time, for 12 to 15 minutes, or until golden brown.

6. Let the cookies set up on the baking sheets for 2 minutes, then carefully remove the cookies to racks to cool completely.

Makes 4 to 5 dozen cookies

Sweetheart Sandwiches

—THE CEREAL MURDERS—

Many people have tried to duplicate the fantastic combination of chocolate and frosting that is the esteemed Oreo cookie. This is Goldy's (and my) crack at it.

Cookies:

8 tablespoons (1 stick) unsalted butter

1¼ cups sugar

2 large eggs

1 teaspoon vanilla extract

½ cup Dutch-process unsweetened cocoa powder

2 cups all-purpose flour

½ teaspoon salt

1 teaspoon baking powder

½ teaspoon baking soda

Filling:

4 tablespoons (½ stick) unsalted butter

1 teaspoon vanilla extract

4 cups powdered sugar

Heavy (whipping) cream

For the cookies:

1. In a large bowl, with an electric mixer, cream the butter with the sugar until light. Beat in the eggs and vanilla. Sift the cocoa, flour, salt, baking powder, and baking soda together. Stir the dry ingredients thoroughly into the butter mixture. Cover the bowl with plastic wrap and refrigerate at least 2 hours, preferably overnight.

2. Preheat the oven to 375°F. Butter 2 baking sheets or line them with silicone baking mats.

3. Using a teaspoon measure, roll level teaspoons of the chilled dough into balls and place them 2 inches apart on the baking sheets. Bake, 1 sheet at a time, for 10 to 15 minutes, or until the cookies are puffed and the surfaces are slightly dry and cracked. Cool *completely* on racks.

For the filling:

1. In a bowl, with an electric mixer, cream the butter until light. Beat in the vanilla and powdered sugar. If the filling is not creamy, beat in heavy cream a bit at a time and continue to beat until the consistency is like creamy frosting.

2. To assemble the cookies, carefully spread about ½ tablespoon filling all over the flat side of one cookie, then top with the flat side of another cookie. Serve immediately.

Makes about 3 dozen sandwich cookies

Variation: For half a batch of vanilla-filled and half a batch of peppermint-filled cookies, divide the filling in half. Add ⅛ teaspoon peppermint extract to half the filling. Tint the peppermint filling pink or green before filling half the sandwiches.

Canterbury Jumbles

—THE LAST SUPPERS—

Ever been to a cookie exchange? I haven't heard of any being held lately, so maybe they are a relic of the middle part of the twentieth century. Back then, you and a hypothetical nineteen others—all equally daft—would make twenty dozen (you read that right) of the same cookie, bag each dozen up separately, then come in and take one dozen from each of nineteen others. If it worked right, you would each walk away with nineteen dozen different types of cookie, plus your own dozen, all of which you could take home and freeze. This would give you twenty dozen different *Christmas cookies stashed in your freezer. This really only works well if four conditions are met:*

1. *Everyone uses at least some butter in her/his cookies*
2. *There are no interlopers*
3. *Nobody screws up the math, and*
4. *You wrap your stash in opaque butcher paper and on the outside scrawl,* Lake Trout, August 1999

Canterbury Jumbles began as a date-and-fruit cookie that I received at a cookie exchange. I changed the recipe somewhat to make it work for us (I used butter and omitted the nuts). Jim and the kids loved them, so now I make them every year at Christmas. (The recipe I came up with is in the Mystery Writers of America Cookbook, *available from your local bookstore or library.)*

But for Canterbury Jumbles, I wanted to play around with the ingredients. My goal was to come up with a cookie that tasted like a candy people of my generation adored. It was called the "Chunky." Chunkies were small, square hunks of chocolate dense with raisins and nuts. Just using chocolate chips, raisins, and nuts didn't seem like enough in my tests, so I added coconut and switched over to macadamia nuts for added richness. Now I usually substitute chopped dried tart cherries for the raisins, as one of our children does not like raisins. (Heresy! But that's family for you.)

- ½ cup solid vegetable shortening
- 8 tablespoons (1 stick) unsalted butter, at room temperature
- 2 cups packed dark brown sugar
- 2 large eggs
- ½ cup buttermilk
- 2 teaspoons vanilla extract
- 3½ cups all-purpose flour
- 1 teaspoon baking soda
- 1 teaspoon salt
- 1 cup sweetened flaked coconut
- 1 cup coarsely chopped macadamia nuts
- 1½ cups raisins or dried tart cherries
- 3 cups semisweet chocolate chips

1. In a large bowl, with an electric mixer, beat the shortening, butter, and brown sugar together until smooth. Beat in the eggs, then stir in the buttermilk and vanilla.

2. In a small bowl, blend together the flour, baking soda, and salt. Stir the flour mixture into the butter mixture until incorporated. Stir in the coconut, nuts, raisins or cherries, and chocolate chips. (If you have time, cover the bowl with plastic wrap and refrigerate overnight. When you are ready to make the cookies, let the dough come to room temperature.)

3. Preheat the oven to 400°F. Butter baking sheets or line them with silicone baking mats.

4. Using a ½-tablespoon measure, measure out leveled spoonfuls of dough onto the baking sheets, 2 inches apart. Bake, 1 sheet at a time, for 7 to 10 minutes, or until the cookies are puffed and lightly browned. Cool on a rack.

Makes 11 dozen cookies

Lemon Butter Wafers

—THE LAST SUPPERS—

The flavors of finely grated lemon zest mixed with ground almonds is delightful in a cookie. The combination is even more delectable if some raspberry flavor is thrown in. I sometimes make these as lemon/raspberry sandwiches, but have to wait until just before serving to spread the jam. Otherwise, they wilt, even in a dry climate.

1½ sticks (6 ounces) unsalted butter, at room temperature

1 cup sugar

2 large eggs

1¼ cups sifted all-purpose flour

2 tablespoons very finely minced lemon zest (see Note)

⅓ cup ground almonds (see Note)

1. In a large bowl, with an electric mixer, beat the butter until smooth and add the sugar, beating until creamy. Beat in the eggs. Add the flour, beating just until combined. Add the lemon zest and almonds, stirring until well incorporated. Cover the bowl with plastic wrap and place in the refrigerator until well chilled, at least 3 hours and preferably overnight.

2. Preheat the oven to 350°F. Butter a baking sheet or line with a silicone baking mat.

3. Using a ½-tablespoon measure, measure out leveled spoonfuls of chilled cookie dough onto the baking sheet, placing them 3 inches apart. Bake, 1 sheet at a time, for about 10 minutes, or until the cookies have just flattened and are lightly browned around the edges. Cool the cookies on racks. Store in a covered tin.

Makes a generous 5 dozen cookies

Note: It is best to grind the almonds and mince the lemon zest in a small electric grinder such as a coffee grinder that you do not use for coffee. The result is superior to that obtained with an ordinary food processor.

Variation: Just before serving, spread 1 tablespoon best-quality seedless raspberry jam on the flat bottom of one cookie, then place the flat bottom of another cookie on top. This makes a divine lemon-raspberry cookie sandwich. *Makes about 32 sandwich cookies.*

Blondes' Blondies

—PRIME CUT—

The blondie, once a staple dessert of school lunch programs, seems to have fallen out of favor, which is a pity. There is a TED talk on the decline of public school lunches, and the theory is that it began with the retirement of the venerable lunch ladies. These women, wearing their hairnets and white uniforms, cooked us and our children lunch fresh, every day. They also baked the desserts. The women were professionals, and the lunches were delicious and nutritious. But then Big Ag got involved, ketchup was listed as a vegetable, and school lunches went to hell. There's a movement on now to make school lunches delicious and nutritious again, and I hope that happens.

Goldy's newfangled blondie contains chopped apple and spices. But the butterscotch flavor of the old-fashioned blondie shines through, and the citrus frosting provides a bright contrast.

2 cups peeled and diced Granny Smith apples

1 cup packed dark brown sugar

1 large egg

8 tablespoons (1 stick) unsalted butter, melted and cooled

1½ cups cake flour (high altitude: add 1 tablespoon)

1 teaspoon baking soda

1 teaspoon ground cinnamon

½ teaspoon salt

½ teaspoon ground allspice

1. Preheat the oven to 325°F. Butter a 9 x 13-inch baking pan (be sure to use metal, not glass).

2. In a large bowl, mix the chopped apples with the brown sugar.

3. In a small bowl, beat the egg slightly. Whisk the melted and cooled butter into the egg. Stir this mixture into the apple mixture.

4. Sift together the flour, baking soda, cinnamon, salt, allspice, and nutmeg. Stir the flour mixture into the apple mixture, mixing just until incorporated. Stir in the nuts and raisins. (The batter will be thick.) Spread the batter in the baking pan.

½ teaspoon freshly grated nutmeg

½ cup chopped pecans or walnuts

½ cup raisins

Creamy Citrus Frosting (recipe follows)

5, Bake for 18 to 22 minutes, or until a toothpick inserted in the center comes out clean or with just a crumb or two attached. Cool the blondies in the pan, then frost with creamy Citrus Frosting. Cut into 32 pieces.

Makes 32 blondies

Creamy Citrus Frosting

2 tablespoons unsalted butter, at room temperature

2 tablespoons orange juice

1 to 1½ cups powdered sugar, sifted

In a small bowl, beat together the butter and orange juice until the butter is very soft (they will not mix completely). Beat in the powdered sugar until you reach a creamy consistency.

Keepsake Cookies

—PRIME CUT—

Prime Cut *is dedicated to Ann Blakeslee, who was our wonderful, loving Director of Religious Education at our former parish. She made a cookie very similar to this for our family one Christmas.*

Cookies:

⅔ cup slivered almonds

1 pound unsalted butter, at room temperature

1 cup powdered sugar, sifted

2 teaspoons very finely minced orange zest

¼ cup Grand Marnier liqueur

3⅓ cups all-purpose flour

½ teaspoon salt

Granulated sugar, for preparing the cookies

Filling:

8 tablespoons (1 stick) unsalted butter, at room temperature

3 cups powdered sugar, sifted

3 tablespoons heavy (whipping) cream

1 tablespoon Grand Marnier liqueur

For the cookies:

1. Grind the almonds in a food processor until they resemble large bread crumbs. Transfer to a small bowl.

2. In a large bowl, with an electric mixer, cream the butter until it is very smooth and creamy. Slowly add the powdered sugar and beat until the mixture is very smooth. Beat in the orange zest and liqueur.

3. Stir the flour and salt into the ground almonds. Stir the flour mixture into the butter mixture until very well combined.

4. Cover the bowl and refrigerate for at least 3 hours or overnight.

5. Preheat the oven to 375°F. Butter 2 baking sheets or line them with silicone baking mats.

6. Using a ½-tablespoon measure, scoop out the chilled cookie dough and roll into balls. Place the balls 2 inches apart on the baking sheets. Butter the flat bottom of a glass, then dip the glass bottom in granulated sugar. Flatten each

cookie with the buttered and sugared glass bottom to a diameter of 2¼ inches. (Do not make the cookies too thin.) Dip the glass into the sugar each time before flattening a cookie.

7. Bake, 1 sheet at a time, for 7 to 10 minutes, or until the cookies are just cooked through but *not at all browned.* Allow the cookies to cool for 1 minute on the baking sheets, then transfer to racks to cool completely.

For the filling:
In a large bowl, with an electric mixer, beat the butter until smooth. Add the powdered sugar, cream, and liqueur and beat until very smooth and creamy. Spread about 1 teaspoon of filling on the flat underside of half the cookies. Make a sandwich with the flat underside of the other half of the cookies. Serve immediately or store tightly covered.

Makes about 5 dozen sandwich cookies

Queen of Scots Shortbread

—STICKS AND SCONES—

The first time I tasted true Scottish shortbread, I fell in love with it. I tried numerous different ways of making this buttery, crumbly cookie that satisfied my picky taste-testers, and this one was their favorite. The key with this recipe is beating the dry ingredients into the wet ones only until they are combined, and handling the dough as little as possible. If you cannot find rice flour, all-purpose flour works fine.

- 2 sticks (½ pound) unsalted butter, at room temperature
- ½ cup powdered sugar
- ¾ teaspoon vanilla extract
- 1½ cups all-purpose flour
- ½ cup rice flour (available at health food stores) or all-purpose flour
- ¼ teaspoon baking powder
- ¼ teaspoon salt

1. Preheat the oven to 350°F. Have two 8-inch round cake pans at the ready.

2. In a large bowl, with an electric mixer, beat the butter until it is very creamy. Add the powdered sugar and beat well, about 5 minutes. Beat in the vanilla. Sift the flours with the baking powder and salt, then add them to the butter mixture, beating only until well combined.

3. With floured fingers, gently pat the dough into the ungreased pans. Using the floured tines of a fork, score (i.e., make superficial cuts into but not through) the shortbreads so that they are marked in eight equal wedges. Press the tines around the edges of each shortbread to resemble fluting, and prick the shortbread with a decorative design, if desired.

4. Bake for 20 to 25 minutes, or until the edge of the shortbread is just beginning to brown. Allow to cool for 10 minutes in the pan on a rack. While the shortbread is still warm, gently cut through the marked-off wedges. Using a pointed metal spatula or pie server, carefully lever out the shortbread wedges and allow them to cool completely on a rack.

Makes 16 wedge-shaped cookies

Chocolate Snowcap Cookies

—THE WHOLE ENCHILADA—

I had tried to make the chocolate cookies that you roll in powdered sugar so that after baking, they come out looking like a resort with various crooked ski runs . . . but nothing ever tasted chocolatey enough. Thanks to Marty O'Leary and the staff at Sur La Table in Sarasota, Florida, I found the perfect answer: adding chocolate extract to the batter. Voilà! This is the cookie I took out on the road for The Whole Enchilada.

4 ounces extra-bittersweet or bittersweet chocolate, such as Lindt, chopped

8 tablespoons (1 stick) unsalted butter

4 large eggs

2 cups packed dark brown sugar

2 cups all-purpose flour

⅓ cup Dutch-process unsweetened cocoa powder

2 teaspoons baking powder

½ teaspoon kosher salt

¼ teaspoon baking soda

2 teaspoons vanilla extract

1 teaspoon chocolate extract

1 cup powdered sugar, for rolling

1. In the top of a double boiler, over simmering water, melt the chocolate and butter. When the mixture is just melted, set aside to cool.

2. In a large bowl, with an electric mixer, beat the eggs until well combined. Add the brown sugar and beat until very well combined.

3. Sift together the flour, cocoa, baking powder, salt, and baking soda.

4. When the chocolate mixture is no more than lukewarm, stir it into the egg mixture. Using a wooden spoon, gently stir in the extracts and the flour mixture.

5. Cover the bowl tightly with plastic wrap and chill overnight. (The dough must be very well chilled.)

6. When you are ready to bake the cookies, preheat the oven to 350°F. Line 2 baking sheets with silicone baking mats.

7. Place the powdered sugar in a large bowl. Remove the bowl of dough from the refrigerator. Using a 1-tablespoon scoop, measure out a dozen level scoops of chilled dough. (Put the plastic wrap back over the bowl of dough and return to the refrigerator, to keep the rest well chilled. As the dough warms up, it becomes too sticky to work with.)

8. Roll the first dozen scoops into balls, then drop them one at a time into the bowl of sugar, rolling them around until they are white. Place the cookies in even rows on the first baking sheet, 2 inches apart. Bake for about 10 minutes, or until the "cracks" in the dough no longer appear wet. Watch carefully, as you do not want the cookies to overbake and dry out. Remove the sheet from the oven.

9. Let the cookies set up for 5 minutes on the baking sheet. Carefully transfer the cookies to racks to cool completely.

10. Remove the bowl of dough from the refrigerator and repeat with the other baking sheet. Repeat this process until all the dough is used up.

11. These cookies can be messy to eat, because of the powdered sugar. Serve them on plates.

Makes 3½ to 4 dozen cookies

Fatally Flaky Cookies

—FATALLY FLAKY—

I had a lot of fun testing this recipe on young relatives, who were equally divided over using ice cream or buttercream frosting as a filling. (One queried, "If I say I like both, does that mean I get more cookies?")

8 tablespoons (1 stick) unsalted butter

¾ cup packed dark brown sugar

1 tablespoon best-quality Dutch-process unsweetened cocoa powder

1½ cups quick-cooking oats

1 tablespoon all-purpose flour (high altitude: add 2 tablespoons)

1 teaspoon baking powder

¼ teaspoon kosher salt

1 large egg

2 teaspoons vanilla extract

Vanilla Buttercream Frosting (recipe follows)

1. Preheat the oven to 350°F. Line 2 baking sheets with silicone baking mats.

2. In a large heavy-bottomed saucepan, melt the butter over low heat. Add the brown sugar and increase the heat to medium. Using a wooden spoon, stir until the mixture bubbles, 3 to 5 minutes. Remove from the heat, pour into a heatproof bowl, and set aside to cool while you prepare the rest of the ingredients.

3. In a large bowl, stir together the cocoa, oats, flour, baking powder, and salt until well combined.

4. In another bowl, beat together the egg and vanilla. Stir into the oat mixture until well combined. Add the cooled butter-sugar mixture and stir well.

5. Using a 1-tablespoon scoop, measure out the dough and place the cookies at least 2 inches apart on the baking sheets (they spread and you need all the cookies to be a uniform size).

6. Bake the cookies, one sheet at a time, for 10 to 12 minutes, or until the cookies are completely cooked. Allow to cool on the sheets for 5 minutes. Then, using a wide, nonstick spatula, carefully transfer the cookies to cooling racks. Allow to cool completely.

7. When you are ready to serve, spread 2 tablespoons of buttercream on the flat side of one cookie, then top with the flat side of a second cookie. Serve immediately.

Makes about 12 sandwich cookies

Vanilla Buttercream Frosting

- 8 tablespoons (1 stick) unsalted butter, at room temperature
- 2 cups powdered sugar, sifted
- Heavy (whipping) cream or milk, preferably whole
- 1 teaspoon vanilla extract

In a large bowl, with an electric mixer, beat the butter on medium speed until it is very creamy. Slowly add the powdered sugar, ¼ cup at a time, beating each time until the sugar is completely blended into the butter. If the frosting begins to get too stiff, add a tablespoon of cream or milk. Beat in the vanilla, and if the frosting is still too stiff, add another tablespoon of cream or milk. You want the frosting to be fairly stiff so the sandwich cookies stay together. Cover and refrigerate any unused frosting.

Chocolate Coma Cookies

—TOUGH COOKIE—

It was a great day for yours truly when a Godiva store opened in the Cherry Creek Mall in Denver. I loved going there to buy bittersweet chocolate, although Lindt and other premium brands like Valrhona also work well. For this recipe, I wanted to try adding oats to a chocolate chip cookie. My sister Lucy was remodeling her house at that point, and I needed to test the recipe at sea level. Lucy invited me to Baltimore to do my testing, so off I went. Lucy's construction workers were eager taste-testers, although they kept saying they just needed me to make one more batch *to tell if the recipe was right.*

1 cup slivered almonds

1 cup dried tart cherries

12 ounces semisweet chocolate chips

2 cups old-fashioned rolled oats

2 cups all-purpose flour

1 teaspoon baking powder

1 teaspoon baking soda

½ teaspoon salt

2 sticks (½ pound) unsalted butter, at room temperature

1 cup packed dark brown sugar

1 cup granulated sugar

2 large eggs

1½ teaspoons vanilla extract

1. In a nonstick skillet, toast the almonds over medium-low heat, stirring constantly, until they have *just* begun to turn brown and give off a nutty aroma, 5 to 10 minutes. Turn out onto a plate to cool.

2. In a large bowl, combine the cherries, chocolate chips, and oats and set aside.

3. Sift together the flour, baking powder, baking soda, and salt and set aside.

4. In a large bowl, with an electric mixer, beat the butter until creamy. Add the sugars and beat until light and fluffy, about 4 minutes. Add the eggs and vanilla. Beat the mixture until well combined, about 1 minute. Add the flour mixture to the butter mixture and beat at low speed until well combined, less than a minute. Add the chocolate chips, cherries, nuts, oats,

4 ounces best-quality bittersweet chocolate, chopped into chunks no larger than large chocolate chips

and chopped chocolate. Using a sturdy wooden spoon, mix well by hand, until all the ingredients are thoroughly incorporated.

5. Cover the bowl with plastic wrap and refrigerate overnight. When you are ready to make the cookies, let the dough come to room temperature.

6. Preheat the oven to 350°F. Butter 2 baking sheets or line them with silicone baking mats.

7. Using a 1-tablespoon scoop, measure out dough and place the cookies 2 inches apart on the baking sheets (about a dozen per sheet). Bake each sheet, one at a time, for 12 to 14 minutes, or until the cookies have set and are slightly flattened and light brown. Cool the cookies on the sheets for 2 minutes, then transfer to racks to cool completely.

Makes 6 dozen cookies

Chocolate Comfort Cookies

—THE GRILLING SEASON—

I worked on this recipe to see if using cream cheese in a chocolate cookie would give it a bit of tartness. It did. Once again, the flavor is enhanced by allowing the dough to chill overnight in the refrigerator.

1 cup skinned hazelnuts (aka filberts)

2 cups extra-large semisweet chocolate chips (11.5-ounce package of Nestlé's mega-morsels also known as "chocolate chunks") or regular semisweet chocolate chips

½ cup dried cranberries

2 ounces bittersweet chocolate, melted

2 sticks (½ pound) unsalted butter, at room temperature

1 cup sugar

3 ounces cream cheese, at room temperature

1 large egg

2 tablespoons milk, preferably whole

1½ teaspoons vanilla extract

1. Preheat the oven to 325°F.

2. Spread the hazelnuts on an ungreased baking sheet and roast for 7 to 12 minutes, or until they are lightly browned. Set aside to cool. (Turn off the oven, as you will not be making the cookies until the next day.) Once the nuts are cool, chop them.

3. In a large bowl, combine the chocolate chips, cranberries, and cooled nuts and set aside.

4. In the top of a double boiler, over simmering water, melt the chocolate.

5. In a large bowl, beat together the butter, sugar, cream cheese, and egg until very creamy and smooth. Beat in the melted chocolate, milk, and vanilla. Sift together the flour, cocoa, baking powder, and salt. Add the flour mixture to the butter mixture. Blend in the marshmallow crème, stirring until thoroughly combined. Add the chips, cranberries, and nuts. Stir until well mixed. The dough will be thick.

2 cups plus 2 tablespoons all-purpose flour (high altitude: add 2 tablespoons)

¼ cup Dutch-process unsweetened cocoa powder

½ teaspoon baking powder

½ teaspoon salt

1 cup marshmallow crème

6. Cover the bowl with plastic wrap and refrigerate overnight. When you are ready to make the cookies, let the dough come to room temperature.

7. Preheat the oven to 325°F. Butter 2 baking sheets or line them with silicone baking mats.

8. Using a ¼-cup measure or a 4-tablespoon ice-cream scoop, place the dough 2 inches apart on baking sheets, placing no more than 6 cookies per sheet. Bake, 1 sheet at a time, for 13 to 17 minutes, or until puffed and cooked through. Cool on the sheet for 1 minute, then transfer to racks to cool completely.

Makes 2 dozen cookies

Chocoholic Cookies

—THE MAIN CORPSE—

At this point, you may be wondering why there are so many chocolate cookie recipes in this book (apart from the fact that people like them). Chocolate cookies were far and away the favorite among readers who came to bookstore events. So for each book, I would work on a different chocolate cookie to take. Then Jim, bless him, would make batch after batch of the cookies and send them overnight to whatever city I was going to be in next. For this cookie, while I know white chocolate is not really chocolate, I love it anyway. So does our youngest son, whose soccer team also taste-tested one of my cheesecake recipes (see page 266). These are his favorite chocolate cookies.

2 cups old-fashioned rolled oats

One 12-ounce package semisweet chocolate chips

2 sticks (½ pound) unsalted butter, at room temperature

1 cup packed dark brown sugar

½ cup granulated sugar

1½ cups all-purpose flour

¼ cup Dutch-process unsweetened cocoa powder

½ teaspoon baking soda

½ teaspoon salt

1 tablespoon milk, preferably whole

1. *Do not alter the order in which the ingredients are combined.* In a large bowl, combine the oats and chocolate chips and set aside.

2. In another large bowl, beat together the butter and sugars until creamy. Sift together the flour, cocoa, baking soda, and salt. Add the flour mixture to the butter mixture, stirring until thoroughly combined. The dough will be very stiff. Stir the milk and vanilla into the eggs, then stir this mixture into the butter mixture until thoroughly combined. Add the chips and oats and stir until well mixed.

3. Cover the bowl with plastic wrap and refrigerate overnight. When you are ready to make the cookies, let the dough come to room temperature.

1½ teaspoons vanilla extract

2 large eggs, lightly beaten

9 ounces white chocolate

1½ tablespoons solid vegetable shortening

4. Preheat the oven to 350°F. Butter 2 baking sheets or line them with silicone baking mats.

5. Using a 2-tablespoon scoop, measure out dough and place 2 inches apart on baking sheets. Bake, one sheet at a time, for 9 to 12 minutes, or until cooked through. Cool the cookies on the sheet for 1 minute, then transfer to racks to cool completely.

6. Place a cooling rack over wax paper. In the top of a double boiler, over simmering water, melt the white chocolate with the vegetable shortening. Holding a cooled cookie between your thumb and forefinger, dip the edge into the warm white chocolate to cover the top third of the cookie. Place it on the rack to dry completely.

7. Store between layers of wax paper in an airtight container in a cool place.

Makes 5 dozen cookies

Strong-Arm Cookies

—DARK TORT—

It does indeed take a strong arm to mix this cookie batter. And as I have learned, the results are improved if you chill the batter overnight. But the results are worth it. This recipe makes a lot *of cookies (8 dozen). I have tried to bake 2 sheets at a time in several ovens that we've owned, without good results. So you may want to spread the baking over a couple of days.*

2 cups pecan halves

1½ sticks (6 ounces) unsalted butter, at room temperature

¼ cup solid vegetable shortening

2 cups packed dark brown sugar

2 large eggs

½ cup buttermilk

3¼ cups all-purpose flour

1 teaspoon baking soda

1 teaspoon salt

2 cups dried cherries

2 cups extra-large semisweet chocolate chips (sometimes called "mega-morsels" or "chocolate chunks") or regular chocolate chips

1. In a large, dry skillet, toast the nuts over medium-low heat, stirring, until they give off a nutty scent and have turned slightly darker, about 10 minutes. Turn out onto paper towels and allow to cool completely.

2. In a large bowl, with an electric mixer, beat the butter and shortening on medium speed until well blended, about 2 minutes. Add the brown sugar and beat until thoroughly creamed into the butter mixture, about 5 minutes. Thoroughly beat in the eggs, then stir in the buttermilk.

3. Sift together the flour, baking soda, and salt. Gently stir into the butter mixture until you can see no more flour. Stir in the nuts, cherries, and chocolate chips. Chill the dough, tightly covered with plastic wrap, for at least 1 hour and up to overnight.

4. Preheat the oven to 375°F. Line a baking sheet with a silicone baking mat.

5. I have found that these cookies are easier to scoop if the dough is *not* brought to room temperature. Using a ½-tablespoon scoop, measure out 12 cookies and place them 2 inches apart on the first baking sheet. Using the heel of your hand, gently push on each cookie to flatten slightly. Bake for 8 to 11 minutes, or until you can touch them lightly and leave almost no imprint. While the first dozen is baking, measure out the second dozen.

6. Allow the cookies to cool 1 minute on the baking sheet, then transfer to a rack to cool completely. You can either bake all 8 dozen in this way, or bake the number you want, then rewrap the dough and chill it until you are ready to finish the baking. The batter keeps, well-wrapped, in the refrigerator for a week.

7. Store the cookies at room temperature in an airtight container.

Makes 8 dozen cookies

Babsie's Tarts

—THE GRILLING SEASON—

I am a linzertorte fanatic. But they can be messy to slice and serve. If you've ever catered an event that involves pieces of pie, cake, torte, or tart for dessert, you will notice that a subtle (or sometimes not so subtle) competition goes on between the guests. They eye the other slices at the table: Was her slice bigger than mine? Did he get a (smaller) end piece from the pound cake, or a bigger one from the middle?

You can also be told: "I only want half a slice." So you serve half a slice. Then you hear a grumbled, "Well, I wanted more than that."

This is all by way of saying that for Babsie's Tarts, my aim was to develop individual *linzertortes, of equal size. My problem then became one of stability. Every time I picked up a tart, the filling would fall through the middle and land on the floor. That is why I finally wrote that one should* indent the center of the crust only slightly. *Any more than a very slight concavity, and your tarts will not hold up. You may serve them plain, or sprinkle with powdered sugar, and serve with a scoop of best-quality vanilla ice cream.*

- 2 sticks (½ pound) unsalted butter, at room temperature
- ¾ cup sugar
- 2 egg yolks, from large eggs
- 1 teaspoon vanilla extract
- 2 teaspoons finely grated lemon zest (see Note)
- 1½ cups all-purpose flour (high altitude: add 1 tablespoon)

1. In a large bowl, beat the butter until creamy. Add the sugar and beat until thoroughly incorporated. In a separate bowl, beat the egg yolks slightly with the vanilla and lemon zest. Add to the butter mixture, stirring thoroughly. Sift the flour, baking powder, cinnamon, cloves, and salt together. Stir the flour mixture into the creamed mixture. Stir in the almonds.

2. Preheat the oven to 350°F. Coat the cups of 2 nonstick muffin tins with cooking spray. Using a 2-tablespoon scoop (or measuring out in two

1 teaspoon baking powder

1 teaspoon ground cinnamon

¼ teaspoon ground cloves

¼ teaspoon salt

1¼ cups blanched slivered almonds, ground (see Note)

Cooking spray

1 to 1¼ cups best-quality *seedless* red raspberry jam

Powdered sugar, optional

1-tablespoon increments), press one scoop of dough gently to cover the bottom of each muffin cup. Only *slightly* indent the dough to form a "tart shell." Any more than a slight indentation will mean that the jam that is to be cooked in the center will leak through. Place 2 teaspoons of jam in the center of each tart.

3. Bake for about 15 minutes, or until the dough has risen and turned golden brown around the jam. After the pans have been removed from the oven, use a sharp knife to loosen the edges of each tart. Allow the tarts to cool in the pan until cool to the touch, at least 1 hour. Using a butter knife, gently lever the tarts out onto racks to cool completely.

Makes 24 tarts

Note: Citrus zests and nuts are easily ground in a coffee grinder used only for that purpose.

Goldy's Nuthouse Cookies

—DOUBLE SHOT—

When my sisters and I were little, we used to answer the phone, "Motts' Candy Shop, which nut do you want?" Needless to say, we found this hilarious. Our parents did not.

The great thing about these cookies is that you can roll the dough into logs and freeze them, then slice and bake whenever you want fresh cookies.

1½ cups slivered almonds

½ teaspoon baking soda

½ teaspoon salt

1¼ cups cake flour

1 cup all-purpose flour

2 sticks (½ pound) unsalted butter, at room temperature

2⅔ cups sifted powdered sugar

1 large egg

1 teaspoon vanilla extract

1. In a wide skillet, toast the almonds over low heat, stirring frequently, until they turn slightly brown and give off a nutty scent, about 10 minutes. Turn out onto paper towels and allow to cool completely.

2. In a bowl, mix together the almonds, baking soda, salt, and flours. Set aside.

3. In a large bowl, with an electric mixer, beat the butter until creamy, about 5 minutes. Add the powdered sugar and beat on medium-low speed until very creamy, about 5 minutes. Reduce the speed to low and beat in the egg and vanilla. Continue to beat until well blended. Stir in the flour mixture just until well combined. Do not overbeat.

4. Divide the dough into 3 equal pieces and place them in the bottom of 3 zippered plastic freezer bags. Roll each section of the dough into logs. Zip the bags closed and place them in the freezer overnight.

5. Preheat the oven to 350°F. Line 2 baking sheets with silicone baking mats.

6. Remove one log at a time from the freezer. Take it out of the bag. While each log is still frozen, place it on a cutting board and use a large, sharp knife to divide it in half. Put the rest of the log back in the freezer. Divide the half roll into 12 equal slices. Place them on one of the baking sheets. Flatten each cold cookie slightly with the palm of your hand. When the first dozen cookies is baked and cooling, you may remove the rest of the roll from the freezer and start on it. (The cookies hold together better, cook more evenly, and develop a better texture if they are placed in the oven while they are still frozen.)

7. Bake one sheet at a time for about 10 minutes, or until the cookies have turned golden brown at the edges. Rotate the baking sheets from front to back after 5 minutes. Cool completely on racks.

Makes 6 dozen cookies

Crunch Time Cookies

—CRUNCH TIME—

If you like toffee and chocolate the way Goldy fans do, you're going to love this recipe. This is the cookie I took out on the road when I visited bookstores for Crunch Time.

- 1 cup pecan halves
- 1¼ cups all-purpose flour
- ½ teaspoon baking powder
- ½ teaspoon baking soda
- ½ teaspoon kosher salt
- 2 sticks (½ pound) unsalted butter, at room temperature
- 2 ounces (¼ cup) cream cheese, at room temperature
- 1 cup packed dark brown sugar
- ¾ cup granulated sugar
- 2 large eggs, at room temperature
- 1 teaspoon vanilla extract
- 2½ cups old-fashioned rolled oats
- 1½ cups (8 ounces) semisweet chocolate chips
- ⅔ cup (4 ounces) toffee chips (aka almond brickle chips)

1, In a large skillet, toast the pecans over low heat, stirring frequently, or until the nuts begin to change color and give off a nutty scent, about 10 minutes. Turn the nuts out onto paper towels and allow them to cool, then chop them roughly and set aside.

2. Sift or whisk together the flour, baking powder, baking soda, and salt. Set aside.

3. In a large bowl, with an electric mixer, beat the butter and cream cheese on medium speed until the mixture is very creamy. Add the brown sugar and beat very well, until the mixture is creamy and uniform. Add the granulated sugar and again beat very well, until you have a uniform, creamy mixture. Add the eggs, one at a time, and beat well after each addition. Stir in the vanilla.

4. Using a large wooden spoon, stir in the flour mixture just until combined. Then stir in the cooled pecans, oats, chocolate chips, and toffee bits, blending only until thoroughly mixed.

5. Cover the bowl with plastic wrap and put it in the refrigerator until thoroughly chilled, 3 hours or overnight. When you are ready to make the cookies, take the bowl out of the refrigerator and allow the dough to warm slightly while the oven is preheating.

6. Preheat the oven to 375°F. Line 2 baking sheets with silicone baking mats.

7. Measure out the dough by tablespoons and place the cookies 2 inches apart on the baking sheets. Place no more than a dozen cookies on each sheet. Bake, one sheet at a time, for 9 to 11 minutes, or until the edges of the cookies are very browned and the centers are no longer soft.

8. Let the cookies set up for 2 minutes on the baking sheet. Then transfer the cookies to racks to cool completely. Store in airtight containers or in zippered freezer bags. These cookies freeze well.

Makes 4 dozen cookies

Dungeon Bars

—CATERING TO NOBODY—

This was the first recipe I ever developed. I took it to my writers' critique group, and they said I had to put the recipe into whatever book I ended up writing.

- 1 cup all-purpose flour (high altitude: add 2 tablespoons)
- ½ teaspoon salt
- ¼ teaspoon baking soda
- 2 sticks (½ pound) unsalted butter
- ½ cup packed dark brown sugar
- ½ cup granulated sugar
- 2 large eggs
- 2 teaspoons vanilla extract
- 1 cup old-fashioned rolled oats
- 1 cup raisins
- Vanilla or cinnamon ice cream, for serving

1. Preheat the oven to 350°F. Butter a 9 x 13-inch baking pan.

2. Sift together the flour, salt, and baking soda.

3. In a large bowl, with an electric mixer, cream the butter with the sugars until the mixture is light and fluffy. Turn the mixer to low and beat in the eggs and vanilla until well combined. Carefully stir in the flour mixture, oats, and raisins until well combined.

4. Spread in the baking pan. (The batter will be thick.) Smooth the top. Bake for 20 to 30 minutes, or until the batter has puffed and flattened, is browned around the edges, no longer appears wet in the center, and a toothpick inserted in the center comes out clean. Cool slightly, but while still warm, cut into 32 bars. Allow to cool completely in the pan on a rack.

5. Serve with best-quality vanilla or cinnamon ice cream.

Makes 32 bars

Lethal Layers

—DYING FOR CHOCOLATE—

These easy-to-make chocolate-chip bars feature a crust. I was playing around with cookies with crusts, and came up with this recipe, which proved to be not only easy, but an instant hit with the kids.

Crust:

8 tablespoons (1 stick) unsalted butter

½ cup packed dark brown sugar

1 cup all-purpose flour

Filling:

1 cup pecan halves

2 large eggs

1 cup packed dark brown sugar

1 teaspoon vanilla extract

½ teaspoon salt

1 teaspoon baking powder

About ¼ cup all-purpose flour

1 cup semisweet chocolate chips

For the crust:

1. Preheat the oven to 375°F. Butter a 9 x 13-inch baking pan.

2. In the bowl of a food processor fitted with the metal blade, combine the crust ingredients and process until crumbly. This can also be done with 2 knives or a pastry cutter. Pat the mixture into the baking pan. Bake for 10 minutes. Let cool.

For the filling:

1. When the crust is cool, preheat the oven to 375°F. Spread the pecans evenly over the surface of the crust. In a bowl, beat the eggs with the brown sugar until thick. Add the vanilla. Put the salt and baking powder in the bottom of a ¼-cup measure; fill the rest of the measure with flour. Stir the flour mixture into the egg mixture. Pour this mixture over the crust. Sprinkle the chocolate chips evenly over the top.

2. Bake for 20 minutes, or until checking with a toothpick reveals the center is cooked through. Cool in the pan, then cut into 32 pieces.

Makes 32 bars

Bleak House Bars

—SWEET REVENGE—

Raspberry and chocolate: That's a marriage made in heaven. Add some cream cheese, and you're way up there in the celestial realms. This recipe drew inspiration from a dessert made by a wonderful man who won a "dessert recipe" contest for which I, unfortunately, was the sole judge. I wish I could remember his name, so I could give him credit for the original idea. Sorry. But I was in such a sugar stupor by the time the contest was over that all I can remember is that the marvelous bookstore where the competition took place was Mysterious Galaxy in San Diego.

¾ cup pecan halves

2 sticks (½ pound) unsalted butter, at room temperature

½ cup packed dark brown sugar

2 cups all-purpose flour

¾ teaspoon salt

Contents of one 14-ounce can sweetened condensed milk (1⅓ cups)

3 cups (18 ounces) semisweet chocolate chips

8 ounces cream cheese, at room temperature

⅓ cup granulated sugar

1 large egg

½ teaspoon vanilla extract

½ cup seedless raspberry jam

1. In a large skillet, toast the nuts, stirring, until they are slightly browned and give off a nutty scent, about 10 minutes. Remove them from the pan to cool, then coarsely chop.

2. Preheat the oven to 350°F. Butter a 9 x 13-inch baking pan.

3. In a large bowl, with an electric mixer, beat the butter until it is very soft and creamy. Keeping the mixer on medium speed, beat in the brown sugar. Remove the beaters from the bowl and scrape it. Stir in the flour, ½ teaspoon of the salt, and the nuts until very well combined.

4. Measure out 2¼ cups of the butter-nut mixture and press into the bottom of the baking pan. (Set the rest of the butter-nut mixture aside.) Bake for about 10 minutes, or until the edges are golden brown.

5. Meanwhile, in a heavy-bottomed saucepan, combine the condensed milk and 2 cups of the chocolate chips. Cook, stirring, over low heat until the chocolate is melted.

6. Remove the crust from the oven and immediately pour the chocolate mixture over the hot crust. Set on a rack to cool slightly. Leave the oven on.

7. In a large bowl, with an electric mixer, beat the cream cheese until it is very smooth. Add the granulated sugar and beat once more until smooth. Finally, add the egg, vanilla, and remaining ¼ teaspoon salt and beat until very smooth.

8. In a small bowl, stir the jam until it is smooth.

9. Now you are ready to make the rest of the layers. Sprinkle the remaining butter-nut mixture over the chocolate. Using a soup spoon, ladle the jam evenly over the butter-nut mixture. Using another soup spoon, ladle the cream-cheese mixture over the jam layer. Finally, sprinkle the remaining 1 cup chocolate chips over the cream cheese.

10. Bake for 30 to 35 minutes, or until the cream-cheese layer is set and no longer liquid in the middle. Cool on a rack before cutting into bars.

Makes 32 bars

Got-a-Hot-Date Bars

—SWEET REVENGE—

In my unending desire to use toffee bits and chocolate chips in dessert, I came up with this recipe, which I took with me when I went to visit bookstores for Sweet Revenge.

1 cup pecan halves

½ cup chopped dates

½ cup raisins

2 tablespoons buttermilk

2 cups all-purpose flour

¾ teaspoon baking powder (high altitude: ½ teaspoon)

½ teaspoon baking soda

½ teaspoon salt

2 sticks (½ pound) unsalted butter, at room temperature

2 cups packed dark brown sugar

2 large eggs

1 teaspoon vanilla extract

1 cup semisweet chocolate chips

1 cup toffee chips (aka almond brickle chips)

1. In a large skillet, toast the pecans over medium-low heat, stirring constantly, until they begin to turn a darker brown and give off a nutty scent, about 10 minutes. Immediately remove the pan from the heat and turn the pecans out onto paper towels. When they are just cool enough to touch, roughly chop them. Set aside.

2. In a small saucepan, combine the dates, raisins, and buttermilk. Bring to a boil over medium heat, then immediately remove the pan from the heat and scrape the date mixture into a shallow bowl to cool. Set aside.

3. Position an oven rack in the middle of the oven and preheat to 325°F. Butter a 9 x 13-inch baking pan.

4. Sift together the flour, baking powder, baking soda, and salt. In a large bowl, with an electric mixer, beat the butter until it is very creamy. Add the brown sugar and beat well, until the mixture is light and fluffy, about 3 minutes. Add the eggs one at a time, beating well after each addition.

Mix in the vanilla. Using a wooden spoon, stir in the flour mixture, date mixture, nuts, chocolate chips, and toffee chips, stirring only until combined. Turn the mixture into the prepared pan and smooth the top.

5. Bake for 35 to 40 minutes, or until a toothpick inserted into the center comes out clean. Cool on a rack before cutting into 24 bars.

Makes 24 bars

Scout's Brownies

—DYING FOR CHOCOLATE—

I worked on Dying for Chocolate *for most of 1991. (When it was published in 1992, a bookstore owner laughingly announced that with the title* Dying for Chocolate, *I could put the Yellow Pages in the middle, and people would read it.) Anyway, during that year, a fellow who'd read* Catering to Nobody *wrote and said Goldy definitely needed a cat.*

As often happens with these things, not long afterward, a terrified stray cat took up residence inside a cardboard construction drum in our yard. It took us exactly one night to figure out where the horrible yowling was coming from.

Jim (a dog person) looked me square in the eye after I'd coaxed the cat out with a dish of milk. He said, "We are not keeping that cat."

So after he left for work, I brought the literally skin-and-bones feline inside and snuggled him inside a blanket. I called our local veterinarians and checked with the paper to see if anyone had reported a cat that was missing or had run away. Nobody had.

I called Jim at work and told him we at least *had to take the poor, starving cat to the veterinarian. There was a long silence, because he really loves all animals, no matter what he claims about the superiority of dogs.*

The veterinarian said "my cat" (you see how these things work?) was so thin, she couldn't even give him shots. So Jim, the kids, and I fattened him up for a while, then took him back to the vet and got the shots. And then we had a cat. (I named him Cappuccino. He has since died, but not until he'd lived a long life, much of it spent twining through my legs while I worked in the kitchen.)

After that, Jim said, "No more cats." And we have remained steadfast dog people, but Goldy has Scout, and she named the brownies after him.

- 2 sticks (½ pound) unsalted butter
- 3½ ounces best-quality bittersweet or unsweetened chocolate, such as Godiva, Lindt, Callebaut, or Valrhona, cut into 1-inch pieces
- 3 tablespoons Dutch-process unsweetened cocoa powder
- 1½ cups all-purpose flour (high altitude: add 2 tablespoons)
- ½ teaspoon baking powder
- 1 teaspoon salt
- 4 large eggs
- 2 cups sugar
- 1 teaspoon vanilla extract
- 1 cup semisweet chocolate chips

1. Preheat the oven to 350°F. Butter a 9 x 13-inch baking pan.

2. In the top of a double boiler, over simmering water, melt the butter with the bittersweet or unsweetened chocolate, stirring occasionally. Set aside to cool.

3. Sift together the cocoa, flour, baking powder, and salt.

4. In a large bowl, with an electric mixer, beat the eggs until creamy. Gradually beat in the sugar, beating constantly. Stir in the vanilla and the cooled chocolate-butter mixture. Stir in the flour mixture just until combined.

5. Spread the batter in the prepared pan. Sprinkle the chips over the surface.

6. Bake for 20 to 25 minutes, watching carefully. Check the center with a wooden toothpick for doneness, and if the center has not cooked, bake for an additional 5 minutes. If the toothpick emerges with only a crumb or two adhering to the surface, the brownies are done.

7. Cool in the pan on a rack, then cut into 32 pieces.

Makes 32 brownies

Spicy Brownies

—THE WHOLE ENCHILADA—

Despite the fact that adding chili powder to any type of chocolate is in vogue now, my tasters pronounced every experiment weird. But ginger proved a winner. You add it to these brownies in both crystallized and ground form. Serve with best-quality vanilla ice cream, and enjoy!

2 sticks (½ pound) unsalted butter

4 ounces (see Note) best-quality extra-bittersweet (85% cacao) chocolate, such as Lindt

1 tablespoon minced crystallized ginger or "ginger chips"

3 tablespoons Dutch-process unsweetened cocoa powder

1¼ cups cake flour, measured by gently spooning into measuring cups and leveling (high altitude: add 2 tablespoons)

1 teaspoon ground ginger

½ teaspoon baking powder

1 teaspoon kosher salt

4 large eggs

2 cups granulated sugar

1 teaspoon vanilla extract

½ teaspoon chocolate extract

1. Preheat the oven to 325°F for dark or nonstick pans, 350°F for glass pans. Butter a 9 x 13-inch baking dish or pan.

2. In the top of a double boiler, over simmering water, melt the butter and chocolate, stirring occasionally. When the mixture is melted, stir in the crystallized ginger or ginger chips and set aside to cool slightly.

3. Sift together the cocoa, flour, ground ginger, baking powder, and salt.

4. In a bowl, beat the eggs until thoroughly combined. Beat in the sugar until thoroughly combined. Add the cooled chocolate mixture and the extracts and stir until thoroughly combined. Gently stir in the cocoa-flour mixture, stirring only until thoroughly combined, 30 to 40 strokes.

5. Spread the batter in the baking pan. Bake for 25 to 35 minutes, or until a toothpick inserted 1 inch from the edge of the pan comes out clean. (Check after 25 minutes; brownies may take longer at high altitude.)

6. Cool completely in the pan on a rack. To serve, place the pan in the freezer for 10 to 15 minutes. Using a sharp knife, gently slice the brownies and lever out of the pan with a spatula.

Makes 16 large brownies

Variations: To make even spicier brownies, add 1 tablespoon minced fresh ginger to the chocolate mixture. To make Chile-Flavored Brownies, omit all the ginger ingredients and add 1 to 1½ teaspoons ground chipotle chile powder to the dry ingredients.

Note: Check that you are using the full 4 ounces, which may involve using a digital scale to weigh it.

Goldy's Terrific Toffee

—CATERING TO NOBODY—

Making candy can be a challenge, because it overcooks in a flash. It can cause particular headaches at 8,000 feet above sea level, because water boils at 202°F, instead of the 212°F of sea level. So keep stirring, and pay close attention that you don't undercook or overcook the toffee.

- 2 cups coarsely chopped pecans
- 2 pounds best-quality milk chocolate, such as Lindt
- 2 pounds (8 sticks) unsalted butter, plus more for the pans
- 4 cups packed dark brown sugar

1. Preheat the oven to 375°F.

2. Spread the pecans in a 9 x 13-inch pan and roast about 10 minutes, or until the nuts have turned slightly darker and are well toasted. Stir once or twice during the roasting process to ensure even browning. Remove the pecans from the oven, spread out to cool on paper towels, and set aside until you finish the toffee.

3. Butter two 9 x 13-inch glass baking dishes and set aside.

4. Unwrap the chocolate and divide it between two plates. Break all the chocolate into squares and set aside.

5. Using a deep, heavy-bottomed pan, melt the butter with the brown sugar and cook over medium to medium-high heat, *stirring constantly,* until a candy thermometer hits 285°F to 290°F (high altitude: 300°F), the soft-crack stage (see Note). The candy will be *very* hot, so be sure to protect all your skin and clothing

through the cooking and pouring processes. Pour the toffee into the prepared pans and immediately place the squares of chocolate in rows across the toffee (1 plateful of chocolate per pan). When the chocolate has softened, spread it to the edges of the toffee. Sprinkle 1 cup of the toasted pecans over the chocolate in each pan. Allow to cool, then cover with foil and chill.

6. Using a large, heavy-duty knife, break the toffee into 1- to 3-inch pieces.

Makes about 6 dozen pieces

Note: A candy thermometer is essential for this recipe. At high altitude, the traditional soft-crack stage is not reached until the thermometer reaches 300°F, at which point the toffee is in danger of burning. Therefore, at high altitude, if you are close to 300°F, detect a burning smell, and stir up a darker substance from the bottom of the pan, stop stirring immediately, remove the toffee from the heat, and quickly pour it into the prepared pans *without scraping the bottom of the cooking pan.* If you have managed not to stir in any of the burnt candy, the toffee will still be delicious. It will be chewier than that made at sea level, but proper refrigeration will maintain a good candy texture.

Labor Day Flourless Chocolate Cake with Berries, Melba Sauce, and White Chocolate Cream

—PRIME CUT—

I received my first recipe for a flourless chocolate cake many years ago from a lovely lady who worked at a delightful store in Charlottesville called The Very Thing! My mother had told her I adored cooking, so she'd written out the recipe, which she gave to me on my next visit. I thanked her and promised to make the cake when I returned to Colorado. Once home, I pulled out the recipe, read it, and thought, She left out the flour and leavening. *So I didn't try it.*

Years later, my sister Lucy made me a flourless chocolate cake, and I begged her for the recipe. (The following recipe is a version of that cake, which I played around with for a while.) Still, when I read Lucy's recipe, I realized it was almost exactly the same recipe I'd received years before from the nice saleslady at The Very Thing!

I put this recipe here because it, too, is a great one if you ever have to cook for TV. Remember, the people watching that TV show—in this case, a fund-raiser for our Denver PBS station—are not interested in you, *they're interested in your* food. *And once again, the people both behind and in front of the camera are hungry.*

So I "made" this cake in a five-minute segment. When you "make" a cake for TV, you actually have to show up at the station with your ingredients, your script (which, if it's public television, you write yourself), and a finished cake. I was interviewed by a very agreeable woman while I was mixing the cake batter, and managed not to lose my temper when she asked if viewers could use margarine instead of butter. (No, I replied, then and now: You should never use margarine, for any purpose.) After I mixed the ingredients and put them on the shelf below the counter (the "magic oven" of television), I pulled out my finished cake, so the camera could focus on it.

When the PBS lady moved on to the next person who was making a recipe for the fund-raiser, I took the finished cake, a knife, and a couple of forks and plates over to the two people who were telling home viewers—between recipes—how they were doing with the appeal. And if you think people who work for network *television are hungry, you have no idea how ravenous public television volunteers are. So when the camera cut back to the pair of ladies informing the viewing public how Channel 6 was doing . . . well! There they were, devouring Labor Day Flourless Chocolate Cake, and telling viewers that if they ordered the channel's cookbook—in which the cake recipe could be found—then they, too, could be made extremely happy.*

Who says Goldy doesn't put the fun *in fund-raising?*

14 tablespoons (1¾ sticks) unsalted butter

7 ounces best-quality bittersweet or semisweet chocolate, such as Lindt or Godiva, cut up

1 tablespoon brewed espresso or strong coffee

5 large eggs, separated

2 tablespoons Dutch-process unsweetened cocoa powder

7 tablespoons sugar

1 tablespoon vanilla extract

One 6-ounce package fresh blueberries

One 6-ounce package fresh raspberries

Melba Sauce (recipe follows)

White Chocolate Cream (recipe follows)

1. Position an oven rack in the middle to lower (not the lowest) part of the oven and preheat to 350°F. Butter the bottom and sides of a 10-inch springform pan. Make sure you have the bottom of another 10-inch springform pan on hand.

2. In the top of a double boiler, over simmering water, melt the butter, chocolate, and coffee together. Transfer to a bowl and allow to cool slightly, then stir in the egg yolks and whisk until smooth. Sift the cocoa and sugar together, then sift this mixture directly into the chocolate mixture and stir until smooth. Stir in the vanilla and set aside.

3. In a bowl, with an electric mixer, beat the egg whites to soft peaks. Fold half the egg whites into the chocolate mixture to lighten it, then pour the chocolate mixture on top of the remaining egg whites and fold in. Pour the batter into the prepared pan and bake for 25 minutes, or until the cake is puffed and the center no longer appears moist.

4. Remove the cake from the oven and immediately press another springform pan bottom onto the cake to deflate it. Take off the pan bottom you have used to deflate the cake, and allow the cake to cool in the pan on a rack.

5. When the cake is cool, remove the springform sides and place the cake on a pretty cake platter. Decorate the top with concentric rings of blueberries and raspberries. When serving, ladle large dollops of Melba Sauce and White Chocolate Cream on top of each slice.

Makes 8 to 12 servings

Melba Sauce

Two 6-ounce packages fresh raspberries

½ cup currant jelly

2 teaspoons cornstarch

7 tablespoons sugar

1. Sieve the raspberries. You should have 1 cup. Discard the seeds.

2. In the top of a double boiler, combine the jelly and sieved raspberries. Place the double boiler top directly on a burner over medium heat and heat until bubbling, 4 or 5 minutes.

3. Meanwhile, bring water in the double boiler bottom to a boil.

4. Place the double boiler top over the boiling water. In a small bowl, stir together the cornstarch and sugar. Stir the cornstarch mixture into the jelly mixture and cook and stir until thickened and clear. Remove from the heat, cool, and chill at least 1 hour before serving.

White Chocolate Cream

6 ounces best-quality white chocolate, such as Lindt or Godiva, coarsely chopped

1¾ cups heavy (whipping) cream, divided

1. In a medium saucepan over low heat, melt the chocolate with ¾ cup of the cream, stirring constantly. When the mixture is melted and smooth, remove from the heat. Pour into a bowl and, stirring occasionally, allow the mixture to come to room temperature.

2. In a bowl, whip the remaining 1 cup cream with an electric mixer until soft peaks form. Whisking constantly to ensure smoothness, whisk into the chocolate mixture. Chill before serving.

Happy Endings Plum Cake

—THE CEREAL MURDERS—

If you want to make this cake portable—for a potluck, say—just cool the cake in the pan, cover with plastic wrap, and take the cake plus a small bag of powdered sugar to the event in question. Then remove the plastic when you get to the party and sift some powdered sugar on top.

This recipe is dedicated to all those writers of literary fiction who think their books must have downbeat conclusions to be taken seriously. Eat cake, and be happy.

2 sticks (½ pound) unsalted butter, at room temperature

¾ cup sugar

¾ cup packed dark brown sugar

2 large eggs

1 teaspoon vanilla extract

2½ cups all-purpose flour (high altitude: add 2 tablespoons)

2 teaspoons baking powder (high altitude: 1½ teaspoons)

1 teaspoon baking soda

½ teaspoon salt

2 teaspoons ground cinnamon

One 16-ounce can syrup-packed purple plums, well drained, syrup reserved and the plums chopped

Powdered sugar

1. Preheat the oven to 375°F. Butter a 9 x 13-inch baking pan.

2. In a large bowl, with an electric mixer, beat the butter until creamy and light, then gradually add the sugars, beating until creamy and smooth. Beat in the eggs, then the vanilla.

3. Sift the flour, baking powder, baking soda, salt, and cinnamon together. Alternating with the reserved plum syrup, stir the flour mixture into the butter mixture, beginning and ending with the flour mixture. Stir in the plums. Pour the batter into the baking pan.

4. Bake for 25 to 30 minutes, or until a toothpick inserted in the center of the cake comes out clean. Allow the cake to cool completely on a rack, then dust with powdered sugar.

Makes 12 to 16 servings

Chocolate Truffle Cheesecake

—THE LAST SUPPERS—

For one entire soccer season, I volunteered to be the postgame Snack Lady for our youngest son's team. I wanted to get nine-year-olds' takes on the different cheesecakes I was trying out. This was their favorite, and I mentioned them in the acknowledgments section of The Last Suppers. *Chocolate will make anyone thirsty, especially after soccer practice, so be sure to supply lots of water.*

Crust:

9 ounces chocolate wafer cookies, broken up

6 tablespoons unsalted butter, melted

Filling:

½ pound unsweetened chocolate

1½ pounds cream cheese, at room temperature

3 large eggs

1 cup sugar

¼ cup amaretto liqueur

1½ teaspoons vanilla extract

½ cup heavy (whipping) cream

For the crust:

1. In a food processor, whirl the chocolate cookies until they form crumbs. Mix with the melted butter. Press into the bottom and sides of a buttered 10-inch springform pan and refrigerate until you are ready to fill and bake.

2. Preheat the oven to 350°F.

For the filling:

1. In the top of a double boiler, over simmering water, melt the chocolate. Set aside to cool.

2. In a large bowl, with an electric mixer, beat the cream cheese until smooth. Add the eggs and sugar and beat until well incorporated. Stir a small amount of this mixture into the chocolate to loosen it. Add the chocolate mixture to the cream cheese mixture and stir well. Stir in the amaretto, vanilla, and cream. Stir until all ingredients are mixed well.

3. Pour the filling into the prepared crust and bake for 50 to 55 minutes, or until the cheesecake is puffed slightly and no linger jiggles in the center.

4. Cool on a rack to room temperature, then refrigerate until chilled, preferably overnight.

5. Take the cheesecake out of the refrigerator 30 minutes before serving for ease in slicing. Remove the sides of the pan and cut pieces with a sharp knife. If the cheesecake is hard to slice, hold a long, unflavored piece of dental floss in 2 hands and carefully saw through the cake to cut even pieces.

Makes 16 servings

Fudge Soufflé

—KILLER PANCAKE—

When I was trying to make low-fat desserts, this one emerged as a winner. Now I use whole milk instead of skim, and serve with real whipped cream flavored with vanilla or sweetened with a bit of powdered sugar.

½ cup Dutch-process unsweetened cocoa powder

½ cup powdered sugar

1 cup skim or whole milk

⅓ cup semisweet chocolate chips

5 egg whites, from large eggs

¼ cup granulated sugar

½ teaspoon vanilla extract

Store-bought whipped topping or whipped cream (optional)

1. In the top of a double boiler, over simmering water, whisk together the cocoa powder, powdered sugar, and milk and cook until smooth. Add the chocolate chips and stir until the chips are melted. Stir and reduce the heat to a simmer.

2. In a large bowl, with an electric mixer, beat the egg whites until soft peaks form. Gradually beat in the granulated sugar, beating until stiff peaks form. Fold the vanilla and ½ cup of the chocolate mixture into the egg white mixture.

3. Bring the water in the bottom of the double boiler back to a boil. Stir the chocolate–egg white mixture into the mixture in the top of the double boiler. Using a handheld mixer or a whisk, beat this mixture for a minute, or until it is well combined. Cover the double boiler and continue to cook over simmering water (watch that the bottom pot does not run out of water) for 25 to 30 minutes, or until the soufflé is puffed and set. Serve immediately with whipped topping or whipped cream, if desired.

Makes 4 servings

Big Bucks Bread Puddings with Hard Sauce

—PRIME CUT—

To understand why I made these individual, see the explanation in Babsie's Tarts (page 242). There used to be a fabulous bakery on Connecticut Avenue in Chevy Chase, Maryland, called Schuppes. They made an outstanding bread pudding in loaves that they would slice thickly and serve on small paper doilies. I carried the memory of that bread pudding for many years. So when our youngest son's fifth-grade class was studying the Caribbean, he decided his project would be "Food of the Caribbean." (You see where this is going.)

He and I did work on various indigenous dishes together, and the only one he liked was the bread pudding. His class at Bethlehem Lutheran School in Denver then put on a Caribbean Festival. I schlepped our son all over Denver looking for a costume to rent for the festival, a search that seemed to take longer than developing the bread pudding recipe. But we finally found one he liked. The morning of the festival, he put on a straw hat and his costume, and balanced the tray of puddings in his lap all the way to school. The puddings were a hit, so I put the recipe into Prime Cut.

5 tablespoons unsalted butter, at room temperature

½ cup Demerara sugar (sometimes sold as "raw sugar") or granulated sugar

2 large eggs

1 cup milk, preferably whole

½ cup heavy (whipping) cream

¼ teaspoon freshly grated nutmeg

1 teaspoon vanilla extract

8 slices white bread, torn up (9 to 10 ounces)

⅓ cup raisins

Hard Sauce (recipe follows)

12 fresh mint sprigs (optional)

1. Preheat the oven to 325°F. Butter 12 cups of a nonstick muffin tin.

2. In a bowl, with an electric mixer, cream the butter until fluffy. Add the sugar and beat until well combined. Beat in the eggs, then beat in the milk and cream. Stir in the nutmeg and vanilla. Thoroughly stir in the bread pieces. The mixture will look like mush. Stir in the raisins.

3. Using a ⅓-cup measure, ladle out a full scoop of batter into each muffin cup. Bake for 15 minutes. Remove from the oven and, using a nonstick-coated spoon (so as not to scratch the coating of the muffin tin), quickly stir each cup of half-risen batter to break up the crust on the sides. Return to the oven for an additional 15 to 20 minutes, or until the puddings are set and browned.

4. Quickly unmold the puddings onto a rack and set upright like cupcakes to cool slightly. The puddings can be served hot, warm, or at room temperature.

5. Make the hard sauce. Chill the mixture until it is easily scooped out. Using a small ice-cream scoop, measure out even scoops of the chilled sauce onto a plate covered with wax paper. Cover with plastic wrap and refrigerate the scoops until ready to serve the bread puddings.

6. Top each pudding with a scoop of Hard Sauce. Using a toothpick, insert the stem of a mint sprig into the top of each scoop of Hard Sauce. (This makes them pretty.)

Makes 12 servings

* * *

Hard Sauce

5 tablespoons unsalted butter, at room temperature

¼ cup heavy (whipping) cream, or more as needed

2 cups powdered sugar, sifted

¼ teaspoon rum extract

In a bowl, beat together the butter and heavy cream until thoroughly combined. Add the powdered sugar slowly and beat until thoroughly blended. Stir in the rum extract. If the mixture is too stiff, add a little more cream. If making to serve with bread puddings, chill the mixture until it is easily scooped out (see bread pudding recipe). The hard sauce can also be thinned with cream and used to frost cookies or cake.

Damson-in-Distress Plum Tart

—STICKS AND SCONES—

Jim loves the small Italian plums that usually become available in September, so I end up making this tart for the family every fall. The cream topping over the rows of plums makes this dessert look as luscious as it tastes. Because this is a custard, you will need to refrigerate any unused portion. When you do serve it, though, be sure to offer best-quality vanilla or cinnamon ice cream to go with it.

Crust:

14 tablespoons (1¾ sticks) unsalted butter, cut into chunks

2¼ cups all-purpose flour

3 tablespoons plus 1½ teaspoons regular or light sour cream

¾ teaspoon salt

Filling:

9 damson or other fresh plums (20 or more if the plums are small, like Italian variety), pitted and cut into quarters

2 large eggs

1½ cups sugar

½ cup regular or light sour cream

3 tablespoons all-purpose flour

Preheat the oven to 325°F. Butter the bottom and sides of a 9 x 13-inch glass baking dish.

For the crust:

In a food processor combine the butter, flour, sour cream, and salt. Process until the dough pulls into a ball. Gently pat the dough into an even layer on the bottom of the baking dish.

For the filling:

1. Cover the prepared crust with rows of plum quarters to completely cover the crust in a single layer. In a bowl, beat together the eggs, sugar, sour cream, and flour until well blended. Pour this beaten mixture carefully over the rows of plums.

2. Bake the tart for 45 to 60 minutes, or until the top is golden brown and the custard is set in the middle. (Use a spoon to check the middle of the tart. The custard should be set, not soupy.)

3. Allow the tart to cool completely on a rack. Cut into rectangles to serve.

Makes 16 servings

Shoppers' Chocolate Truffles

—CHOPPING SPREE—

I'll never forget when my friend Karen Johnson Kennedy suggested, on about my tenth working trip to the caterer's kitchen, "Let's go graze in the truffle case." Ha! My fate to make truffles was sealed. The challenging aspect of making truffles is to allow time to let the chocolate cool properly, first before you beat in the butter, then before you scoop it to go into the refrigerator, where it chills overnight before being coated. Be sure to use the best-quality bittersweet chocolate you can afford. (I once accidentally used unsweetened chocolate while making a double batch of this recipe, and had to throw it all away.)

Ganache:

½ cup heavy (whipping) cream

1 tablespoon Grand Marnier liqueur

¼ teaspoon vanilla extract

11 ounces best-quality bittersweet chocolate, such as Valrhona, very finely chopped

2 tablespoons unsalted butter, at room temperature

Dutch-process unsweetened cocoa powder, for dusting

For the ganache:

1. Pour the cream into a heavy 1-quart or larger saucepan. Add the liqueur and vanilla and heat over medium to medium-high heat until the mixture reaches 190°F. Remove the mixture from the heat, add the chopped chocolate, stir vigorously until the chocolate melts and the mixture is shiny. If all the chocolate does not melt, you can *briefly* return the pan to the burner over low heat, stirring constantly, *just* until the chocolate melts, at which point the pan needs to be immediately removed from the heat. Scrape the ganache into a bowl and allow it to cool at room temperature. (Do not attempt to hasten the cooling in any way.) When the ganache reaches 90°F, beat in the butter. Allow the ganache to cool until it is firm.

Note: You will need a digital thermometer to make this recipe properly.

Coating:

6 ounces best-quality bittersweet chocolate, such as Godiva Dark

1 to 2 tablespoons clarified butter or solid vegetable shortening

2. Using a 1-tablespoon scoop, measure out the firm ganache into balls and place them on a baking sheet lined with a silicone baking mat. Cover loosely with plastic wrap. Chill overnight in the refrigerator.

3. Remove the chocolate from the refrigerator and dust your hands with cocoa powder. Roll each mound into a smooth ball, then place it back on the baking sheet. When all the ganache mounds have been rolled, return the baking sheet to the refrigerator.

For the coating:
In the top of a double boiler, over simmering water, melt the chocolate with 1 tablespoon of the clarified butter or shortening. Whisk it well until thoroughly combined and melted. Line a baking sheet with foil. Working one at a time, drop a chilled ball of ganache into the coating chocolate, roll it around gently with a fork until it is completely covered, then lift it out of the pan. Scrape off the excess chocolate on the side of the pan, and place the truffle on the foil. Work in this way until all the truffles are coated. If the coating chocolate begins to seize and become recalcitrant, add a bit more clarified butter or shortening to it and stir and melt as before. Work until all the truffles are coated. Allow the coating to set up and cool on the truffles. (This usually takes over an hour.) Serve.

Makes 12 to 15 truffles

Super Spenders' Strawberry-Rhubarb Cobbler

—CHOPPING SPREE—

This is my favorite cobbler. It is also our family's favorite cobbler . . . if I substitute sliced peaches for the rhubarb. Once, while taste-testing the cobbler on a group of children, they all said they loved it, but then left neat, pyramid-shaped piles of chopped rhubarb on their plates. Lesson learned.

The most important aspect of making this dish is to check that the very center of the topping has cooked through and is cakelike. This will save you the embarrassment of taking the dish out when it only looks *ready. Then when you plunge a serving spoon into the center of the dish, yellow batter gushes out. To avoid this fate, scoop some of the center when the timer goes off. Bake until it is like* cake.

Fruit:

½ to ⅔ cup sugar, depending on the sweetness of the strawberries

2 tablespoons cornstarch

1½ pounds strawberries, halved

½ pound rhubarb, cut into 1-inch pieces

1 teaspoon vanilla extract

Preheat the oven to 375°F. Butter a 9 x 13-inch baking pan or 2-quart gratin dish.

For the fruit:

In a small bowl, mix the sugar with the cornstarch. Place the fruit in a large bowl and pour the sugar mixture and vanilla over it. Mix together gently and pour into the prepared pan.

Topping:

¾ cup all-purpose flour

⅜ teaspoon baking powder (high altitude: ¼ teaspoon)

⅛ teaspoon salt

11 tablespoons (1 stick plus 3 tablespoons) unsalted butter, at room temperature

¾ cup sugar

1 large egg

½ teaspoon vanilla extract

Vanilla ice cream or heavy (whipping) cream, for serving

For the topping:

1. Sift together the flour, baking powder, and salt and set aside.

2. In a large bowl, with an electric mixer, beat the butter until creamy and light. Add the sugar gradually, beating until light and smooth. Beat in the egg until thoroughly combined, then mix in the vanilla. With a large wooden spoon, stir in the flour mixture just until all the ingredients are well combined.

3. Using an ice-cream scoop or other large spoon, drop the dough in large, even spoonfuls onto the fruit in the pan. Bake for 35 to 45 minutes, or until the topping is golden brown and the fruit is bubbling. Test for doneness by spooning up a small section of the middle of the topping. If it is like cake, it is done. If the topping is still liquid yellow, bake until it is like cake. Serve warm with best-quality vanilla ice cream or heavy cream, either poured or whipped.

Makes 6 large or 8 small servings

In-Your-Face Strawberry Pie (I)

—DOUBLE SHOT—

I knew there would come a time when Goldy shoved a pie in somebody's face—not at a catered function, mind you, much as she might be tempted—but on her own porch. I liked the idea so much I developed two recipes for Strawberry Pie. This one contains a cream filling.

Crust:

1 cup chopped skinned hazelnuts (aka filberts)

2 sticks (½ pound) unsalted butter, melted

2 cups all-purpose flour

Topping (see Note):

6 pounds fresh strawberries, trimmed, hulled, and divided

2 cups sugar

2 tablespoons cornstarch

1 cup spring water

Filling:

8 ounces cream cheese, at room temperature

1 cup powdered sugar, sifted twice before measuring

2 teaspoons vanilla extract

2½ cups chilled heavy (whipping) cream

For the crust:

1. In a large dry skillet, toast the nuts over medium-low heat, stirring until they give off a nutty scent and have turned a very light brown. Turn out onto paper towels and allow to cool completely.

2. Preheat the oven to 350°F. Butter a 9 x 13-inch or 10 x 14-inch glass baking dish.

3. In a bowl, mix the nuts, melted butter, and flour until thoroughly combined, then press this mixture evenly onto the bottom of the pan.

4. Bake the crust for 20 to 30 minutes, or until it is set and has turned a very light brown. Set aside on a rack to cool completely before filling.

For the topping:

Set aside 2 pounds of the strawberries. Mash the remaining strawberries with a potato masher until they are crushed. Measure them; you should have about 2 cups. (Add or subtract strawberries to make 2 cups. Although you may not use all the topping, this is to keep the proportions correct.) Transfer to a large saucepan. Mix the sugar with the cornstarch and add it to the pan along with the water. Heat over medium heat, stirring until the sugar has dissolved. Stirring constantly with a wooden spoon or heatproof silicone spatula, increase the heat to medium-high (low altitude) or high (high altitude) and bring to a boil. (The mixture will be *very* hot, so be careful of splatters.) Stirring constantly, boil the mixture for about 1 minute, or until it is very thick and begins to clear. (It will not clear completely.) Remove from the heat and pour into a heatproof bowl. Allow to cool completely.

For the filling:

1. In a large bowl, beat the cream cheese with the powdered sugar and vanilla until smooth. In a separate bowl, with an electric mixer, whip the cream until it holds soft peaks. (Do not overbeat.) Fold the whipped cream thoroughly into the cream cheese mixture.

2. To assemble the pie, spread the cream filling over the cooled crust. Place the 3 pounds of reserved strawberries in even rows over the top. Set aside any remaining strawberries for another use. Carefully spoon the cooled strawberry topping over the strawberries until the pie is completely covered.

3. Chill the pie thoroughly, at least 4 hours and preferably overnight, before serving. If you are chilling the pie overnight, cover it with plastic wrap, which you remove just before cutting.

Makes 24 servings

Note: For the topping that goes between the fresh strawberries on top of the pie, it is best to start with about 3 pounds of strawberries before trimming and hulling. You will end up with about 2½ pounds of strawberries. Also, you should prepare the topping before starting on the filling, because it needs to cool completely before being spread on the filling. Finally, this recipe may make more strawberry topping than you need for the pie. Leftover topping must be refrigerated and used within 2 to 3 days. It is delicious on vanilla ice cream or on toasted, buttered English muffins.

In-Your-Face Strawberry Pie (II)

—DOUBLE SHOT—

This recipe contains no cream filling, just strawberries! Serve with best-quality vanilla ice cream.

Crust:

2½ cups all-purpose flour

1 tablespoon powdered sugar

1 teaspoon salt

2 sticks (½ pound) cold unsalted butter, cut into 1-tablespoon pieces and chilled

¼ cup lard, cut into 1-tablespoon pieces and chilled

⅓ cup iced spring water, plus 1 to 3 tablespoons more if needed

Filling:

½ cup all-purpose flour

¼ cup cornstarch

1½ to 2 cups sugar, depending on the sweetness of the strawberries

6 cups halved strawberries

1 egg white from a large egg, lightly beaten

Sugar, for sprinkling

Note: A kitchen scale is helpful in making this recipe.

For the crust:

1. In a large bowl (or in a food processor), whisk together the flour, sugar, and salt until thoroughly combined, about 10 seconds. Drop the first 4 tablespoons of chilled butter on top of the flour mixture, and cut in with 2 sharp knives (or pulse in the food processor), *just* until the mixture looks like tiny crumbs. (In the food processor, this will take less than a minute.) Repeat with the rest of the butter and the lard in batches, keeping the unused portions well chilled until it is time to add it to the flour. The mixture will look like large crumbs when all the butter and lard have been incorporated.

2. Sprinkle the ⅓ cup water over the top of the mixture and either mix with a spoon (or pulse in the food processor) until the mixture *just* begins to hold together in clumps. If the mixture is too dry to hold together, add 1 to 3 tablespoons additional water until it does. Place a little less than half (12 ounces) of this mixture into a 2-gallon zippered plastic bag. (This will be the top crust.) Put the remaining 15 ounces (just more than half) into

another 2-gallon zippered plastic bag. (This will be the bottom crust.) Pressing *very* lightly through the plastic, quickly gather each mixture into a rough round *in the center of the bag.* Refrigerate the bags of dough until they are *thoroughly* chilled.

3. When you are ready to make the pie, position a rack in the lower third of the oven and preheat to 425°F. Have a 9-inch deep-dish pie plate and a rimmed baking sheet at the ready.

4. Remove the bag with the larger amount of dough from the refrigerator. Unzip the bag to ventilate it, then quickly roll out the larger crust (still inside the bag) to a round about 10 inches in diameter. Using scissors, cut the plastic all the way around the bag and gently lift one side of the plastic. Place the bag, dough side down, in the pie plate. Gently remove the remaining piece of plastic so that the dough falls into the plate. Refrigerate while you make the filling.

For the filling:

1. In a small bowl, whisk together the flour, cornstarch, and sugar. Place the strawberries in a large bowl and sprinkle the flour mixture over it. Mix thoroughly.

2. Take the pie shell out of the refrigerator.

3. Fill the pie with the strawberry mixture, then repeat the rolling-out process with the other crust, and place it on top of the filling. Seal the two crusts together around the edges, and flute the crust. Using a sharp knife, cut four or five 2-inch slits in the top crust, to ventilate the pie. Using a pastry brush, brush the top of the pie with just enough of the beaten egg white to cover it. Sprinkle the top crust with a small amount of sugar.

4. Bake the pie for 20 minutes, then quickly take the pie out of the oven and put it on the baking sheet. Put the pie and the sheet back in the oven, and reduce the heat to 350°F. Continue to bake for 35 to 45 minutes, or until *thick* juices bubble out of the slits.

5. Remove the baking sheet and place the pie on a rack. Allow it to cool *completely.* (Do not serve the pie hot or warm.)

Makes 10 to 12 servings

Double-Shot Chocolate Cake

—DOUBLE SHOT—

Once I'd gotten over the hurdle of worrying that flourless chocolate cakes wouldn't rise, I became obsessive about experimenting with them. I'd read somewhere that you could bake one in a pan of water, as long as you used a solid (i.e., not springform) pan that is at least 2 inches in depth, and guarded the cake well from splashes by not putting more than an inch of hot water in the outer pan. After baking, the cake will come out cleanly if you have buttered both the pan and the parchment. My friend and recipe-tester Carol Alexander made a stencil for me to decorate the top of this cake (you can buy stencils at virtually any kitchen supply store). You place the stencil on top of the cooled cake, just before serving, and sift powdered sugar on top. Carefully remove the stencil and you have a dark/light design. But be sure you wait until just before serving. Otherwise, a puff of breeze will bring your efforts to naught.

2¼ sticks (9 ounces) unsalted butter

10 ounces best-quality bittersweet chocolate, broken into small pieces

¾ cup plus 3 tablespoons extra-fine ("super fine") granulated sugar

2 tablespoons Dutch-process unsweetened cocoa powder

8 large eggs

1 teaspoon vanilla extract

Powdered sugar, for decorating

Sweetened whipped cream or best-quality vanilla ice cream, for serving

1. Preheat the oven to 350°F. Butter the bottom and sides of a 10-inch heavy-duty round cake pan that is 2 inches in height. (*Do not use a springform pan.*) Line the bottom with a round of parchment paper and butter the parchment.

2. Fill a 16 x 11-inch roasting pan with 1 inch of hot water, place the roasting pan on a baking sheet, and put it into the oven.

3. In the top of a double boiler, over simmering water, melt the butter with the chocolate. When the ingredients are melted, remove the pan from the heat and remove the double boiler top from the bottom. Allow the butter-chocolate mixture to cool slightly. Sift the sugar with the cocoa twice, then whisk it into the melted chocolate mixture.

4. In a large bowl, beat the eggs until they are foamy. Add the vanilla and the chocolate mixture. Blend with a spatula until very well mixed.

5. Carefully pour the batter into the cake pan. Gently place the cake pan into the water-filled roasting pan, taking care not to splash the water onto the cake.

6. Bake for 40 to 50 minutes, or until the cake begins to shrink slightly from the sides and a toothpick inserted in the center comes out clean. Remove the cake pan from the pan of water. (Discard the pan of water.) Place the cake on a rack to cool for 15 minutes, then gently invert onto a cake plate and peel off the paper. Allow to cool completely.

7. Just before serving time, carefully place a 9- or 10-inch cake stencil on top of the cake and sift powdered sugar over the stencil (then remove the stencil). Serve immediately with sweetened whipped cream or vanilla ice cream.

Makes 16 servings

Deep-Dish Cherry Pie

—SWEET REVENGE—

Our family loves cherry pie, and I used to make it every summer with fresh tart cherries. A writer friend in Boulder had two massive cherry trees in her front yard and would invite me over to pick bags full every summer. But the birds discovered her trees, and pretty soon she went from having an abundant crop to no crop. Jim and I optimistically planted two Montmorency cherry trees in our own yard, and for a couple of years, he would go out once a week and pick enough cherries for a pie. Then the elk discovered our trees, and ate them down to the nub—they left no fruit, no leaves, no branches, no tree trunks. So now I use canned cherries. I also always bake the bottom crust first. This keeps it from becoming soggy. Serve alone or with vanilla ice cream.

Crust:

3½ cups all-purpose flour

1 tablespoon plus 1 teaspoon powdered sugar

1 teaspoon kosher salt

3 sticks (¾ pound) cold unsalted butter, cut into 1-tablespoon pieces and chilled

¼ cup plus 2 tablespoons lard or solid vegetable shortening, cut into 1-tablespoon pieces and chilled

½ cup iced spring water, plus 1 to 2 tablespoons more if needed

For the crust:

1. In a large bowl (or in the bowl of a food processor fitted with the metal blade), whisk together the flour, sugar, and salt until thoroughly combined, about 10 seconds. Drop the first 8 tablespoons of chilled butter on top of the flour mixture, and cut in with 2 sharp knives (or pulse in the food processor), *just* until the mixture looks like tiny crumbs. (In the food processor, this will take less than a minute.) Repeat with the rest of the butter and the lard or vegetable shortening in batches, keeping the unused portions well chilled until it is time to add it to the flour. The mixture will look like large crumbs when all the butter and lard have been incorporated.

2 egg whites, from large eggs, kept in separate bowls and lightly beaten

Filling:

2 cups granulated sugar

¼ cup plus 1 tablespoon cornstarch

1 cup reserved cherry juice

Contents of two 14½-ounce cans sour pitted cherries (4 cups), drained, juice reserved

1 tablespoon unsalted butter, melted

1 teaspoon fresh lemon juice

Granulated sugar or crushed sugar cubes, for sprinkling

Best-quality vanilla ice cream, for serving (optional)

2. Sprinkle the ½ cup water over the top of the mixture and either mix with a spoon (or pulse in the processor) until the mixture *just* begins to hold together in clumps. If the mixture is too dry to hold together, add 1 to 2 tablespoons more water until it does. Divide the mixture into 2 pieces, one slightly larger than half (the bottom crust), the other slightly less than half (the top crust). Place each piece into a 2-gallon zippered plastic storage bag.

3. Pressing very lightly through the plastic, quickly gather the mixture into rough rounds in the center of each bag. Refrigerate the bags of dough until they are thoroughly chilled.

4. When you are ready to make the pie, preheat the oven to 400°F. Have a 9-inch deep-dish pie plate ready. Have a rimmed baking sheet ready to place underneath the pie.

5. Remove the bag with the larger portion of dough from the refrigerator. Unzip the bag, then quickly roll out the dough (still in the bag) to a round about 10 inches in diameter. Using scissors, cut the plastic all the way around the bag and gently lift back one side of the plastic. Place the bag dough side down into the pie plate. Gently remove the remaining piece of plastic so that the dough falls into the plate. Trim the edge of the crust. Gently line the crust with parchment paper and weight down the crust with rice, dried beans, or pie weights.

6. Bake for 10 minutes. Remove from the oven and remove the parchment with the weights. Brush the bottom and sides of the crust with one of the beaten egg whites. Return the crust to the oven to bake for 10 minutes more. If the edges begin to brown too quickly, it can be covered with pieces of foil until the crust is baked. Remove the crust from the oven and allow it to cool slightly while you prepare the filling and the top crust. Leave the oven on.

For the filling:

1. In a medium saucepan, combine the sugar and cornstarch and stir until well mixed. Stir in the reserved cherry juice. Cook the mixture over medium heat, stirring frequently, until it thickens and bubbles, then cook a minute or two longer, until the mixture begins to clear. Remove from the heat and stir in the cherries, melted butter, and lemon juice.

2. Spoon the cherry mixture into the cooked crust. Remove the second chilled bag of pie dough from the refrigerator. Roll the dough following the process used for the bottom crust. After cutting the plastic, gently lift the plastic from one side of the dough. Center the bag, dough side down, over the cherry filling and gently remove the remaining piece of plastic. Press the dough around the edge of the baked crust to seal the 2 crusts as much as possible (you will not be able to seal them completely; this is okay). Cut slits in the top crust to create vents. Brush the top crust with the second egg white. Sprinkle the granulated sugar or crushed sugar cubes lightly over the top. Place the pie onto the rimmed baking sheet before it bakes.

3. Bake for 40 to 45 minutes, or until the top crust is browned and *thick* juices are bubbling out of the pie. Cool the pie on a rack for at least 2 hours, so the pie can set up.

Makes 12 servings

Door-Prize Gingerbread

—SWEET REVENGE—

Whoever thought putting black pepper into gingerbread would add a certain je ne sais quoi *to the result? When I finally hit on this combination of ingredients, Jim pronounced it his favorite gingerbread ever. I have somehow collected a number of castle cake molds, so I make three of these gingerbreads every Christmas. The grandchildren then sprinkle on powdered sugar, or place dabs of frosting here and there on top, with jimmies or colored sugar on top of that. They used to take great pride in their creations, but except for the youngest one, they're becoming a little too cool to decorate gingerbread castles.* Tempus fugit.

Baking spray (with flour)

4⅔ cups all-purpose flour (high altitude: add ¼ cup plus 2 tablespoons)

2 teaspoons baking soda

2 teaspoons ground ginger

½ teaspoon ground cinnamon

¼ teaspoon freshly grated nutmeg

⅛ teaspoon ground cloves

½ teaspoon freshly ground black pepper

¼ teaspoon salt

1 pound unsalted butter

2 cups molasses

2 large eggs

2 cups sugar

1. Preheat the oven to 350°F. Take out three 8- or 9-cup tall nonstick castle cake molds and baking spray, but do not spray the pans until just before you are going to pour the batter into them.

2. Sift together the flour, baking soda, spices, pepper, and salt. In a saucepan, melt the butter with the molasses and set aside to cool.

3. In a stand mixer fitted with the paddle attachment, beat the eggs with the sugar until they are very thick and almost white. Add the butter mixture and beat on low speed, just until combined. Add the flour-spice mixture and beat on low speed, just until combined. Add the boiling water, sour cream, ginger, and orange juice and beat 3 minutes. Scrape down the sides of the bowl and the paddle attachment, making sure all the ingredients are well incorporated.

1½ cups boiling spring water

1⅓ cups regular or light sour cream

1 teaspoon freshly grated peeled fresh ginger, minced

3 tablespoons orange juice (high altitude: add 3 tablespoons)

Best-quality vanilla ice cream, for serving

4. Coat the 3 castle molds with baking spray until every surface inside the mold is completely covered. Immediately pour the batter into the molds, dividing it evenly. Bake for 25 to 30 minutes, and check with a toothpick to see if the gingerbread is done. If necessary, allow another 5 to 10 minutes for the gingerbread to bake, until a toothpick inserted into the center of each gingerbread comes out clean.

5. Grease 2 large or 3 smaller cooling racks. Cool the gingerbreads, still in their pans, on the racks for 20 minutes. Carefully invert them to unmold onto the greased racks. Cool completely, then carefully slide onto serving plates. Serve with the ice cream.

Makes 3 gingerbreads, 4 to 6 servings each

Dark Torte

—DARK TORT—

I thought it was a great idea to use the legal term tort, *which at its base means a* wrong, *with* torte, *which is a* dessert. *I thought (mistakenly, as it turned out) that most readers would think it was a great idea, too. Yet many people who had not read the book, which involves both torts and tortes, indignantly told me at signings that a word in my title was spelled incorrectly, and that what I meant was t-o-r-t-e. My rigid-smile response became, "Please read the book."*

That aside, I did enjoy experimenting with t-o-r-t-e-s, and learning about t-o-r-t-s. This recipe uses finely ground zwieback crumbs and finely chopped pecans. The syrup moistens the layers. A trick I learned while catering is that pouring liquid *gelatin into whipped cream helps hold its shape.*

6 large eggs, separated

1 cup sugar

1½ cups ground zwieback crumbs (one 6-ounce box)

1 teaspoon baking powder

½ teaspoon ground cinnamon

½ teaspoon ground cloves

(High altitude: Add 1 tablespoon cake flour)

⅛ teaspoon salt

⅛ teaspoon cream of tartar

1 cup finely chopped pecans

Sherry Syrup (recipe follows)

Whipped Cream Topping (recipe follows)

1. Position an oven rack in the middle of the oven and preheat to 375°F. Butter two 9-inch cake pans. Butter two cooling racks.

2. In a large bowl, beat the egg yolks until they are light and lemon-colored. Remove 2 tablespoons of sugar from the cup of sugar and set aside. Gradually beat the rest of the sugar (1 cup minus 2 tablespoons) into the egg yolks.

3. In another large bowl, combine the crumbs, baking powder, cinnamon, and cloves (and flour if cooking at high altitude), stirring to combine well. Stir this mixture into the egg-yolk mixture (the dough will be very stiff). Set aside.

4. In another large bowl, using a wire whip or whip attachment, beat the egg whites until they

are foamy. Add the salt and cream of tartar, and continue beating until stiff peaks form. Gradually beat in the reserved 2 tablespoons sugar.

5. Fold one-third of the egg-white mixture into the egg-yolk mixture. Fold in half of the nuts. Fold in another one-third of the egg-white mixture, then fold in the last of the nuts. Fold in the remaining egg-white mixture until there are no traces of white in the batter. Spread the batter evenly in the prepared pans.

6. Bake for 15 to 25 minutes, or until the layers have browned slightly, a toothpick inserted in the center comes out clean, and the layers have begun to shrink from the sides of the pans.

7. Cool the layers for 5 minutes in their pans. Place large pieces of foil underneath the buttered racks and fold them up all the way around so as to catch the syrup. (This makes your clean-up easier.) Turn the layers out onto the separate buttered cake racks. Allow the layers to cool while you make the sherry syrup.

8. Using a skewer or ice pick, evenly poke holes all over the tops of the layers. (Take care not to poke the holes all the way through the cake. The holes should go down about three-fourths of the way through the layers.) Carefully and slowly pour the hot sherry syrup evenly over the layers, until it is all gone.

9. When the layers are cool, make the whipped cream topping. Discard the foil and carefully turn the first layer onto a cake plate. Spread a thick layer of whipped cream topping over this layer. Then top with the second layer. Spread the rest of the topping on the top and sides of the torte.

10. The torte may be served immediately or it may be chilled. Because of the whipped cream, leftovers must be kept in the refrigerator.

Makes 12 servings

Sherry Syrup

2 cups sugar

2 cups spring water

½ cup dry sherry

1. In a large saucepan, combine the sugar and water. Bring to a boil over medium-high heat. Allow the mixture to boil until it reaches the soft-ball stage (234° to 240°F) on a candy thermometer.

2. *Immediately remove the pan from the heat.* Using a wooden spoon, carefully and slowly swirl in the sherry until well combined.

Whipped Cream Topping

1 tablespoon spring water

1 teaspoon vanilla extract

1 teaspoon unflavored gelatin powder

2 cups (1 pint) heavy (whipping) cream, well chilled

2 tablespoons powdered sugar

1. Pour the water and vanilla into a small saucepan. Sprinkle the gelatin powder over the surface of the liquid and allow the gelatin to soften for 2 minutes. Turn the heat on under the pan to medium-low. Swirling the mixture frequently, cook and stir the mixture until the gelatin is completely dissolved. Keep the heat on very low to maintain the *liquid* gelatin mixture.

2. In a large bowl, whip the cream until it forms soft peaks. Beat in the powdered sugar and whip until stiff peaks form.

3. With the beater running, pour the liquid gelatin mixture into the cream and beat until completely combined.

All-American Deep-Dish Apple Pie

—DARK TORT—

This recipe has been honed over the years, and is our family's favorite apple pie. (We planted an apple tree in our yard and, as with the cherry trees, the elk ate that *one down to the ground.) Serve with best-quality vanilla or cinnamon ice cream.*

Crust:

1¾ cups plus 2 tablespoons all-purpose flour

2 teaspoons powdered sugar

½ teaspoon salt

1½ sticks (6 ounces) cold unsalted butter, cut into 1-tablespoon pieces and chilled

3 tablespoons lard or vegetable shortening, cut into 1-tablespoon pieces and chilled

¼ cup iced spring water, plus 1 to 2 tablespoons more if needed

1 large egg, lightly beaten

Filling:

1¼ teaspoons ground cinnamon

¾ cup sugar

8 peeled, cored, and thinly sliced Granny Smith apples

Topping:

1¼ cups all-purpose flour

½ cup sugar

10 tablespoons (1¼ sticks) chilled unsalted butter, cut into 1-tablespoon pieces

For the crust:

1. In a large bowl (or in the bowl of a food processor fitted with the metal blade), whisk together the flour, sugar, and salt until thoroughly combined, about 10 seconds. Drop the first 4 tablespoons of chilled butter on top of the flour mixture, and cut in with 2 sharp knives (or pulse in the food processor) *just* until the mixture looks like tiny crumbs. (In the food processor, this will take less than a minute.) Repeat with the rest of the butter and the lard (or vegetable shortening) in batches, keeping the

unused portions well chilled until it is time to add it to the flour. The mixture will look like large crumbs when all the butter and lard have been incorporated.

2. Sprinkle the ¼ cup water over the top of the mixture, and either mix with a spoon or pulse in the food processor until the mixture *just* begins to hold together in clumps. If the mixture is too dry to hold together, add 1 to 2 tablespoons additional water until it does. Place the mixture into a 2-gallon zippered plastic bag. Pressing very lightly through the plastic, quickly gather the mixture into a rough round in the center of the bag. Refrigerate the bag of dough until it is thoroughly chilled.

3. When you are ready to make the pie, preheat the oven to 400°F. Have a 9-inch deep-dish pie plate and a rimmed baking sheet at the ready.

4. Remove the bag of dough from the refrigerator. Unzip the bag, then quickly roll out the dough (still inside the bag) to a round about 10 inches in diameter. Using scissors, cut the plastic all the way around the bag and gently lift one side of the plastic. Place the bag, dough side down, into the pie plate. Gently remove the remaining piece of plastic so that the dough falls into the plate. Trim and flute the edge of the crust. Using the tines of a fork, prick the pie crust in several places to allow for steam to evaporate. Gently line the crust with parchment paper and weight down the crust with ceramic pie weights or uncooked rice or beans.

5. Bake for 10 minutes. Remove from the oven, take out the parchment and weights, and brush the bottom and sides of the crust with the beaten egg (you will not use all of the egg). Return the crust to the oven and bake for 10 minutes more. If the fluted edge begins to brown too quickly, it can be covered with pieces of foil until the crust is baked. Remove the crust from the oven and allow it to cool slightly while you prepare the filling and topping.

For the filling:
In a small bowl, combine the cinnamon and sugar. Place the apple slices in a large bowl. Sprinkle the apples with the cinnamon-sugar mixture and set aside while you prepare the topping.

For the topping:

1. In a large bowl (or in the bowl of a food processor fitted with the metal blade), whisk together the flour and sugar for 10 seconds. Drop the pieces of butter on top of the flour mixture and cut in with 2 sharp knives (or pulse in the food processor) just until the mixture resembles large crumbs. Do not overblend.

2. Place the apple mixture in the crust. It may seem very tall, but the fruit will cook down. Take the time to get all the apple slices in, even if you have to cut some of the slices in half. (Discard any liquid that has accumulated in the bottom of the bowl.) Evenly spread the topping over the apples.

3. Place the pie on the rimmed baking sheet, place in the oven, and reduce the oven temperature to 375°F. Bake for 40 to 45 minutes, or until the topping is browned and the apples are cooked. (If it seems as if the topping is burning, reduce the oven temperature even more, to 350°F.)

4. Cool the pie on a rack for at least 2 hours so it can set up.

Makes 8 large servings

Chocolate-Lovers' Dipped Fruit

—DARK TORT—

At holiday time, I make these dipped dried fruits for family and friends. My own favorite is dipping glacé apricots, but in summer, the family loves the dipped long-stemmed strawberries. Considering how much commercial enterprises charge for these confections (producing an inferior product), this recipe is a gold mine.

8 ounces best-quality bittersweet chocolate, such as Godiva Dark, chopped

1 tablespoon unsalted butter

11 to 12 ounces dried fruit (apricots, strawberries, peaches, pears, etc.)

In the top of a double boiler, over simmering water, melt the chocolate and butter, stirring frequently. Line a baking sheet with wax paper. When the chocolate and butter are thoroughly melted and blended, turn down the heat under the double boiler. Holding the top of a piece of fruit between your thumb and forefinger, gently dip the bottom end into the hot chocolate. Immediately raise the fruit, shake it gently to loosen any stray drops, then place it on the wax paper to cool completely. Repeat with the rest of the fruit.

Totally Unorthodox Coeur à la Crème

—FATALLY FLAKY—

This recipe is unorthodox because it has a crust. But people like crusts, so have at it. Brushing the apricot preserve mixture over the fruit at serving time makes the dessert look spectacular.

- 2½ cups heavy (whipping) cream, chilled
- 16 ounces mascarpone cheese, at room temperature
- 1 cup powdered sugar, sifted
- 2 teaspoons vanilla extract
- Hazelnut Crust (recipe follows)
- 1 pound fresh strawberries, rinsed, patted dry, and halved
- 1 pound fresh blueberries, rinsed and patted dry
- 1 cup apricot preserves
- ½ cup spring water

1. In a large bowl, with an electric mixer fitted with the whip attachment, beat the cream until stiff peaks form, 2 to 3 minutes.

2. In another large bowl, with an electric mixer, beat the mascarpone on low speed just until blended. Add the sugar and vanilla and beat only until well blended.

3. Using a rubber spatula, fold the whipped cream into the cheese mixture.

4. Cut 2 pieces of 2-ply cheesecloth large enough to line a large sieve with enough cheesecloth left over to fold up over the combined mixture. Wet the cheesecloth pieces and wring them out. Line a strainer or mold with the cheesecloth.

5. Gently spoon the mixture into the lined sieve. Fold the ends of the cheesecloth up over the mixture. Suspend the sieve over a bowl and put into the refrigerator. Allow to drain overnight.

6. To assemble the coeur, make the hazelnut crust and allow to cool completely. Spoon the chilled and drained mascarpone mixture into

the cooled crust and spread it evenly. (You may cover the coeur with plastic wrap at this point and chill for up to 4 hours.)

7. Just before serving time, arrange the strawberries and blueberries in rows on top of the mascarpone mixture. In a small pan, heat the apricot preserves with the water over low heat. Remove from the heat, strain, and cool slightly. Brush over the fruit. (You will not use all of the apricot mixture.)

Makes 12 servings

* * *

Hazelnut Crust

- 1½ cups skinned hazelnuts (aka filberts)
- 2 cups all-purpose flour
- 3 tablespoons powdered sugar
- 2 sticks (½ pound) unsalted butter, melted

1. In a large skillet, toast the hazelnuts over medium-low heat, stirring constantly, until they give off a nutty scent, 10 to 15 minutes. Place the nuts on paper towels to cool. When they are cool enough to touch, place the nuts on a cutting board and roughly chop.

2. Preheat the oven to 350°F. Generously butter the bottom of a 9 x 13-inch glass baking dish.

3. Sift the flour with the powdered sugar and place it in a large bowl. Using a wooden spoon, mix in the melted butter and chopped hazelnuts. Pat the mixture into the bottom of the prepared pan.

4. Bake for 10 to 15 minutes, or until the edges of the crust begin to brown. Place on a rack to cool completely before filling.

Black-and-White Cake

—FATALLY FLAKY—

When I was a young teen, the coolest place to get dessert was Gifford's, in Bethesda, Maryland. There, I would always order a slice of an ice-cream cake that I tried to duplicate here. When I tested this recipe (those young relatives again), one group confessed that their mother had never allowed them to have Häagen-Dazs ice cream. I quickly corrected that oversight. In the original cake recipe, I used milk, but after later experiments, the family insisted I change it to water. Either works.

Note: This is an ice-cream cake and should be kept frozen until ready to serve.

1 quart best-quality vanilla ice cream, such as Häagen-Dazs

3 cups all-purpose flour (high altitude: add ¼ cup)

2 cups sugar

¼ cup plus 2 tablespoons Dutch-process unsweetened cocoa powder

2 teaspoons baking soda

1 teaspoon salt

½ cup plus 2 tablespoons safflower, canola, or corn oil

2 tablespoons distilled white vinegar

1 tablespoon vanilla extract

2 tablespoons dark rum

2 cups spring water or milk, preferably whole (high altitude: add 1 tablespoon)

Chocolate Glaze (recipe follows)

1. Preheat the oven to 350°F.

Butter a 9-inch round cake pan and a large cooling rack. Butter and flour 2 more 9-inch round cake pans.

2. Soften the ice cream in a microwave oven, just until it is spreadable. Spread it evenly in the buttered pan and place it in the freezer.

3. Sift together the flour, sugar, cocoa, baking soda, and salt. Sift it again into a large bowl. Add the oil, vinegar, vanilla, rum, and water or milk

and with an electric mixer beat on low speed for 1 minute, then scrape the bowl. Beat on medium speed for 1 to 2 minutes, or until the batter is completely mixed.

4. Pour the batter into the buttered and floured pans and bake for 25 to 35 minutes, or until a toothpick inserted in the cake comes out with only a crumb or two adhering to it. Cool in the pans for 10 minutes, then turn out onto the buttered rack to cool completely.

5. When you are ready to assemble the cake, soften the ice-cream layer slightly by dipping the pan quickly into hot water. Unmold it onto a plate. Place one cake layer on a serving plate. Place the ice-cream layer on top. Carefully place the second cake layer on top of the ice cream. Loosely cover the whole thing with foil and put back in the freezer. Freeze until firm, at least 3 hours.

6. Make the chocolate glaze and allow it to come to room temperature.

7. When you are ready to serve dessert, remove the cake from the freezer. Slowly pour the glaze over the cake, smoothing over the tops and sides. Using a serrated knife dipped in hot water and wiped dry, cut the cake.

8. Refreeze any unused portions.

Makes 12 large servings

Chocolate Glaze

- 10 ounces best-quality bittersweet chocolate, such as Godiva Dark, chopped
- 2½ sticks (10 ounces) unsalted butter
- 3 tablespoons light corn syrup

In the top of a double boiler, over simmering water, melt the butter and chocolate, stirring until melted. Remove the top pan of the double boiler from the bottom pan and whisk in the corn syrup. Allow to come to room temperature before using.

Breakfast Bread Pudding with Rum Sauce

—CRUNCH TIME—

This rich pudding could also be served after dinner, of course. But when we have guests for breakfast, this is what I make. I usually serve it with a spiral-sliced ham.

Bread pudding:

1 teaspoon ground cinnamon

1½ cups sugar

1½ pounds raisin bread, torn into bite-size pieces

4 tablespoons (½ stick) unsalted butter, at room temperature

4 large eggs, at room temperature

4 cups half-and-half

2 tablespoons vanilla extract (see Note)

Rum sauce:

8 tablespoons (1 stick) unsalted butter

1 cup packed light brown sugar

⅓ cup best-quality dark or light rum

¼ teaspoon freshly grated nutmeg

1 large egg

For the bread pudding:

1. In a small bowl, mix the cinnamon into the sugar until well combined and set aside. Butter a 9 x 13-inch glass baking dish and place the torn-up bread into it.

2. In a large bowl, with an electric mixer, beat the butter until it is creamy. Mix in the cinnamon-sugar mixture and beat until very creamy. Add the eggs, one at a time, and beat until well combined. Mix in the half-and-half and vanilla and beat well. (The mixture will be thin and will not be completely combined; this is normal.) Stop the beaters and use a spatula to mix as well as possible.

3. Pour the butter mixture over the torn-up bread. Cover the pan with plastic wrap and place in the refrigerator overnight.

4. In the morning, remove the pan from the refrigerator and discard the plastic wrap.

5. Preheat the oven to 350°F.

6. Bake the pudding for 30 minutes, then remove from the oven and stir with a wooden spoon, smoothing the pudding out evenly to the edges of the pan. Place the pudding back in the oven and bake for an additional 30 minutes, or until it is puffed and golden. While the pudding is baking, prepare the rum sauce.

For the rum sauce:

1. In a medium sauté pan, melt the butter over low heat. Add the brown sugar, rum, and nutmeg and stir carefully with a wooden spoon or heatproof silicone spatula until the sugar dissolves and the mixture is well blended. Remove from the heat and allow to cool slightly, still in the pan.

2. In a small bowl, beat the egg until it is very frothy. Beat the egg into the butter mixture until well combined. Place the pan back on the stove and cook, stirring, over medium-low heat, until the mixture thickens.

3. Remove the pudding from the oven, place on a cooling rack, and carefully pour the rum sauce over it. Allow the sauce to soak into the pudding (2 to 3 minutes) and then serve. The pudding will be very hot.

Makes 8 servings

Note: If possible, use Mexican vanilla, or you can use 1 tablespoon vanilla extract and 1 tablespoon vanilla bean paste.

Sugar-Free Vanilla Gelato

—THE WHOLE ENCHILADA—

I have tried baking with sugar substitutes and have never had much luck producing a worthy product. But making a cold sugar-free dessert worked.

- 4 egg yolks, from large eggs
- ½ cup sugar substitute for baking, such as Splenda for Baking
- 1½ cups whole milk
- 1½ cups heavy (whipping) cream
- 1 teaspoon vanilla extract

1. Follow the manufacturer's instructions for freezing the bowl of your ice-cream or gelato maker.

2. In a large bowl, whisk the egg yolks with the sugar substitute until thoroughly combined. Set aside.

3. Place the milk and cream in a medium heavy-bottomed saucepan and place over low heat, stirring occasionally, until the mixture comes to a simmer (bubbles appear around the outside of the mixture). Remove from the heat and pour into a 4-cup glass measuring cup.

4. Whisking the egg yolk mixture constantly, pour in the hot milk mixture very gradually. (The key here is not to cook the eggs. You are beginning to make a custard, not scrambled eggs.) Whisk until completely combined.

5. Pour the egg-milk mixture back into the pan and place over medium-low heat. Put a thermometer into the pan so that it is not touching the bottom (you can usually clip a candy thermometer to the side of the pan).

Stir constantly with a wooden spoon until the mixture thickens and covers the spoon. The thermometer should read just above 170°F. Once the mixture thickens, immediately remove it from the heat. It is now a custard. (If bits of cooked egg begin to appear before the thermometer reaches 170°F, immediately remove from the heat.)

6. Using a paper towel, wipe out the 4-cup glass measuring cup. (You will be pouring the cooked custard back into it.)

7. Pour the thickened custard mixture through a sieve back into the 4-cup glass measuring cup. Stir in the vanilla. Place a large piece of plastic wrap directly onto the custard to cover completely. (This is to prevent a skin from forming as the custard cools.)

8. Chill the custard in the refrigerator until it is thoroughly cold, usually 2 hours or overnight.

9. Following the manufacturer's instructions, turn on the gelato maker and scoop the chilled custard mixture into the frozen rotating bowl. With most gelato makers, the soft gelato will be ready after 25 minutes. If you desire a firmer gelato, scoop it into a hard plastic container with a lid and freeze, covered, for 20 minutes or so.

10. After serving the gelato, freeze any leftovers, covered, in a hard plastic container with a lid. Allow to soften at room temperature for about 15 minutes before serving again.

Makes about 2 cups

Chocolate Tartufi Diana

This is a bonus recipe. It is not in any of the books. But after I finished writing this cookbook and submitted it for editing, I took a fabulous online class through Coursera: Roman Imperial Architecture, *taught by Yale's phenomenal Professor Diana Kleiner. During the class, Professor Kleiner occasionally mentioned her favorite gelato places in Rome. She raved about Tre Scalini, where she always ordered the* tartufo. *I decided to try to figure out how to make this frozen chocolate truffle (a restaurant secret). I made several recipes for chocolate gelato, which was fun, and finally hit on a combination of flavors we liked. Making* tartufi, *though, proved quite demanding, mainly because molding the gelato into balls was challenging. Then I hit on trying the round molds used for freezing ice cubes (made by Tovolo and available online). The molds come in sets of 2, and to be on the safe side, I ordered 3 sets. I describe the mold-filling in detail in the recipe, but it is really quite easy. My taste-testers invariably said, "Whoa, that's intense!" (before their eyes rolled upward). To moderate the intensity, I found that it was important to serve each* tartufo *with a very large dollop of the whipped cream garnish as well as the cookie. If you crave what Professor Kleiner calls a "chocolate bomb," I hope this recipe meets your expectations.*

Centers:

5 glacé cherries (available either at your grocery store during holiday time or year-round online)

1 to 2 tablespoons, or more as needed, best-quality dark rum, such as Clément or Appleton Estate

For the centers:

Place the cherries in a narrow glass or plastic container and pour the rum over them to completely cover. (Make sure the rum completely covers the cherries.) Place a piece of plastic wrap over the cherries and allow them to sit at room temperature while you work on the gelato. (They can remain at room temperature for at least a day. Longer is fine.)

Gelato:

2¼ cups whole milk

¾ cup extra-fine (also called "Superfine") sugar, divided

1 cup Dutch-process unsweetened cocoa powder

⅓ cup heavy (whipping) cream

2 ounces bittersweet chocolate, such as Godiva Dark, chopped

4 egg yolks, from large eggs

1 tablespoon Grand Marnier liqueur

1 tablespoon amaretto liqueur

1 teaspoon vanilla extract

⅛ teaspoon salt

For the gelato:

1. In a large saucepan, heat the milk and ½ cup of the sugar over medium heat, stirring with a wire whisk until the sugar dissolves and the milk begins to simmer (bubbles appear around the rim of the pan). Add the cocoa and whisk vigorously, until smooth. Set aside.

2. In the top of a double boiler, over simmering water, heat the cream and the chopped chocolate, stirring until the chocolate melts. Remove the top of the double boiler from the bottom pan.

3. Pour the milk mixture into a 4-cup glass measuring cup. Pour the mixture slowly into the cream-chocolate mixture (still in the double boiler top), whisking until well combined. Pour the mixture back into the glass measuring cup. Set aside.

4. In a large bowl, with an electric mixer, beat the egg yolks with the remaining ¼ cup sugar on high speed for 4 minutes, or until the mixture is lemon-colored and very thick. Turn the mixer to low speed, then pour the combined milk-cream mixture slowly into the egg yolk mixture. Beat well to combine.

5. Pour this mixture back into the saucepan and clip a candy thermometer onto the side of the pan. Make sure the thermometer does not touch the bottom of the pan. Cook over medium-low

heat, stirring constantly, until the mixture thickens into a custard and covers a spoon. The thermometer should register at least 170°F when the mixture thickens. (At high altitude, you may have to stir until the thermometer registers 180° to 183°F.) Remember: You are making a custard, not scrambled chocolate eggs, so although you do need to allow the mixture to thicken, you do not want to allow the mixture to boil.

6. Pour the mixture through a sieve into a glass bowl. Stir in the liqueurs, vanilla, and salt. Place a piece of plastic wrap directly onto the custard (this is to prevent a skin from forming). Chill completely, preferably overnight.

7. Meanwhile, follow the manufacturer's instructions for prepping the bowl of a gelato or ice-cream maker.

8. Following the manufacturer's instructions, pour the custard mixture into the bowl of the gelato maker or ice-cream maker. Process about 25 minutes, until the gelato is soft set. Turn off the gelato maker and remove the bowl of gelato.

9. Follow the directions that come with the spherical ice molds for filling them, *except* you will not be filling the molds to the fill line, but just below it, so as not to lose too much gelato when you place the tops on the molds. Using a rubber spatula, scrape the gelato into the bottom half of the first mold, to just below the fill line. Drop 1 rum-soaked cherry into the mold. Using a toothpick, gently push the cherry into the center of the gelato. Carefully place the silicone cap on the top of the first mold. If you have filled the mold to just below the fill line, you should not have much gelato squirting out the hole in the top of the mold. If you do have gelato squirt out the top of your first mold, fill the next molds even less. (Even if you do have gelato squirt out the hole in the top, do not worry, you will rinse it off later.) Depending on how well you can manage the mold-filling, you will have 4 or 5 molds filled. Freeze the molds until rock-hard, usually 4 to 6 hours, or overnight. If there is gelato left over after you fill the molds, you can freeze it in a hard plastic container for another use.

Coating:

8 tablespoons (1 stick) unsalted butter, plus 1 to 2 tablespoons more as needed

7 ounces best-quality bittersweet chocolate

For the coating:

1. When you are ready to make the globes into *tartufi*, make the coating. In the top of a double boiler, over simmering water, melt the butter with the chocolate, stirring until completely melted. Remove the top of the double boiler and allow the mixture to cool *slightly*, stirring frequently. (If the chocolate seizes up, or is too thick, reheat the mixture over simmering water, and add the additional butter, a tablespoon at a time. Stir well, until the mixture is liquid again.)

2. Once the coating is slightly cool but still quite liquid, unroll a 12-inch square of wax paper and place it on a freezer-proof dinner plate. Remove the molds from the freezer. Working quickly, run each mold under warm tap water, remove the silicone cap from the mold, and unmold the whole globe onto the wax paper. (If you have run the mold under warm tap water and the globe still will not release, you may have to coax the chocolate globe out of the bottom half of the mold with a fork. This is okay.)

3. Using tongs, quickly dip each frozen globe into the butter-chocolate mixture, and roll it around until it is completely covered. Place the chocolate-coated globes back on the wax paper–covered plate and place in the freezer. These are now *tartufi*, or truffles. (You may not use up all the coating, in which case you can dip large fresh strawberries into it. Place these on wax paper until firm.)

Garnish:

1 cup heavy (whipping) cream

½ teaspoon vanilla extract

1 teaspoon powdered sugar, or more to taste

5 to 10 Pirouline or Pirouette cookies

For the garnish:

When you are ready to serve the *tartufi*, whip the cream with the vanilla and powdered sugar. Place each *tartufo* into a pretty individual serving bowl, top with a very large dollop of whipped cream, and put 1 or 2 cookies on top.

Makes 4 or 5 large tartufi

Chapter 7

Enfin! Low-Carb Recipes *or* How I Lost Thirty Pounds and Kept It Off

These days, nutrition experts repeatedly tell us—and after all my experiments with low-fat food, which yielded me nothing, I now believe them—that the problem with Americans' diet is that it contains too many simple carbohydrates. The enemy comes in the form of sugar, flour, white bread, pasta, chips, etc. Even more of an issue is that sugar and wheat are both addictive. Some people call them "the heroin of the grocery store." If one is trying to lose weight, it might be good to keep that in mind.

Losing weight and keeping it off is a long, slow marathon, not a sprint. With all the food-testing I did over the years, plus hours sitting at my desk working, the pounds crept on. Eating so-called low-fat food made no difference. So I finally decided to try something new, and to do it systematically, for weight loss.

I tried one diet after another and exercised endlessly, all of which proved

unsuccessful. Finally I hit on two wonderful books: Gary Taubes's *Why We Get Fat* and *Neris and India's Idiot-Proof Diet: A Weight-Loss Plan for Real Women*, by Neris Thomas and India Knight. (Unfortunately, the last time I checked the latter, it was out of print. You could try your local library, or if you want to buy it, The American Book Exchange at abe.com.)

I had two strict requirements going in. First, I didn't want to feel deprived or bored. Second, having a husband and three sons with healthy appetites, I didn't want to have to do a lot of extra cooking just for *me*. So I read the books, tried out the suggestions, and decided these were eating plans with enough variety and actual food that I enjoyed. I took the books to my doctor to see if I was a good fit, health-wise, for the eating plans the books described. He said I was. If you want to lose weight, I recommend talking to your doctor.

So I reread the books, went on the eating plan, lost thirty pounds, and have kept it off for over five years. I began each day with a hard-boiled egg, or egg salad, or tuna salad, or cheese in any number of guises. (No juice! Fruit oxidizes quickly in juice, so a glass of orange juice is like a glass of sugar.) I would have espresso with cream, not milk, and certainly no fat-free milk (thank God). Lunch was a tunafish (or other protein source) salad made with real mayonnaise over arugula and sliced tomatoes, lettuce, and guacamole (woo-hoo!). For lunches with friends, there was always shrimp or fish or other protein, and green vegetables such as spinach, green beans, and broccoli. I avoided bread, rice, pasta, and potatoes. For dinner I would prepare the usual family meal, making sure there was plenty of meat or chicken or fish for everyone. Here, too, I had no rice, potatoes, pasta, bread, or sweets. After a week, I didn't miss them. I don't like store-bought desserts, so I told the family that while I was on my new eating plan, they would have to endure grocery-store desserts. And they did. When I craved something sweet, I would have berries, sometimes lightly sprinkled with Splenda, or the Berries with Yogurt Cream (page 323).

Once the weight came off, I began to enjoy other fruits in moderation, plus the occasional cracker, cookie, piece of pie or cake, or even a *tartufo*, with no ill effects. I walk every day and work out in a gym. I feel great in my new body, have much more energy, and my blood tests are astonishingly improved. (The only downside was that I had to spend money having my clothes altered to make them *smaller.* This is one of those good problems.)

Again, if you want to lose weight, I recommend reading the books and talking to your doctor. And speaking of doctors, I do like them. Really. In fact, one of my brothers-in-law, Dave Faison, is a radiologist. Dave helped me when I was trying to figure out who the victim would be in *The Grilling Season.* I knew the Jerk would be a suspect, and I had to figure out who it was my fictitious doctor—the character readers loved to hate—might have killed. So I asked Dave who it was that he, or most doctors, would like to kill.

Dave did not hesitate. "An HMO executive."

When I finished the book (spoiler alert), I proudly told Dave I had killed off an HMO executive.

Dave's voice turned sad. "Only one?"

So there you have it.

There are many low-carb recipes throughout this cookbook, or recipes you can make low-carb. Snowboarders' Pork Tenderloin (page 111) is a particular favorite. You can make Quiche Me Quick (page 47) without the crust, Ferdinanda's Florentine Quiche (page 64) without the crust, and so on. What I've learned is that the main things one needs in a low-carb meal are: protein to bring up one's blood sugar for the long haul to the next meal and lots of dark green vegetables, the more variety in both of those departments, the better.

There is only one appetizer in this chapter. When you are on a low-carb eating plan, your most frequent appetizer will be nuts or a slice of cheese. My favorite nuts are pecans. My mother-in-law, now sadly deceased, gave me this recipe forty-plus years ago.

Fried Pecans

8 tablespoons (1 stick) unsalted butter

1 pound pecan halves

Popcorn salt

1. Line a baking sheet with paper towels.

2. In a large skillet, melt the butter over low heat. Add the nuts and stir to coat them with the butter. Cook very slowly, stirring frequently with a wooden spoon, until the nuts sound hollow. (This can take 30 to 40 minutes.) Once the nuts sound hollow, they will turn brown fast, so watch carefully. As they turn brown, use tongs to remove them to the lined baking sheet. Salt them while they are warm. When they are cool, store in a covered container.

Makes about 2 cups

Luscious Arugula Salad

Unfortunately, balsamic vinegar contains carbohydrates, so while one is on a low-carb eating plan, the vinaigrettes need to be made without balsamic. For the sugar substitute in this recipe, I use a product called Stevia in the Raw. Also, for the vinaigrette here, I splurge and use fleur de sel. This salad meets the strict requirements of looking good and tasting fabulous.

Vinaigrette:

1 tablespoon Dijon mustard

¼ cup best-quality red wine vinegar (or balsamic vinegar, if you are not on a low-carb eating plan)

1 teaspoon sugar substitute (omit this if using balsamic vinegar)

½ teaspoon kosher salt

Freshly ground black pepper

½ cup best-quality extra-virgin olive oil

Salad:

4 ounces baby arugula

16 strawberries, sliced

4 tablespoons (¼ cup) freshly grated best-quality Parmesan cheese

For the vinaigrette:

In a glass bowl or glass measuring cup, whisk the mustard with the vinegar, sugar substitute, salt, and pepper to taste. Whisk well to make sure the sugar substitute and salt are dissolved. Slowly whisk in the olive oil. You are making an emulsion, so keep whisking until the mixture is thick and evenly mixed. You may need to check the sides of the bowl or measuring cup, and use a spatula to scrape all the sugar substitute into the mixture. Set aside while you make the salad, but do not wash your whisk; you will need it again.

For the salad:

Divide the arugula among 4 salad plates. Top the arugula with the sliced strawberries (each serving gets the equivalent of 4 strawberries). Top each serving with 1 tablespoon Parmesan. Whisk the vinaigrette again and sprinkle about 1 tablespoon vinaigrette on top of each serving.

Makes 4 servings

Cauliflower Mash, or How to Get by Without Potatoes

This will fool your brain into thinking you are having mashed potatoes. (You can imagine what our family thought of mashed cauliflower. So I served them baked potatoes when I had the cauliflower mash.)

- 1 head cauliflower (about 1¼ pounds), cut into florets
- 1 teaspoon salt
- 2 tablespoons unsalted butter
- Heavy (whipping) cream
- Kosher salt or fleur de sel and freshly ground black pepper

1. Bring a large pot of spring water to a boil over high heat. Add the florets and salt and reduce the heat to medium-high. Cook, uncovered, until the cauliflower is tender, 10 to 15 minutes. Remove from the heat. *Drain thoroughly in a colander. You may need to shake the colander to remove moisture.* (This is the key to having a mash that is not watery.)

2. When the cauliflower is no longer dripping any water, place it in a large bowl and either use a potato masher to mash it, or beat it on low speed with an electric beater. You can also process it in a food processor.

3. Place the butter in a large skillet and melt it over low heat. Add the mashed cauliflower and stir. Add cream a little bit at a time, until you have reached a consistency you like. Salt and pepper the cauliflower to taste, and heat very gently. Whatever you don't consume that night can be cooled and stored in the refrigerator.

Makes about 6 servings

Garlicky Spinach

Spinach and garlic are yet another marriage made in culinary heaven. To avoid dealing with little bits of burned garlic, use garlic oil, available at specialty food shops or by mail order.

1 pound baby spinach leaves

1 tablespoon garlic oil

Kosher salt or fleur de sel and freshly ground black pepper

1. Wash the spinach, but do not spin it. You want some moisture on the leaves.

2. Pour the oil into a large sauté pan, and heat over medium-high heat. When the oil ripples slightly, put in the moist spinach. It will sizzle, so stand well away from the pan. Using tongs, toss the spinach for a moment, until it cooks down enough to place a lid on the pan. Cook until the spinach is completely wilted, only about a minute or two. Sprinkle with the salt and pepper, to taste. Serve immediately.

Makes 2 to 3 servings

Green Beans Amandine

When I was young and started doing the family cooking, one box of frozen vegetables used to be called "Green Beans Amandine." It was easy to make: Boil a bit of spring water, add the block of frozen sliced beans, cook for a few minutes, then open the teensy-weensy package of sliced almonds that came with the beans, and sprinkle them on top. Now, we are very fortunate to have fresh, slender French green beans (haricots verts) at almost every grocery store. We can also buy roasted, salted Marcona almonds. (At this writing, both are available at Costco.)

1 teaspoon kosher salt

1 pound fresh haricots verts (French green beans), trimmed

Butter, salt, and freshly ground black pepper

¼ cup salted roasted Marcona almonds, chopped

1. Bring a large quantity of spring water to boil. (If you have a pasta pentola, it will work perfectly, because you will not be cooking the beans long, and they need to drain quickly.) Add the 1 teaspoon salt to the cooking water. Have your serving dish ready.

2. Add the beans to the water and reduce the heat. Cook 1 minute. Using tongs, remove one bean from the water, allow it to cool slightly, and taste it. It should be just done. If it still tastes raw, cook the beans another 30 seconds.

3. Quickly drain the beans. You want them to be cooked, but crunchy. Place them in the serving dish, place a large hunk of butter on top, and sprinkle with the salt, pepper, and chopped almonds.

Makes 4 large servings

Hard-Core Prawn Salad

On a low-carb diet, mayonnaise and avocados are a-okay. This recipe is good if you have people over for a summer lunch or dinner. It is similar to a dish from Chopping Spree, *but that dressing contains sugar. The* sauce gribiche *here is full of flavor. (You can also serve it with the Tenderloin of Beef, page 321.) When this dish is sprinkled with paprika, it looks ready for a photo shoot. Use one avocado per person if you are serving this for a main dish. (For the shrimp, I buy the "wheel" of shrimp cocktail from Costco or the grocery store, discard the sauce, and remove all the shells.) I make the* gribiche *first, so the avocados do not have a chance to turn brown.*

Sauce gribiche:

2 teaspoons chopped scallions (including tops)

2 teaspoons chopped gherkins or cornichons

2 teaspoons chopped capers

1 tablespoon chopped fresh parsley

2 teaspoons minced fresh tarragon

1 teaspoon fresh lemon juice

½ teaspoon Worcestershire sauce

1 teaspoon Dijon mustard

¼ teaspoon sugar substitute

1 large egg, hard-boiled, peeled, and chopped

Freshly ground black pepper

1 cup best-quality mayonnaise

Salad:

1 head butter lettuce, washed, dried, trimmed, and carefully separated into leaves

4 avocados

32 large cooked shrimp, peeled and deveined

Paprika

For the sauce gribiche:

In the bowl of a food processor, combine the scallions, gherkins, capers, parsley, tarragon, lemon juice, Worcestershire sauce, mustard, sugar substitute, egg, and pepper to taste. Stir in the mayonnaise. Process until the ingredients are well mixed (but not puréed; you want the distinctive aspects of the sauce to shine through), 10 to 15 seconds. Refrigerate until ready to use. Just before serving, take the sauce out of the refrigerator.

For the salad:

Arrange 4 or 5 lettuce leaves on each of 4 salad plates. Peel, halve, and pit the avocados. Place 2 avocado halves on the arranged leaves, and place 4 shrimp on each avocado half. Spoon about ¼ cup *sauce gribiche* on top of each serving. (Any unused *gribiche*—you may have about ½ cup—can be covered with plastic wrap and refrigerated for 2 days.) Sprinkle each serving with paprika. Serve immediately.

Makes 4 servings

Chicken Tarragon

This was actually one of the very first dishes I made for Jim that wasn't out of a box. Mrs. Tita Peters, an amazing cook and the mother of my maid of honor, Louise, used to make it. Tita sent me the recipe, to which I have made very few changes over the years. Jim loved this dish, as does the family to this day. You make the brine first, so the chicken can soak in it for several hours or overnight before cooking.

¼ cup kosher salt

5 cups spring water

2½ pounds bone-in, skin-on chicken thighs

2 tablespoons unsalted butter, at room temperature

¼ cup fresh lemon juice

¼ cup dried tarragon

Salt and freshly ground black pepper

Parsley, for garnish

1. In a large glass bowl, stir the salt into the water. Stir until it is completely dissolved. Carefully place the thighs in the brine, cover the bowl with plastic wrap, and place in the refrigerator for 4 hours or overnight.

2. When you are ready to make the chicken, line one or two large plates with paper towels and have more paper towels ready. Carefully place the bowl in the sink and drain off the brine. Rinse the chicken pieces with cold water, then fill the bowl with cold water and allow the chicken pieces to sit for 10 minutes, to remove excess salt.

3. Using tongs, place the chicken pieces on the paper towels and pat them dry.

4. Preheat the oven to 350°F.

5. Smear *all* the butter in a 9 x 13-inch glass baking dish. Place the chicken pieces (you should have about 6) into the pan. Pour the

lemon juice over the chicken. Crumble the tarragon over the chicken pieces, so that each piece is thoroughly covered. Salt and pepper the chicken, and place a meat thermometer into one of the pieces, so that it does not touch the bone or the bottom of the pan.

6. Place in the oven and bake for 45 minutes to 1 hour, or until the thermometer reads 170°F. Remove the pan from the oven, tent it with foil, and allow to rest for 10 minutes.

7. Using tongs, place the chicken pieces on an attractive platter. Pour the accumulated juices into a gravy boat. Surround the chicken pieces with large stems of parsley and serve.

Makes 6 servings

Tenderloin of Beef

This is our favorite dish for holiday dinners. The only challenge, if you buy a tenderloin that is untrimmed, is trimming it of the fat and membrane. Once trimmed, you wrestle the beef into a cylinder and use kitchen twine to tie it, so it will cook evenly. You must have a working meat thermometer to prepare this dish properly.

5-pound whole tenderloin of beef, trimmed, preferably prime grade, or a 7-pound whole tenderloin that you trim of fat and membrane yourself (both are usually available at Costco)

¼ cup garlic oil

2 teaspoons kosher salt

½ teaspoon freshly ground black pepper

1 teaspoon dried tarragon

Sauce Gribiche (from Hard-Core Prawn Salad, page 317) or your favorite horseradish sauce

1. If you are using the untrimmed tenderloin, use a sharp knife to carefully trim the beef of fat and visible membrane.

2. *Allow the beef to come to room temperature.* Tuck the slender end underneath the meat. Using four 12-inch pieces of kitchen twine, tie the beef at 2-inch intervals, so that it is in an even cylinder.

3. Preheat the oven to 325°F. Brush some of the garlic oil on the rack of a roasting pan.

4. Place the meat on the roasting rack. Rub the meat with some garlic oil and pour any left over on top. In a small bowl, mix the salt, pepper, and tarragon. Sprinkle this evenly over the roast. Insert a meat thermometer into the beef. (For this and all other recipes using a meat thermometer, I use a digital probe type, set to a certain temperature.)

5. Roast until the meat thermometer reads 125°F for medium-rare (about 1 hour, but watch the

thermometer carefully, or if your thermometer comes with an alarm, set it to beep to remind you when the roast comes to 125°F). Remove the roast from the oven and tent it with foil. Allow to rest for 15 minutes. (The meat will rise 5 degrees in temperature while it is resting.)

6. Place the meat on a platter. Either pour the accumulated pan juices over the meat or serve it separately in a gravy boat. Serve with *sauce gribiche* or horseradish sauce.

Makes 8 to 12 servings

Berries with Yogurt Cream

One of the few guilt-free desserts you can have on a low-carb diet is berries, either sweetened with sugar substitute or served with sugarless yogurt or cream. Still, it's better than nothing, and you can also serve berries with the Sugar-Free Vanilla Gelato (page 301). I originally developed this recipe before Greek yogurt was widely available. I have tested the recipe with Greek yogurt, and it works well. The finished Yogurt Cream will be softer if you use Greek yogurt, but using it means you can skip the overnight draining step. If you choose to drain plain yogurt overnight, the resulting Yogurt Cream will be thicker and more substantial. Either way, you can indulge in a healthful bowl of lusciousness while the family is slicing into pieces of (store-bought) chocolate cake.

1 quart plain full-fat yogurt, such as Wallaby, or 1¾ cup full-fat plain Greek yogurt

1 cup heavy (whipping) cream

1 teaspoon vanilla extract

Sugar substitute, to taste

1 to 2 pounds fresh raspberries, strawberries, or blueberries, or a mixture

1. If you are draining the regular yogurt, cut two 18-inch pieces of cheesecloth, wet them, and wring them out. Use them to line a sieve that you place over a large bowl. Spoon the regular (not Greek) yogurt into the sieve and cover the mixture with plastic wrap.

2. Place the bowl in the refrigerator and allow the yogurt to drain overnight. In the morning, discard the accumulated liquid in the bottom of the bowl. (Again, if you are using the Greek yogurt, there is no need to do the overnight draining.)

3. Just before serving, whip the cream. Stir in the vanilla, then the yogurt. Taste and carefully add sugar substitute, if desired, a small amount (less than a teaspoon) at a time. (A little goes a

long way here, and you cannot take it out once you've put it in. You may find that you like the yogurt-cream mixture as is, and do not want any sugar substitute. But I doubt it.)

4. Place a cup of berries in a bowl and spoon a ½ cup or more of the yogurt cream over it. Enjoy with abandon.

Makes 4 or more servings

Epilogue

Now I'm going to switch hats and say a last few words about writing:

If you want to write books and have them published, first, you must educate yourself. Read as widely as possible in the genre in which you want to publish. Make a notebook. Study those books you like to read. Outline them. How does the book work? How do the characters work? Put all this in your notebook.

Second, ask if you can visit a critique group. While there, see if you agree with the criticisms being offered on the manuscripts. Usually members will bring ten or so pages to be critiqued. Groups that are either too flattering or too harsh are worthless. Groups that see what a manuscript *needs* are like gold. If you can't find a critique group, you can start your own or ask your library to help you get one going.

Third, as I have said, join good writers' organizations and make booksellers your friends. Great booksellers can help you find books that work with your taste. Trust them, and buy the books they recommend while you are in the store. Sorry, but there is no algorithm that will predict correctly "books you might like." But when a bookseller says to me, "Diane, I just finished a book that I think you are going to love," that, too, is gold.

Fourth, there is the extremely important issue of training oneself. This means finding a writing schedule that works. Many authors fit doing their writing into their workday or their family's natural rhythms. Sue Grafton, a great, longtime source of inspiration for me, memorably uses the daily page quota. Gabriel García Márquez would take his sons to school, come home, and write until it was time to pick them up. Anthony Trollope talked about his daily page quota, for which he was roundly ridiculed at the time. But the judgment of history is that his novels are brilliant.

Even if what you produce is terrible, it's a starting place. As Joanne Greenberg, one of our treasured local authors, so wisely says, "The beginning writer says, 'It stinks; toss it.' The professional writer says, 'It stinks; fix it.' "

Finally, it is extremely important to find sources of positive reinforcement, wherever they may be. Write them down. Read them every morning. Tape them to your computer or hang them on your wall. It's hard enough to write a book that a publisher wants to buy, so cherish any positive feedback you receive.

I had a longtime source of inspiration that was the very best: I mentioned at the outset of this cookbook how watching Julia Child on television was revelatory. I put the story about messing up her recipe for Gâteau de Crêpes à la Florentine into *Dying for Chocolate,* which was published in 1992. To my great surprise, after *Dying for Chocolate* came out, *Julia Child herself* wrote me a fan letter! She thanked me for mentioning her as inspiration! She wished me all success with my writing!

I taped that note to my kitchen window. It served as the very best motivation possible.

Then I went on a book tour. Because Jim and I were always tripping over each other in our tiny kitchen, we had decided to have it expanded and remodeled. When I returned, the contractor had installed new kitchen windows . . . and the note from Julia Child had disappeared. High and low searching never uncovered it. (This is one of the reasons I had to kill off a kitchen contractor in the book I was working on.)

I love writing as well as cooking. If I create a novel or a dish, and it doesn't work, I try (and try and try) to fix it. All those years ago, on the night before Jim's and my wedding, I did not need to be sobbing in the front seat of our car. Things worked out. Things will work out for you, too.

Many of you have written asking if there will be more Goldy books. I am taking a break now, but have not given up on the idea of revisiting the Goldy series. Thank you many times over for your support.

Throughout the writing and publication of the Goldy books, you wonderful readers have become my constant source of inspiration and support. I feel blessed to have known you through meeting you in bookstores and through your letters and posts on my Facebook fan page. You have taken Goldy, Arch, Tom, Marla, Julian, and all the rest of the Aspen Meadow gang into your hearts. And you are in mine.

Index

C

D

E

F

G

O

P

Q

R

S

T

U

V

W

Y

Z